A Harvest of Lutheran Dogmatics and Ethics

The Life and Work of Twelve Theologians

1960-2020

Robert W. Bertram
Edward H. Schroeder
Gerhard O. Forde
William H. Lazareth
Robert Benne
Paul R. Sponheim
Philip Hefner
Ted Peters
George A. Lindbeck
Robert W. Jenson
Paul R. Hinlicky
Carl E. Braaten

Carl E. Braaten

ALPB Books
Delhi, New York

Cover image:
Luther's Rose, depicted in the banner which hangs above the altar
at Holy Trinity Lutheran Church, Chenango Bridge, New York
(used by permission)

The American Lutheran Publicity Bureau wishes
to acknowledge with deep appreciation the work of
Carl E. Braaten for the reflective creation, editing and
preparation of this text and Martin A. Christiansen for
layout/design work.

Paul Robert Sauer
Executive Director, ALPB

ISBN 978-1-892921-40-6

American Lutheran Publicity Bureau
PO Box 327
Delhi, NY 13753

A Harvest of Lutheran Dogmatics and Ethics:
The Life and Work of Twelve Theologians 1960-2020
(Delhi, NY: ALPB Books, 2021), 288 pp.

Contents

Introduction

After the Second World War Lutherans in America witnessed a remarkable surge of theological productivity in all fields of theology — biblical, both Old and New Testaments, church history, ancient, medieval, and modern, with particular emphasis on the Reformation, Christian dogmatics and ethics, as well as various areas of practical theology, such as homiletics, liturgics, and pastoral counseling. This was an unprecedented and surprising development. Our teachers at the various Lutheran seminaries for the most part had not earned doctorates at any of the ranking divinity schools such as Harvard, Yale, Chicago, Union or Princeton. As seminary students in the 1950s the theological books we read were not written by our professors. The course bibliographies included books written mostly by German or Swedish scholars, and a few by Danish, Finnish or Norwegian. This is understandable because all Lutherans in America were of immigrant descent and only gradually emerged from their respective ethnic heritage after the first World War. At that time the seminaries of the various Lutheran Churches or Synods taught the kind of theology they imported from the country from whence they came. That changed dramatically after the Second World War. While our standard textbooks were not yet ecumenical, they had definitely become pan-Lutheran. Books authored by Gustaf Aulén, Anders Nygren, Regin Prenter, Hermann Sasse, Helmut Thielicke, Ernst Troeltsch, C. F. W. Walther, Joachim Jeremias, and Oscar Cullmann among others had become available in English translation.

Most seminary students after World War II graduated from Lutheran Colleges — such as Muhlenberg, Gettysburg, Wittenberg, Valparaiso, St. Olaf, Luther, Concordia, Augsburg, Augustana (Sioux Falls, SD), Augustana (Rock Island, IL), and others — whose philosophy and religion departments prepared their pre-sems to become serious students of theology. I will focus on twelve such Lutheran college students who went on to become professors of dogmatics and ethics and prolific authors of monographs, as well as hundreds of articles and book reviews in the leading journals of theology. I came to know these scholars and their works in my capacity as the editor of two journals of theology. The first one was *dialog — A Journal of Theology*, founded in 1961 and the second was *Pro Ecclesia — A Journal of Catholic and Evangelical Theology*, founded in 1991, together with my friend and collaborator, Robert W. Jenson. Jenson and I then became co-editors of *Christian Dogmatics* (Fortress Press, 1984), a textbook to which five of these twelve theologians each contributed two Loci. The twelve theologians I have chosen to write about represent a diversity of methods and interests. Lutheran theology in America has never been monolithic. A word about the number twelve is in order. Why only twelve? Four of the twelve are of Norwegian ethnicity — Paul R. Sponheim, Gerhard O. Forde, Robert W. Jenson, and Carl E. Braaten; six are of German background — William H. Lazareth, Robert W. Bertram, Edward H. Schroeder, Philip Hefner, Robert Benne, and Ted Peters; one of Swedish — George A. Lindbeck — and one of Slovak origin — Paul R. Hinlicky. The omission of theologians from the Danish, Finnish, and Icelandic traditions means either that their teaching theologians specialized in fields other than dogmatics and ethics or that they did not write theological books.

Rev. Dr. Robert W. Bertram was a pastor and theologian in the Lutheran Church–Missouri Synod. He was born on Easter Sunday March 27, 1921 in Fort Wayne, Indiana. Bertram grew up in the world of the Missouri Synod. He attended its educational institutions—a B.A. from Concordia Senior College in Ft. Wayne, Indiana and in 1946 an M.Div. from Concordia Seminary in St. Louis. Bertram was ordained into the Lutheran ministry in 1953. He chose not to do his graduate theological degree at Concordia Seminary, unusual for a budding Missouri theologian at that time. He received his Ph.D. in 1964 from the Divinity School of the University of Chicago, mentored by two famous Lutheran theologians, Paul J. Tillich and Jaroslav J. Pelikan. He taught philosophy and theology at Valparaiso University for fifteen years. In 1963 he accepted a call to teach at his alma mater, Concordia Seminary in St Louis. Together with his friend and colleague, Edward Schroeder, he founded the Crossings Community. In 1974 he joined the faculty of a "seminary in exile," Christ Seminary-Seminex, which merged with the Lutheran School of Theology at Chicago, where he taught for eight years until his retirement. Bertram died March 12, 2003 in Webster Groves, Missouri.

Rev. Dr. Edward H. Schroeder was born on an Illinois farm November 6, 1930 and died in St. Louis on March 1, 2019. He was educated at Valparaiso University in Indiana and earned a theological doctorate from the University of Hamburg in Germany. He taught theology at Valparaiso University and Concordia Seminary, and led seminars in overseas seminaries in Australia, Ethiopia, and Lithuania. Edward H. Schroeder, together with Robert W. Bertram, founded the Crossings Community, a worldwide network of Christians committed to connect the Word of God with daily life under the motto, "Crossing Life with the Promise of Christ." They heard the plea of some lay persons who asked, "Can you help us connect Sunday worship with our lives the other six days of the week?" The teaching method of the Crossings Community is to relate Scripture to everyday existence by drawing the proper distinction of the law and gospel of God. Bertram and Schroeder held weekend workshops and also offered semester-long courses in seminaries and other venues, dealing with the many areas of secular life — politics, economics, education, health care, family life, media, technology, etc.

One

Robert W. Bertram and Edward H. Schroeder

Confessing Lutheranism

R obert W. Bertram (1921-2003) and Edward H. Schroeder (1930-2019) were two of the most prominent theologians of the twentieth century, raised and educated to be pastors and professors within the Lutheran Church — Missouri Synod. They met at Valparaiso University where Bertram was teaching theology in the philosophy department and Schroeder was his student. Thereafter they became life-long friends, colleagues, and collaborators. Of this period in their life together Schroeder wrote, "Where my life intersected Bob's theology was well over half a century ago in 1949 in the classroom at Valparaiso University. He was a Young Turk prof, age 28, and, at 18, I was just young. My baccalaureate major was philosophy, and that's where Bob was teaching — alongside colleagues Jaroslav Pelikan and Richard Luecke, equally youngish and possibly even more Turkish. At Valparaiso in those days, university and church politics being what they were, serious theology was being taught in the philosophy department."[1] Bertram moved to Concordia Seminary in St. Louis where he became Professor of Historical and Systematic Theology. There he taught until the majority of

---

1. Edward Schroeder, "Foreword," *A Time for Confessing*, Robert Bertram, ed. Michael Hoy (Eerdmans, 2008), vii.

the faculty went into exile to found Christ Seminary-Seminex. The Seminary in Exile merged with the Lutheran School of Theology at Chicago, where Bertram concluded his teaching career. For ten years he was my colleague with an office next door to mine. Schroeder followed Bertram to become his colleague both at Concordia Seminary and Christ Seminary-Seminex.

1. The Crossings Community

Bertram and Schroeder were not only colleagues at Concordia Seminary and Seminex, early in the 1970s they co-founded the Crossings Community, which they described as "a worldwide network of Christians dedicated to connecting the Word of God and daily life under the motto, 'Crossing Life with the Promise of Christ.' What makes our approach distinctive is our commitment to a theological outlook called the *proper distinction between law and gospel*."[2] They developed the "Crossings Method" to help Christians to connect their Christian faith and everyday life, to relate the Word of God to the world in which they live — political, economic, science, technology, family and social life, quite a tall order. The Crossings Method is a theological orientation well known to Lutherans as "Law and Gospel," or more accurately, drawing the proper distinction between Law and Gospel. This type of theology is, of course, not original with Bertram and Schroeder. By adopting it they proved to be faithful to the signature theme of the theological brain trust of the confessional Saxon Lutherans who settled in Missouri, Carl Wilhelm Ferdinand Walther, the author of an enormously influential book entitled, *The Proper Distinction Between Law and Gospel*. In addition to this the Law/Gospel Theology of the German Lutheran theologian, Werner Elert, was admittedly key to the Crossings Method of interpreting Scripture. According to Elert the original "point of departure" in Luther's experience and understanding of the Christian faith, which he called "*der*

---

2. https://crossings.org/about/

evangelischer Ansatz," was "the proper distinction between law and gospel." Bertram and Schroeder knew this Lutheran history and theology well. Schroeder received his doctorate in theology from the University of Hamburg, and Bertram, according to Schroeder, likely had the proper distinction between law and gospel in his DNA. This is what Schroeder wrote of his buddy, "Bob might already have learned that before his years of Luther-probing at the University of Chicago; it could have been in his DNA. How so? His maternal grandfather, William H. T. Dau, had translated the Missouri Synod patriarch's classic work into English: C. F. W. Walther's *The Proper Distinction between Law and Gospel.* Bob's father, a Germanics professor, later translated Werner Elert's dogmatics (in which the law/gospel distinction is the fundamental axiom for Lutheran theology) into English. Though Bob could read and speak German, and thus didn't need these translations, might such Lutheran theology have been transmitted at the family table (or even from mother's milk)?"[3]

Law/Gospel theology is something taught by other Lutheran theologians featured in this book. As a first year seminarian at Luther Seminary in Professor Herman Preus' homiletics class, I was required not only to read but to outline chapter by chapter C. F. W. Walther's book, *The Proper Distinction between Law and Gospel,* which modeled for me what preaching is all about. This distinction is paramount also in the dogmatics of William H. Lazareth, Gerhard O. Forde, Robert W. Jenson, and Paul R. Hinlicky, but not so much in the others. What is different about the use of Law/Gospel theology by Bertram and Schroeder is that it became the one controlling theme of virtually everything they taught and wrote. Neither of them published a book, let alone a book of dogmatics or systematic theology. The scuttlebutt was that Missouri Synod theologians didn't write books of dogmatics because they assumed that all true theology had already been written. They were accused by other Lutheran

---

3. Edward Schroeder, "Foreword," *A Time for Confessing,* Robert Bertram, ix.

theologians of practicing the method of repristination. New theology is likely to be heterodox, even heretical. When Robert W. Jenson and I co-edited two volumes of *Christian Dogmatics*, members of Concordia Seminary in St. Louis reviewed them; the authors did not conform strictly to the *Book of Concord* and seventeenth century Lutheran scholastic orthodoxy.

As important as the Law/Gospel dialectic is in the Lutheran tradition, it is not possible to derive all the contents of Christian doctrinal theology, from the alpha of creation to the omega of eschatology, simply by rightly distinguishing law and gospel. The Trinitarian and Christological doctrines of the ancient Creeds of the Church were constructed from the pattern of God's self-revelation in the biblical history of salvation, which the law/gospel theology presupposes.

Just what is Law/Gospel theology, according to Bertram and Schroeder? First of all, it is a hermeneutical method for understanding the two contrasting ways of God acting in the world, by the Law and the Gospel. The Law refers to the demands that God places on all human beings, as summarized in the two parts of the Great Commandment: "You shall love the Lord your God with all your heart, and with all your soul, and with all your mind, and with all your strength.... And you shall love your neighbor as yourself" (Mark 12:30-31). The irreducible demand of God's Law reveals that all have fallen short and live as condemned sinners under the wrath of his judgment. The Gospel, moving in the opposite direction, refers to the gracious love of God by which he reconciles sinners to himself on account of the life, death, and resurrection of Jesus Christ. By faith sinners are adopted into the new family of God — the communion of saints — and are made new creatures by the power of the Holy Spirit. This is the prime principle of Lutheran catechetics 101.

The emphasis on the *proper* distinction between Law and Gospel is a warning that there are improper ways of relating them, one by confusing them and another by separating them. The Law should not be treated as Gospel, and the Gospel should not be treated as Law. Every person stands before God under his law and is judged to be guilty of sin, estranged and alienated from the Creator. Only the Gospel has the power to transfer a person from the state of being under the Law to the state of being accepted by God on account of Christ's sacrificial death on the cross. Making the proper distinction between Law and Gospel is credited with some of the historic examples of discerning the difference between orthodoxy and heresy, as Irenaeus did against the Gnostics, Athanasius against the Arians, Augustine against the Pelagians, Luther against the Antinomians, Elert against the Barthians, and Bonhoeffer against the pseudo-Lutherans.[4]

As an educational tool for interpreting biblical texts in order to properly distinguish Law and Gospel Bertram and Schroeder developed what they called the "Crossings Template." The Bible is treated as a "problem-solving" literature. The first step is called "diagnosis," that is, to diagnose what is wrong with human existence, to discover its predicament in light of God's Law, and the second step is called "prognosis," that is, to identify the solution to the problem in light of the Gospel of God. The problem of the sinner's estrangement from God is matched by the solution of the sinner's reconciliation through faith in the crucified and risen Lord Jesus Christ.[5] The salvation the Gospel gives heals the deadly sickness that universally afflicts the human condition. In sermon preparation, for example, the "Crossings Template" begins its exegesis of the biblical text by asking the question, "What is the problem, what is the particular sickness that the people in the text are experiencing?" If there is no problem, there is no need for a solution, and hence no point at all in preaching a sermon. This would make sense to a lot of preachers other than Lutheran.

The Law/Gospel theology was reinforced for me by the way Paul Tillich appropriated it for his apologetic theology, which he

---

4. https://crossings.org/about/lawgospel-theology/
5. https://crossings.org/about/the-crossings-template/

called the "method of correlation." Edward Schroeder acknowledged that correlation is exactly what the Crossings Method is also aiming to accomplish. Tillich formulated the question of meaning in all spheres of reality and then developed the answer in light of the gospel. Without a point of contact in the correlation, the questions would remain blind and the answers sterile. The Crossings Template asserts that the Gospel-solution fits the Law-problem like hand in glove. For Tillich preaching communicates the eternal truth of the Christian message to the existential conditions of life in the modern world. This is always risky business, as any preacher knows, because it is tempting to shave the bold truth of God's revelation to relate more easily to the human situation, or the opposite can happen, to shout the supreme truth of God's revelation, making no contact with those in the pew. Tillich praised Luther's *Bondage of the Will* — which Luther himself once said was the best of the things he wrote — because it provided radical insight into the depths of the human situation, under the Law and the Wrath of God. Tillich acknowledged that it is impossible to draw salvation answers from the human situation, in bondage to sin, death, and the power of the demonic, lacking faith and the fear of God. The Law cannot provide a solution to the human predicament that it lays bare. "*Lex semper accusat*," said Luther. The Law cannot release a person from its accusations. The Gospel alone is the source of the solution to the problem the Law discloses.

2. Bertram's Paradigm of Confessing Theology

Robert Bertram will be remembered by historians of theology for his persistent emphasis on the calling of Christians to be confessors of Christ in times when they are put to the test, on trial for the faith they confess. Five years after Bertram died (2003), one of his former students, Michael Hoy, edited a book of essays entitled, *A Time for Confessing*. They deal with historic occasions when Christians were challenged to confess their faith in times of persecution. The first one Bertram takes up is what happened at

Augsburg, Germany (1530), when the first Lutheran confessors were on trial before the highest authorities in church and society. The only authority to which they appealed was that of the Word of God, given in trust to the church to communicate to the world in the one gospel and the sacraments. Melanchthon said to their accusers: "Certainly we should not wish to put our own souls and consciences in grave peril before God by misusing his name or Word, nor should we wish to bequeath to our children and posterity any other teaching than that which agrees with the pure Word of God and Christian truth."[6]

Confessors are willing to be martyrs, if necessary, since their accusers have the official authority and power to determine their fate for good or ill. Bertram reminds us that the Augsburg confessors were encouraged by the promise of Jesus in the Gospel of Matthew: "Whosoever therefore shall confess me before men, him will I confess also before my Father which is in heaven. But whosoever shall deny me before men, him will I also deny before my Father which is in heaven."[7] Confessors face an either/or: either fidelity to Christ and his gospel or apostasy. The Augsburg confessors refused to add the observance of ceremonial traditions to the gospel and sacraments as necessary for church unity. They could not have said it more clearly: "For the true unity of the church it is enough (*satis est*) to agree concerning the teaching of the Gospel and the administration of the sacraments. It is not necessary that human traditions or rites and ceremonies, instituted by men, should be alike everywhere."[8] The confessors were not opposing ecclesiastical traditions as such; their opposition was strictly against requiring their observance as essential to preserve the unity of the church. Such traditions were called "*adiaphora*," matters of indifference.[9] The confessors were even

---

6. "The Augsburg Confession," *The Book of Concord*, Tappert Edition (Fortress Press, 1959) 47.

7. Matthew 10: 32-33

8. "The Augsburg Confession," Article VII, 1-3.

9. "The Augsburg Confession," Article XXVII, 27.

willing to observe such *adiaphora*, provided they not be added by church authority to the gospel as necessary for salvation.

The second case study that exhibits Bertram's paradigm of a confessing movement is the civil rights struggle of the Black Churches led by Martin Luther King, Jr. King's "Letter from Birmingham Jail" documents that at stake were not merely some social laws that Black Christians were protesting and disobeying. What was at stake was what he called "the gospel of freedom." King was, Bertram insists, "a defendant, and in that sense, a *martyr,* a *confessor.* What he was confessing to, of all things, was a 'gospel of freedom.' This freedom, whose superiority consists in the power to bear a cross, was for prisoner King a shadow of things to come."[10] King's "Letter from Birmingham Jail" is "public witness to the Christian gospel under fire, a form of martyrological *confessio*.... Such a moment, such a 'time for confessing,' as the *Formula of Concord* called it, has arrived when an oppressive establishment has exalted some favorite feature of its culture to salvational significance, insinuating it into the gospel itself as a condition of human worth, thus nullifying the unconditional grace of God in Christ."[11]

The third case study takes us to South Africa where the confessional movement opposed apartheid not merely as an ethical issue but as an ecclesial case of "heresy."[12] In discussing apartheid Bertram continues to explain the various features of his understanding of *confessio, or a* "time for confessing."

First, confessing is not any declaration of one's faith, say at baptism or confirmation. Rather, "It is *martyria,* in an adversary situation, implying that the confessors — indeed, the whole church — are at that moment on a witness stand (*in statu confessionis*) before a superior critical tribunal, to all appearances

---

10. Robert Bertram, *A Time for Confessing,* 39.

11. Robert Bertram, *A Time for Confessing,* 40, 41.

12. Robert Bertram, *A Time for Confessing,* 57.

18

divinely ordained, from whose authority the witnesses must nevertheless dissent."[13]

Second, a "time for confessing" arises when the confessors deem it necessary to protest against the authorities, whether civil or ecclesiastical, who add this or that to the gospel, such as circumcision in the early church against the Judaizers, or the *adiaphora* (rites and ceremonies) protested by the *Augsburg Confession,* or apartheid in South Africa. The result is always the same — the gospel is subverted or replaced by an "alien gospel."

"Third, the 'time for confessing' is also ecumenical in nature, inviting the whole church to join on the witness stand."[14]

Fourth, to confess in the sense Bertram uses the term is to oppose secular authority when it usurps the spiritual authority of Christ and his gospel.

Fifth, the confessional protest may not be exclusively soteriological but liberationist as well, advocating for the poor and the oppressed.

Sixth, confessors realize that they are acting in an ambiguous situation, "acutely aware that they too do not have clean hands and that even their protest is compromised morally by their own mixed motives."[15] They know that they as much as their opponents are sinners in need of forgiveness.

Apartheid was eventually opposed not only by confessors within South Africa but also by external ecumenical organizations — the World Council of Churches, the Lutheran World Federation, and the World Alliance of Reformed Churches. Their reasoning was clear: Apartheid is in bondage to an alien gospel that divides churches and Christians from one another.

Bertram's fourth case study is focussed on Dietrich Bonhoeffer, martyred at the hands of Hitler's National Socialist regime.

---

13. Robert Bertram, *A Time for Confessing,* 58.

14. Robert Bertram, *A Time for Confessing,* 59.

15. Robert Bertram, *A Time for Confessing,* 60.

Bonhoeffer was Bertram's hero, his favorite example of what it means to confess Christ in a time of persecution. Whenever the church is in danger of exchanging its unique Christ-centered authority for some mess of secular pottage, true Christians must be willing to act boldly in a "time for confessing." The Christian Church in Germany in the 1930s was in grave danger of forfeiting its birthright in the gospel of Christ for allegiance to Hitler's anti-Semitic ideology. In 1934 the *Barmen Declaration* was composed, most of it by Karl Barth, and adopted by a synod of confessing Christians. Bonhoeffer was not present on that occasion, but he became a leading advocate and interpreter of the Declaration.

The first thesis declares that Jesus Christ is the one Word of God which we have to hear, trust, and obey and it rejected as false doctrine any other source of the church's proclamation. The second thesis confesses Jesus Christ as the only Lord of all aspects of personal life and there can be no other authority. The *Barmen Declaration* goes on to declare that the Church cannot be ruled by a "*Führer*" and that it cannot be subordinate to the State. The main purpose of this confessional document was to create a consensus of three churches, Lutheran, Reformed, and United, thus unifying them to establish the Confessing Church to oppose the "German Christians," who took the oath of loyalty to Hitler.[16]

The Confessing Church was not one happy united family of confessors. Lutherans, for their part, criticized the first thesis, Barth's favorite, confessing Jesus Christ to be the one Word of God. Led by Werner Elert, Lutherans insisted on a revision that acknowledged the twofold nature of God's Word, Law and Gospel, each with a different role to play in the Two Kingdoms of God.[17] Bonhoeffer was a Lutheran, but he had his own way of interpreting the doctrine of the Two Kingdoms, repudiating

16. Robert Bertram, *A Time for Confessing*, 65-67.
17. Robert Bertram, *A Time for Confessing*, 69-70.

the tendency of some conservative Lutherans to separate them into two mutually exclusive spheres.[18] This became a sore point between various factions within the Confessing Church, which Bertram discusses at length. Our focus is on the role that Bonhoeffer played in forcefully voicing the claims of the Barmen Confession. He wrote an article in which he stated something many in the Confessing Movement found scandalous. "Whoever knowingly separates himself from the Confessing Church of Germany separates himself from salvation."[19] What was deemed to be offensive is that the Barmen Declaration was being used not only to reject the heresy of the German Christians, but was also condemning every one of them to hell. Bonhoeffer was accused of legalism, of denying evangelical freedom, by claiming that the Confessing Church is the only true Church of Jesus Christ in Germany.

Bertram's chapter on Bonhoeffer's role in the Confessional Movement was written decades after Bonhoeffer's death on Hitler's scaffold. He added his to hundreds of biographies, dissertations, and articles written on the life and theology of Bonhoeffer. Bertram's treatment of Bonhoeffer excels in not only putting the best construction on Bonhoeffer's role in the Confessing Movement, but also in demonstrating that he was being faithful to the idea of a "Time for Confessing" affirmed in Article X of the "Formula of Concord."

Bertram's fifth case study deals with the People Power's Revolution in the Philippines in 1986. This was a bloodless revolution called the miracle of EDSA (*Epifanio de los Santos Avenue*) that occurred over three days between February 22 and February 25. Hundreds of thousands of ordinary people from around the country gathered to protest the corrupt government of Ferdinand Marcos and the rigged election to keep him in power. The revolution was peaceful with no tolerance for violence or

---

18. Dietrich Bonhoeffer, *Ethics* (1955).

19. Robert Bertram, *A Time for Confessing*, 78.

bloodshed. The Marcos government was tyrannical and violated basic human rights. The straw that broke the camel's back was when former Senator Benigno Aquino was shot and killed upon his return to the Philippines from exile in the United States. The cry for democracy erupted. Two of Marcos' top officials withdrew their support for Marcos' government and called upon him to resign. The Archbishop Cardinal Sin along with many priests and nuns called upon all Filipinos to join a protest march of EDSA. The wife of Senator Aquino, Corazon Aquino, took the presidential oath of office on February 25. Marcos, with the support of President Reagan, abandoned his fight to remain in office and with his wife Imelda and entourage fled his palace and flew to Hawaii, with a plane load of money and gold.

Why did Bertram choose the Democratic Peoples' Revolution of 1986 as an example of a "time for confessing?" After all, it was a political revolution with a political purpose and result. Bertram relied for his information about this revolution mainly on some writings of Francisco F. Claver, a Jesuit priest,[20] as well as a few others. Bertram's research led him to believe that the energy behind the revolution was spiritual, in fact, a demonstration of the power of faith, the people's faith which was Christian to the core.[21] This faith was influenced by a prior movement for the liberation of the poor and oppressed by the founding of Basic Christian Communities (BBC). According to Claver, whom Bertram cites approvingly, the BBC movement in the Philippines was inspired by the Second Vatican Council. Bertram writes, "An initial im-

---

20. Francisco F. Claver, S. J., "The Miracle of EDSA: Reflections on the People's Shallow Faith" (March 13, 1986). Unpublished paper. Francisco F. Claver, S. J., "Church Power and the Revolution: Episcopal Reflections," *Pulso* 1, no. 4 (1986). Francisco F. Claver, S. J., "The Church and Revolution: The Philippine Solution," *America* 154, no. 17.

21. Francisco Claver wrote of the people's revolution in "The Miracle of EDSA": "They succeeded. They stopped tanks. They silenced guns. They tumbled an entrenched dictatorship. And their only weapons were rosaries, crucifixes, religious images of the Virgin and the Holy Child — and a vulnerability born of faith."

petus for the BBCs came from Vatican II in its emphasis on the church's task of 'socially transforming the world,' most importantly its emphasis on lay participation."[22] Bertram understands the democratic revolution in the Philippines as a case of "Christian *confessio*." The seeds were sown at Vatican II without which the hundreds of thousands of lay believers who took to the streets of Manila to protest Marcos' evil regime would not have happened. Bertram quotes Claver to make his point: "Faith is what makes or breaks the Basic Christian Community. The faith is the BBC's *raison d'être*, basic to its being and operation. Without Christian faith, these local communities degenerate into purely political groups under the guise of being church."[23]

The conviction that faith was empowering the Philippine's People's Revolution was music to Bertram's ears. No Lutheran theologian has stressed more emphatically that faith alone (*sola fide*), not grace alone (*sola gratia*) and not even Christ alone (*solus Christus*), was the central issue in the controversy on justification between the Lutheran confessors at Augsburg and their Roman Catholic critics. The defenders of Rome's theology might well affirm the unique role that grace and Christ play in salvation, but they could not accept the notion of "faith alone" because that discounts the necessity of good works. However, Bertram does not play "faith alone" against "grace alone" and "Christ alone." All three are important and imply each other. The confession of "faith alone" depends on the soteriological uniqueness of the person in whom it believes.[24]

Robert Bertram became widely known far beyond his home base in the Lutheran Church–Missouri Synod. He was

---

22. Robert Bertram, *A Time for Confessing*, 99.
23. Francisco F. Claver, S. J., "History of Philippine BBCs," a talk he gave in January 1986.
24. Robert Bertram, "Faith Alone Justifies," Luther on *Iustitia Fidei*," in *Justification by Faith, Lutherans and Catholics in Dialogue VII*, edited by H. George Anderson, T. Austin Murphy, and Joseph A. Burgess (Augsburg, 1985), 172-184.

Missouri's representative in ecumenical dialogues and international conferences, such as the World Council of Churches, the Lutheran World Federation, USA Lutheran-Roman Catholic Dialogue, Lutheran-Episcopal Dialogue, and many others. He was a virtual globe trotter representing both his Church and the Crossings Community in many countries in Europe, Africa, Asia, and South America. Bertram was a member of numerous academic societies such as the American Academy of Religion, Society for Reformation Research, Science and Theology Seminar, American Society of Christian Ethics, and others.

Bertram was a prolific writer. His bibliography, too long to be listed here, was composed by one of his students, Steven C. Kuhl, "Bibliography of Robert W. Bertram, *Currents in Theology and Mission,* 14, No. 2 (April, 1987), 140-146. Bertram was a dearly beloved mentor for hundreds of students whom he inspired by his Socratic-like way of teaching. It is fitting to end this tribute to a great Lutheran theologian of the twentieth century with a quotation from a book written by one of his students. "In my final year at seminary, I took two courses with theologian Robert Bertram: one entire course on Luther's interpretation of Galatians, the 'magna carta of Christian freedom,' and the other on the philosophy of history, in which Marxist notions of the future were brought into dialogue with Christian hope. Bertram was as orthodox as they come, but, unlike my prep school teachers, he had a big picture of the world. He knew how to turn every statement of doctrinal truth into a declaration of power that did not exclude those who had come on other boats. He held the tradition up to the light, like a jeweler who patiently turns a stone until it yields its greatest brilliance, and he did it with low-key Socratic presence. By the time one of Bertram's classes ended, we were often passionate about truths we hadn't even suspected at its beginning."[25]

---

25. Richard Lischer, *Open Secrets: A Spiritual Journey through a Country Church* (Doubleday, 2001), 38.

3. Schroeder's Teaching Ministry

Edward H. Schroeder was co-founder with Robert Bertram of the Crossings Community. After Christ Seminary-Seminex left St. Louis and merged with the Lutheran School of Theology at Chicago, Schroeder chose to remain in St. Louis to continue his teaching ministry with the Crossings Community. But he did not confine his teaching to his Crossings students. His ministry became a missionary venture to bring the Lutheran theology of Law and Gospel to many corners of the world. He lectured at Lutheran Seminaries in Adelaide, Australia, Addis Ababa, Ethiopia, Aarhus, Denmark, as well as at the United Seminary in Singapore. He was a passionate preacher of the gospel of Christ and a prolific author of hundreds of journal articles published in the *Cresset, Concordia Theological Monthly, Word and World, Lutheran Forum, Dialog- A Journal of Theology, Currents in Theology and Mission, Missiology,* and many others. Like his colleague Bertram he was conscientiously orthodox by confessional Lutheran standards, although he was one of the professors at Concordia Seminary in St. Louis whom President Jacob Preus and his cronies accused of teaching heresy. Schroeder's bibliography exceeds six hundred titles, which includes sermons, book reviews, syllabi, and articles. Like Bertram he never wrote a book of dogmatics, nevertheless dogmatics and ethics formed the contents of his prolific authorship. His unpublished doctoral dissertation (for Hamburg University) is entitled "The Relationship Between Dogmatics and Ethics in the Thought of Elert, Barth, and Troeltsch." Elert's Law/Gospel theology made an enormous and life-long impact on Schroeder's theology, and became the chief resource of the Crossings Method, to read Scripture and examine daily life through the prism of Law and Gospel.

I cannot end this presentation on the confessional Lutheran theology of Robert Bertram and Edward Schroeder without commenting on a point of difference between us that became public knowledge in my memoirs entitled, *Because of Christ.*

Memoirs of a Lutheran Theologian. Seldom, perhaps never, has a well-published Lutheran dogmatician ended his or her career without getting at some time embroiled in controversy. I wrote in my memoirs, "The idea of a noncontroversial theology is an oxymoron."[26] Both Bertram and Schroeder were deeply involved in the controversy that erupted at Concordia Seminary in St. Louis that led to a schism. After the AELC merged with the ELCA and ten theologians from Christ Seminary-Seminex joined the faculty of the Lutheran School of Theology at Chicago, I noticed a not so gradual shift leftward in matters of theology and policy. The editors of three Lutheran journals, *dialog, A Journal of Theology, Lutheran Quarterly*, and *Lutheran Forum* met in Chicago to plan two theological conferences held at St. Olaf College announced as "A Call to Faithfulness," held in 1990 and 1992. Over a thousand concerned Lutheran clergy and laity attended. The speakers represented the traditional differences among Lutherans on ecclesiology and ecumenism, but they agreed on what was happening in and to the ELCA. This is what I wrote about what the speakers said: "They were united in opposing the main trends in the ELCA, its revisionism bearing on Christology and the Trinity, its abandonment of world missions and evangelization, its exchange of the mark of catholicity as a mark of the church for inclusivity, its confusing of law and gospel (and of the two kingdoms) in social statements, its failure to discipline clergy breaking the rules, and its treatment of the gospel as a marketing product. That is only a partial list."[27]

None of those accusatory generalizations apply directly to Bertram and Schroeder. What did surface was their putative connection with the rise of rampant antinomianism within the ELCA, having to do with their rejection, following Elert, of the third use of the law. What is the third use of the law? Article VI of the "Formula of Concord" declares: "We believe, teach, and

---

26. Carl E. Braaten, *Because of Christ. Memoirs of a Lutheran Theologian* (Eerdmans, 2010), 58.
27. Carl E. Braaten, *Because of Christ*, 131.

confess that the preaching of the law is to be diligently applied not only to unbelievers and the impenitent but also to people who are genuinely believing, truly converted, regenerated, and justified through faith."[28] The Formula acknowledges that "a controversy has arisen among a few theologians concerning the third and last function of the law." That controversy persists until this day, and the theologians we are covering in this treatise are not in accord. That would not in itself be much of a problem, except that they also disagree as to whether it opens the door to antinomianism. Article V of the "Formula of Concord" explicitly states: "Therefore we explicitly condemn the Antinomians or nomoclasts who cast the preaching of the law out of the churches and would have us criticize sin and teach contrition and sorrow not from the law but solely from the Gospel."[29] Antinomianism appeared early in Lutheranism when two of Luther's disciples, Johan Agricola and Nicholaus von Amsdorf, taught that the Old Testament law (e. g., the Ten Commandments) no longer applies to believers who live under the New Testament promise of the gospel. Antinomianism is the mother of "Situation Ethics," the teaching that rules and regulations cannot be formulated in advance to guide ethical decisions and moral actions.

Edward Schroeder reviewed many books written by his fellow Lutheran theologians. He wrote a lengthy review of William Lazareth's *magnum opus*, *Christians in Society: Luther, the Bible and Social Ethics*,[30] the ripe fruit of decades of teaching and writing on the subject. The review is very laudatory of Lazareth's biblical scholarship and his knowledge of Luther's works, but he takes issue at one revealing point. Lazareth uses the law to explain how Christians are to make moral decisions, whereas Schroeder appeals solely to the gospel to motivate Christians to be socially responsible actors. Is this all much ado about nothing,

---

28. Formula of Concord, Epitome, 2.

29. Formula of Concord, Solid Declaration, 561.

30. https://crossings.org/a-review-of-William-Lazareths-Christians-in-society-Luther-the-Bible-and-Social-Ethics/

a lot of sophistry too subtle for ordinary saints to grasp? When I studied and memorized Luther's *Small Catechism*, I took every word of his explanations of the Ten Commandments to heart, and I was led to believe by the Catechism that those words were meant to be taken literally by every believer in Christ and member of his Church.

Rev. Dr. Gerhard O. Forde was born September 10, 1927 in Pope County, Minnesota and died August 9, 2005 in St. Paul. He received his B.A. degree from Luther College in 1950 and attended the University of Wisconsin in Madison for one year. He received an M.Div. from Luther Seminary in 1955. He earned a Th.D. from Harvard Divinity School in 1967. Forde also studied at the University of Tübingen and was the Lutheran Tutor at Mansfield College, Oxford University, 1968-70. He also spent sabbatical years of study at Harvard (1972-73), Strasbourg (1979-80), and at St. John's University Institute for Ecumenical and Cultural Research, Collegeville, Minnesota (1988). Forde began his teaching career at St. Olaf College as instructor of religion in 1955-56. He joined the faculty of Luther Seminary as a lecturer in church history in 1959-61. He taught at his alma mater Luther College as an assistant professor of religion in 1961-63, after which he returned to Luther Seminary where he taught as a professor of systematic theology until his retirement in 1998. Gerhard Forde is an ordained minister in the Evangelical Lutheran Church in America. He served for many years as a Lutheran representative on the USA Lutherans and Catholics in Dialogue.

Two

Gerhard O. Forde

Radical Lutheranism

Gerhard Forde (1927-2005) was best known among his peers for his single-minded concentration on the major theme of Lutheran theology — justification by faith alone (*sola fide*) and all its corollaries, such as the proper distinction between law and gospel, *simul justus et peccator*, the bondage of the will, the two kingdoms, *satis est*, theology of the cross (*theologia crucis*), and the like. Gerhard Forde and Robert Jenson began a life-long friendship when they were students at Luther College and that continued as seminarians at Luther Seminary in the early 1950s. Both were known by their fellow students for their loyalty to *gnesio-Lutheranism*, an anti-Pietist theological tradition Luther College was known to represent. A half century later Jenson wrote a little book entitled, *Lutheran Slogans. Use and Abuse* (American Lutheran Publicity Bureau, 2011). The slogans were: Justification by Faith *Apart from Works*, The Priesthood of All Believers, The Proper Distinction of Law and Gospel, *Theologia Crucis, Sola Gratia, Finitum Capax Infiniti, Sola Scriptura, Simul Justus et Peccator*. For Gerhard Forde these are not mere slogans; they are the vehicles that carry the truths of Luther's reformation to our time five hundred years later. Forde's use of these slogans was indeed radical, according to his own self-understanding. Anticipating the formation of the Evangelical Lutheran Church in America in 1988, Forde wrote an article entitled "Radical Lutheranism," in which he dealt with the question as to what kind of Lutheranism should we in this new church aim to be. He asked, "Shall we be conservative, liberal, confessional, orthodox, charismatic, neo-pentecostal, fundamentalist, or 'evangelical' (perhaps 'fundagelical,' as someone recently put it)?"[31] His answer to this question was crisp and clear: "My thesis is that Lutherans, to be true to their identity, yes, even to reclaim their identity, or rather to be reclaimed by it, should become even more radical proponents of the tradition that gave them birth and has brought them thus far. The crisis in identity indicates the necessity for staking out some turf on the ecclesiastical map. What shall we be? Let us be radicals; not conservatives or liberals, fundagelicals or charismatics... but radicals: radical preachers and practitioners of the gospel of justification by faith without the deeds of the law.... If Lutheranism is to recover a sense of its identity and mission today, it must begin to consider what it means to preach the gospel in radical fashion.... Virtually all the failures and shortcomings of Lutheranism can be seen in the hesitancy to proclaim the gospel in uncompromising, unconditional fashion, to proclaim as though we were in the business of summoning the dead to life, calling new beings into existence.... Either the gospel must be preached in radical fashion, or it is best left alone altogether.... A radical Lutheranism would be one that regains the courage and the nerve to preach the gospel unconditionally"[32]

1. The Bondage of the Will

Radical Lutheranism intends to get to the root (the *radix*) of the identity crisis that ails Lutherans not only in America but in Europe and around the world. The radical gospel of justification by faith without the works of the law calls for an anthropology that fits. Luther provided such an anthropology in his controversy with Erasmus. Luther affirmed the bondage of the will

---

31. Gerhard Forde, "Radical Lutheranism," in *A More Radical Gospel*, eds. Mark C. Mattes and Steven D. Paulson (Eerdmans, 2004), 4.

32. Gerhard Forde, "Radical Lutheranism," *A More Radical Gospel*, 7, 13, 15.

over against Erasmus' defense of free will.[33] Forde agreed with the Luther-interpretation of Hans Joachim Iwand who asserted that the Pauline-Lutheran radical gospel cannot tolerate "the slightest hint of free choice."[34] Iwand maintained that Lutheranism has suffered by its ambivalence on Luther's idea of the enslaved will. Then Iwand wrote: "The doctrine of justification was retained but it was combined with an anthropology which had its entire pathos in a faith in the freedom of the will.... Humanism from Melanchthon to Ritschl indeed permits justification to occur even *sola fide*, but nevertheless breaks off the spearhead by which it would itself be mortally wounded, the bondage of the will."[35]

Gerhard Forde started writing a book on Luther's *Bondage of the Will (De Servo Arbitrio)* when he was doing his doctoral studies at Harvard Divinity School. He did not finish the manuscript until the very end of his teaching career at Luther Seminary, indicating that it was a linch-pin in his understanding of the radical gospel from which he never wavered. Steven Paulson was one of Forde's students who became his colleague teaching systematic theology at the same seminary. He wrote in memory of Forde that he was not only his teacher and colleague but his mentor putting him on the same track. Paulson wrote: "I once asked him if he would ever consider contributing to the *Christian Century* series, 'How I Changed My Mind,' to which Dr. Forde said, 'But I never did.' And that is true. He never veered or blinked when it came to the question of the gospel."[36]

I was one of Forde's classmates at Luther Seminary, graduating in 1955, and after that we were both doctoral students at Harvard Divinity School. I can vouch for the truth of

---

33. Martin Luther, *The Bondage of the Will*, trans. J. I. Packer and O. R. Johnson (Fleming H. Revell, 1957).

34. Gerhard Forde, "Radical Lutheranism," *A More Radical Gospel*, 11.

35. Quoted by Gerhard Forde, "Radical Lutheranism," *A More Radical Gospel*, 11.

36. Marianna Forde, *Gerhard O. Forde, A Life* (Lutheran University Press, 2014), 171-172.

what Steven Paulson wrote in memory of Forde. His friends called him "Bish;" why this nickname I never knew. What I did know and never had any reason to doubt, Forde was from beginning to end the most radical Lutheran I ever came to know. A recent book has been published with the title, *Radical Lutheran/Lutheran Radicals*, ed. Jason A. Mahn, with Contributors Jacqueline Bussie, Lori Brandt Hale, Carl S. Hughes, and Samuel Torvend (Wipf and Stock, 2017). Forde is honored for calling Lutherans to be radical, radically committed to the core principles of Luther's gospel-centered theology. Forde was a "radical Lutheran" as such. However, judged by the theological orientation of these younger scholars who teach at various Lutheran universities, Forde was a radical Lutheran, but he was not a Lutheran radical. He did not get — for him — sidetracked into social, political, economic, and ecological problems that worried many of his contemporaries. Ethics is the discipline that deals with problems such as racial injustice, economic disparity, nuclear threat, and climate change, all of which call for radical action on the part of Christians, Churches, educational institutions, political organizations, and all people of good will. Christian ethics is the discipline that seeks to answer the question what we as believers in Christ and members of his body are to do in the real world beyond the walls of our church.

Forde was once invited to give an address on Luther's ethics. In his introduction he opined, "I tried to beg off. My reputation (which I covet and guard zealously) among friend and foe is that I am weak on sanctification. When questioned about this, I respond that since I have to work so hard to get people to believe in justification, I have no time to bother with sanctification!"[37] He continued, "Put audaciously, perhaps even irresponsibly, one might announce that the problem is that Luther does not have any ethics! ... Luther was not interested in ethics. He was concerned first and foremost about the eternal salvation of

---

37. Gerhard Forde, "Luther's Ethics," *A More Radical Gospel*, 137.

lost sinners. And ethics, at least as he knew it, hindered more than helped in that concern. One is saved by faith and not by works — and dare we say it? — not by ethics?"[38] Forde feared that ethics, which deals with penultimate concerns, things that matter in this world (*coram mundo*) for good or ill, would deflect from the one thing that matters of ultimate concern, how one stands before God (*coram deo*), which is a matter of life or death, of one's eternal destiny. Expressing this worry, Forde stated, "Ethics, one might say, becomes the way of salvation.... Everything, it seems, especially in the church, has to be justified before the bar of ethics."[39]

Forde's fear of good works was so extreme that it produced a jaundiced view of ethics. Once he was given a button that said, "Weak on sanctification," and he was proud to wear it. Having warned about the danger of trusting in good works normed by ethical standards, Forde then puts the best construction on what Luther had to contribute to ethics. Luther's treatise on "The Freedom of the Christian" states that "good works do not make a person good." Forde transposes that to mean that "ethical deeds do not make a person ethical."[40] The discipline of ethics entails an understanding of law and justice. The Lutheran tradition has endured endless controversy on the doctrine of the law. Forde rejects the traditional Lutheran affirmation of a "third use of the law," not only in apparent opposition to the "Formula of Concord," but also to the subsequent dogmaticians of Lutheran Orthodoxy and Pietism. Some modern Luther-scholars contend that Luther taught only two uses of the law, the political use, administered by civil authorities, that restrains evil and punishes evil doers and the theological use that convicts people of their sins, delivers them from the wrath of God, and drives them to Christ the Savior. The third use of the law is addressed to born-

---

38. Gerhard Forde, "Luther's Ethics," 138.
39. Gerhard Forde, "Luther's Ethics," 139, 144.
40. Gerhard Forde, "Luther's Ethics," 141.

again Christians who, in spite of their faith active in love, still need the encouragement of the law to do works of mercy. Some zealous early followers of Luther, Johann Agricola and Nikolaus von Amsdorf, were accused of antinomianism, of being against the law, even teaching that doing good works impedes salvation. Luther wrote a number of disputations against the antinomians, leaving the question open among Luther scholars as to whether he would agree with those who reject the law's usefulness to Christians who delight in hearing and obeying the commandments of God. Forde puts great store on the phrase *"lex semper acusat."* According to a plain reading of Luther's Catechisms, it would be mistaken to believe that the only purpose of the law is to accuse people, to make them feel guilty and doomed with fear of God's wrath. Writing to Christians Luther concludes his explanation of the Ten Commandments with this assurance: "God promises grace and every blessing to all who keep them. We should therefore love him, trust in him, and cheerfully do what he has commanded."[41]

Forde does teach that, according to Luther, Christians do good works, but they ought not trust they'll have any worth for salvation. Having said good works do not make a person good, turn the coin over and you read, "A good person does good works," echoing Matthew 7:17: "Every good tree bears good fruit, but the bad tree bears bad fruit." Taken literally this means that a believer in Christ will do good works spontaneously, period, no ifs, ands, or buts about it. A good tree has no choice in the matter; it will bear good fruit. Persons saved by the gospel of justification by faith alone on account of Christ will automatically do good, not for their own good, but for the good of others, especially those most in need. Pastors who serve congregations, preaching the gospel with all their might, would like to believe that and see evidence of that in their parishioners. But that's not all they do; they teach the Catechism with all

---

41. Martin Luther, "Small Catechism," *The Book of Concord*, Tappert Edition, 344.

the powers of persuasion at their command. And at the end of their ministry they are often tempted to wonder if any of that did any good. The problem is that human beings are not trees.

Be that as it may, whether good works done by Christians are as spontaneous as fruit falling from a tree, Forde invokes Luther's doctrine of the two kingdoms (realms or regiments) to further explicate how Luther expresses his thoughts on ethics. Perhaps at this point it should be noted that when Forde presents Luther's thought on any particular topic, whether on justification by faith alone or on the two kingdoms, readers should understand that Forde intends it as his own view on the subject at hand. This raises two hermeneutical questions. First, is Forde's interpretation of Luther supported by the majority of contemporary Luther-scholars? I am not a Luther-scholar, but Forde does cite some reputable Luther-scholars to support his interpretation, among them, Leif Grane,[42] Hans J. Iwand,[43] Wilhelm Dantine,[44] Wilfried Joest,[45] Lauri Haikola,[46] and Gustaf Wingren,[47] to name a few. A second and even more important question is whether Forde's Luther-interpretation can count on support from contemporary biblical scholars. Like other Lutheran dogmaticians Forde affirms the traditional Lutheran slogan, *sola scriptura*. But how does that work in an age when the academy of biblical scholars is in complete disarray? Anyone who attends the annual conference of the

---

42. Leif Grane, *Modus Loquendi Theologicus: Luthers Kampf um die Erneuerung der Theologie* (1515-1518), trans. E. Groetzinger (Leiden: E. J. Brill, 1975).

43. Hans J. Iwand, *"Um den Rechten Glauben," Gesammelte Aufsätze*, ed. K. G. Steck (Munich: Chr. Kaiser Verlag, 1959).

44. Wilhelm Dantine, *Justification of the Ungodly*, trans. Eric and Ruth Gritsch (St. Louis: Concordia, 1969).

45. Wilfried Joest, *Gesetz und Freiheit*, 2nd ed. (Göttingen: Vandenhoek und Ruprecht, 1956).

46. See Gerhard Forde, *The Law-Gospel Debate* (Minneapolis: Augsburg, 1969), 176.

47. Gustaf Wingren, *Creation and Law*, trans, Ross Mackenzie (Fortress Press, 1961).

Society of Biblical Literature soon learns that its 8000 members agree on virtually nothing. This means that Forde is in the same boat as his fellow dogmaticians; lacking any consensus from the guild of biblical scholars, all are required to do their own exegesis. Karl Barth led the way in demonstrating that theological exegesis of the Bible cannot rely on the cacophony produced by the always conflicting results of historical-scientific criticism.

Robert Jenson and I as co-editors of the two volume work of *Christian Dogmatics* invited Gerhard Forde to contribute two of the twelve *loci*. The first *one* was on "The Work of Christ," and the second on "The Christian Life." These chapters gave thousands of seminarians a good dose of vintage Forde, in my estimation the most creative output of Forde's prolific authorship. The doctrine of the atonement is the place in dogmatics that deals with the salvation God wrought for the world though the death and resurrection of Jesus of Nazareth. In the introduction to his treatment of the doctrine of the atonement Forde rightly states: "There is no official dogma of the work of Christ — not in the sense in which one could speak of the dogmas of the Trinity, or the person of Christ, or even of justification in the churches of the Reformation."[48] The greatest theological minds in church history have addressed the twofold question, *Cur Deus Homo?*, why did God become Man, and why then did Jesus, the Son of God, have to be crucified on a bloody cross to bring about the salvation of the world and all humankind? What was God up to? Forde puts the question this way: "Does God in Jesus do it for us, or does Jesus do it for God on our behalf? Is God propitiated, satisfied, or in some way altered by the event? Does God need 'Christ's work' to become merciful? Or does God act on us through the event, changing us or the situation in which we find ourselves? Does God need the cross, or do we? Who

48. Gerhard Forde, "The Work of Christ," *Christian Dogmatics*, eds. Carl E. Braaten and Robert W. Jenson (Fortress Press, 1984), 5.

is the real obstacle to reconciliation? God? Humans? Or some others —demons, perhaps?"[49]

Such questions are the grist for theologians who have created theories of the atonement, to answer the question, "Why did Jesus have to die on the cross?" The history of the Christian tradition is by no means unanimous in answering the question. Three or four theories, and maybe more to come, have interpreted the relevant Scriptural passages in different ways. Forde begins his treatment of the atonement by quoting a major passage written by the apostle Paul:

> *Therefore, if any one is in Christ, he is a new creation; the old has passed away, behold, the new has come. All this is from God, who through Christ reconciled us to himself and gave us the ministry of reconciliation; that is, in Christ God was reconciling the world to himself, not counting their trespasses against them, and entrusting to us the message of reconciliation. So we are ambassadors for Christ, God making his appeal through us. We beseech you on behalf of Christ, be reconciled to God. For our sake he made him to be sin who knew no sin, so that in him we might become the righteousness of God.* (II Cor. 5:17-21)

2. Theories of the Atonement

Forde discusses the various theories of the atonement, and he treats them as just that, theories. Forde is not a friend of speculative theories; each one fails to do justice to the facts on the ground, what he calls the "brute facts." After critiquing each of the theories, he entitled his own view, "Atonement as Actual Event." The ancient church contributed two scenarios in reflecting on the significance of Christ's life, death, and resurrection. Origen of Alexandria (184-253), for example, taught that the death of Christ was a ransom God paid to the Devil to free the

---

49. Gerhard Forde, "The Work of Christ," 6.

fallen descendants of Adam and Eve from his clutch. God tricked the Devil into accepting Christ's death as a ransom, since the Devil did not know that death could not defeat Christ. When the Devil accepted the deal, justice was supposedly satisfied and God was able to free sinners from Satan's dominion. The recapitulation theory of the atonement was formulated by Irenaeus of Lyons (130-202), which he based on a biblical passage (Ephesians 1:10) that says that in the fulness of time God purposed to sum up all things in Christ, things in heaven and things on earth. "Recapitulate" was the Latin translation of the Greek word for "sum up." In this view Christ is the new Adam who succeeds where Adam failed. Adam's disobedience is undone by Christ's obedience. Forde follows Anselm in regarding both the idea of ransom and recapitulation as inadequate to answer the question why Jesus had to die on the cross.

> Anselm dismisses both the theory of recapitulation and the idea of ransom paid to the devil as insufficient (though not wrong). A recapitulation theology, working with contrapuntal pictures has aesthetic appeal but does not give substantial reasons for the cross.... Talk about the deception and defeat of Satan is equally insufficient, because it does not explain why the Almighty had to go to such trouble to defeat enemies. Could not God simply have crushed Satan and released the captives by divine decree?[50]

Forde's treatment of the atonement has been severely criticized by conservative Evangelicals, including Missouri Synod Lutheran theologians, for his criticism (rejection?) of the theory formulated by Anselm of Canterbury (1033-1109), known as the Latin view, also called the satisfaction or penal theory of the atonement. Anselm's view has been elevated virtually to the status of church dogma by Roman Catholics and biblically inerrant truth by Conservative Evangelical Protestants. The doc-

---

50. Gerhard Forde, "The Work of Christ," 21.

trine of the atonement was not a factor in Luther's controversy with Rome, and there is no article on the atonement as such in the entire Lutheran *Book of Concord*. Anselm's basic idea is that a sacrifice is necessary as a payment to satisfy God's justice. Because human beings are sinners, they are unable to meet the demands of God's law and so they are deeply in debt to him. Reconciliation with God requires that the debt must be paid to make things fair and square measured by the law of justice. Anselm's question was, *Cur Deus Homo?*" God became incarnate in Jesus so that as a perfect sinless human being he could make a sufficient payment to satisfy God's honor. He could offer himself as a vicarious substitute to offset the sins of humanity.

Forde calls into question many of the assumptions inherent in Anselm's view of the sacrificial death of Jesus. The major problem is that the legal order of justice functions as the bedrock assumption of Anselm's theory, placing the unconditional love and mercy of God in a subordinate position. In Forde's words:

> Anselm's doctrine represents an acute juridicizing of Christ's work — some call it Latinizing. To give the actual history rational necessity, Anselm is driven to call on ideas from the realm of law and justice. The relationship between God and God's creatures comes to be understood in terms of legal order.... The more serious problems with Anselm's doctrine are theological rather than legal. The most persistent one is the question of justice versus mercy and its consequences for the doctrine of God. The attempt to prove the necessity of satisfaction leads to the idea that mercy can be exercised only when the demands of justice have been fulfilled. Why cannot God, the Almighty, simply forgive? Indeed, we are enjoined to forgive our debtors, why cannot God?[51]

---

51. Gerhard Forde, "The Work of Christ," 22, 23.

Forde at this point is reiterating Peter Abelard's (1079-1142) criticism of Anselm's theory. "Abelard did not see why justice must be satisfied before God can be merciful. Did not Jesus forgive before his death? ... Abelard shows clearly how the vicarious satisfaction doctrine recoils on God. It restricts the freedom of God and leads to a gruesome and forbidding picture of the deity."[52] But what Abelard put in its place did not pass muster for Forde either. Abelard is famous for his moral influence or moral exemplar theory. Its basic idea is that Jesus' entire life is an inspiring demonstration of God's love. Sinners are moved by Jesus' example and become more loving like him. Forde faults the moral influence view because it is merely subjective, a change in attitude and devotion inside of us. It does not answer the question, "But why did God become man and end up dead on a cross? "It would seem, God sent his Son to a shameful and painful death to provide an example powerful enough to entice us to be reconciled to him as a God of mercy and charity.... How can God possibly be 'justified' in sending his Son into this world to be cruelly murdered at our hands just to provide an example of what everybody knew anyway? If the cross does not accomplish anything new, is not the price too great? Is not a God who would do such a thing be fully as thoughtless and cruel as the God of vicarious satisfaction?"[53]

Next Forde takes up a more recent attempt to construct a theory of the atonement, Gustaf Aulén's publication entitled, *Christus Victor*. Aulén claims that the *Christus Victor* motif is the classical view, with its origin in the New Testament and then further developed by the church fathers of the first five centuries. It was eclipsed by Anselm's satisfaction view in the twelfth century and then rediscovered by Martin Luther in the sixteenth century. Its basic idea is that in Christ God won a victory over the demonic forces that kept people in bondage. The *locus classicus* is what the apostle Paul wrote: "God was in Christ reconciling

52. Gerhard Forde, "The Work of Christ," 23-24.
53. Gerhard Forde, "The Work of Christ," 87.

the world unto himself" (2 Cor. 5:19). In this view God is the reconciler and the reconciled. In Christ God has brought about an objective change in the human situation. God has won a victory over the powers of evil hostile to his will and oppressive of humanity, such as sin, guilt, death, and the devil. That's the gist of the matter, a view that Forde finds preferable to Anselm's satisfaction theory and Abelard's moral influence theory.

Yet, Aulén's *Christus Victor* view, according to Forde, does not succeed in answering Anselm's question, *Cur Deus Homo*? "The troublesome dogmatic question for the victory motif is the one we have been encountering all along: wherein lies the necessity for Christ's death and resurrection? ... If defeat of demonic powers is all that is necessary, why could not the Almighty God have done it some other way? Why subject the Son to such torture?"[54] Forde follows that up with a second caveat. "It is questionable whether the motif in its mythological form can make sustained appeal to the modern mind. The 'cosmic-dualistic battle' tends to appear extraneous to us.... A way must be found to assert the reality of the victory that retains its cosmic scope and still makes it concrete and viable existentially."[55]

Forde prepares the way for his own construction of the doctrine of the atonement by acknowledging the positive contributions made by Friedrich Schleiermacher, Albrecht Ritschl, P. T. Forsyth, and Emil Brunner, though not without some trenchant criticisms of each of them. Forde appreciates their emphasis on the triumph of divine love and their focus on the concrete historical actuality of the life and death of Jesus. A problem with all of them, however, is that their views of the atonement seem to work without taking into account the resurrection. The table is now set for Forde to present his own view of the atonement, that unsurprisingly begins with a chapter on "Luther's Theology of the Cross." Theology of the cross teaches that atonement occurs when

---

54. Gerhard Forde, "The Work of Christ," 37-38.
55. Gerhard Forde, "The Work of Christ," 40.

God in Christ overcomes our human predicament described as living under his wrath and oppressed by the law, sin, death, and the devil. "God is satisfied, placated, when his move toward us issues in faith. A 'happy exchange' takes place: Jesus takes our sinful nature and gives us his righteous and immortal life."[56]

The sacrificial death of Christ is the "actual event" by which God vindicates his unconditional love and mercy in the act of forgiving sinners and through the creation of faith. "Christ's work, therefore, 'satisfies' the wrath of God, because it alone creates believers, new beings who are no longer under wrath. Christ actualizes the will of God to have mercy unconditionally in the concrete and thereby 'placates' God."[57] Forde concludes his view of the atonement by summing up what it means in relation to the other theories of the atonement. "Atonement conceived as an actual event thus does justice to the concerns of all the various theories. It is objective; it comes from without entirely. God's wrath is satisfied in the sense that God's resolve to have mercy breaks through the abstractions, the bondage in which we are implicated, to create faith. Just so, it is also intensely 'subjective.' When faith is created, a new subject emerges, the historical being who, as a member of the body of Christ, the crucified and resurrected one, has become an historical being who waits, follows, and hopes. What Schleiermacher and Ritschl wanted can be seen to have come to fruition. The divine love establishes an actual historical community. But this is the body of believers who have died and who look to the resurrection, who bear that stamp, who follow Christ, not a community of religious or moral idealists. Actual atonement is also the divine victory. The victory, however, is not abstract and mythological. Sin, death, the law, the devil— all the powers — are defeated in us. The new covenant is established."[58]

---

56. Gerhard Forde, "The Work of Christ," 47.

57. Gerhard Forde, "Caught in the Act: Reflections on the Work of Christ, *A More Radical Gospel*, 97.

58. Gerhard Forde, "The Work of Christ," 98.

3. The Christian Life: Justification by Faith

Forde was the author of a second dogmatic locus on "The Christian Life" in the two volumes of *Christian Dogmatics* referred to above. All four chapters are an extended exposition and defense of the Lutheran doctrine of justification by faith alone. More attention is given to justification as the foundation of the Christian life than to sanctification as its unfolding in daily life, in their Christian calling as family members, citizens of a nation, and members of the church. Actually, the doctrine of sanctification is absorbed into justification. For Forde it does not merit any distinctive treatment of its own since, as noted above, he has no use for the third use of the law. "*Lex temper accusat*" is the mantra which holds steady throughout. The law cannot have any positive role to play in guiding or instructing Christian behavior. Admittedly, Forde is right to insist that the law is not and never can be a way of salvation. Yet, that does not necessarily nullify the role of the law in guiding and instructing Christian behavior, or there would have been no point for Luther to write his *Small* and *Large Catechisms*, whose purpose was not evangelism but pedagogy.

Forde strongly argues for a radically "forensic" concept of justification, which he says is the only way to be true to Luther's teaching, even though scholars cannot find that Luther ever used the word. Melanchthon used the word forensic in a legal sense to acquit a guilty person and to declare him righteous, on account of the righteousness of another, namely Christ, attributed to that person by faith. The righteousness of Christ is imputed in such a way that a person becomes totally righteous while simultaneously remaining totally sinful. This brings into play Luther's important idea of *simul iustus et peccator*. God's imputation declares sinners righteous while they are still sinners. This is an idea that seems to contradict Thomas Aquinas' understanding of justification as a process that starts with an infusion of grace to move the will toward God in faith, away from sin, resulting in the remission of guilt and the forgiveness of sins. It is conceived as a process;

persons become more righteous as they become less sinful, rather than totally both at the same time. This is what Forde writes: "For the reformers, justification is 'solely' a divine act. It is a divine judgment. It is an imputation. It is unconditional. All legal and moral schemes are shattered. Such justification comes neither at the beginning nor at the end of a movement; rather, it establishes an entirely new situation. Since righteousness comes by imputation only, it is absolutely not a movement on our part.... The judgment can be heard and grasped only by faith. Indeed, the judgment creates and calls forth faith that hears and grasps it.... Imputed righteousness as a divine act brings with it the *simul justus et peccator* (simultaneously justified and a sinner) as a simultaneity of total states."[59]

4. Theology Is For Proclamation

Theology Is For Proclamation is one of Gerhard Forde's most popular books that clearly discloses the beating heart of his career as a systematic theologian. In the Preface of this book Forde writes:

> "The thesis of this book is straightforward. Systematic theology, whatever else it might be for, has to be for proclamation. Not, heaven forbid, that systematic theology is what is to be proclaimed! That, I contend, is precisely one of the more persistent misadventures. Systematic theology, whether good or bad, gets substituted for and displaces proclamation. I contend here that systematic theology, while itself not to be confused with proclamation, should be the kind of thinking that advances, fosters, and drives to proper proclamation of the gospel of Jesus Christ; it should be a systematic reflection that promotes the speaking of the promise. Such a systematic theology should be for proclamation in a double sense; it insists on proclamation; and it

---

59. Gerhard Forde, "The Christian Life," 407.

recognizes such insistence to be its ultimate purpose. That is, if systematic theology is done properly it will leave its practitioners in a position where they can, in order to complete their own task, do no other than proclaim."[60]

After Forde died, Luther Seminary created a Memory Book to which colleagues and students wrote expressions of gratitude for his life and teaching. James Nestingen wrote: "His classes were his form of evangelism. The goal was always, relentlessly, to declare the justifying word as clearly as possible.... Over and over again, students described what happened as a conversion, and that is what it was."[61] Steven Paulson wrote this in his appreciation: "Dr. Forde taught me the gospel. One would think he would not have had to do that, since I grew up Lutheran and went to school at a Lutheran college, but through it all I did not know the gospel. No doubt some of that ignorance was age, experience, and personal cussedness but the testimonies are endless from students who tell the same story; they did not hear the gospel of Jesus Christ until Gerhard Forde put it in their ears.... Once you find such a preacher and teacher, as I did, you don't ever let go. Gerhard taught me the gospel, and I am only one among thousands, even tens of thousands."[62]

5. *Satis Est* Ecumenism

Gerhard Forde served as a participant in the USA Lutheran-Roman Catholic Dialogues for over twenty years. The dialogues between churches were initiated after the Second Vatican Council. Lutherans engaged in such bi-lateral dialogues both at the international and the national levels. The ostensible purpose of the dialogues was to achieve doctrinal consensus on the historic

60. Gerhard Forde, *Theology is for Proclamation* (Fortress, 1990), vii.
61. Marianna Forde, *Gerhard O. Forde: A Life*, 167.
62. Marianna Forde, *Gerhard O. Forde: A Life*, 175, 179.

church-dividing issues since the Reformation. The consensus was deemed essential in order to pave the way for churches to bring about "full communion" and possibly even "visible unity." Most theologians engaged in ecumenical dialogues knew that to attain such goals would not be easy, perhaps even out of reach, yet the investments of time, money, and labor are still worth doing. Indeed, they have already brought about a new ecumenical situation in which churches no longer condemn each other but relate to each other as sisters and brothers in Christ.

From Forde's point of view the purpose of the dialogues is for churches to bring their respective theological and ecclesial gifts to the ecumenical round table, and not to compromise what they truly believe and confess in order to reach a lukewarm consensus that is soon forgotten. Rather uncharacteristically for a self-avowed confessional Lutheran, Forde wrote: "Basically, I have come to reject the principle of making exhaustive agreement in doctrine and polity a condition for intercommunion. From reading Luther and the Reformers, that is a quite un-Lutheran idea. Indeed, in most instances of churches confessing the triune God, there exists enough common ground for us to declare ourselves to be in the fellowship that already exists. This is especially true in those instances where we have had considerable dialogue and have arrived at mutual understandings. Certainly this is the case in light of the Lutheran-Reformed dialogue and the Lutheran/Roman Catholic dialogue.[63] That goes far to explain why Forde sees no point in engaging in dialogue to achieve church unity and intercommunion. He appeals to the "*satis est*" principle in Article VII of the *Augsburg Confession*. "Our churches also teach that the one holy church is to continue forever. The church is the assembly of saints in which the Gospel is taught purely and the sacraments are administered rightly. For the true unity of the church it is enough (*satis est*) to agree

---

63. Gerhard Forde, "Lutheran Ecumenism: With Whom and How Much?" *A More Radical Gospel*, 172.

concerned the teaching of the Gospel and the administration of the sacraments." Church unity that matters already exists — even though the institutional churches are governed in different ways — that is, wherever the gospel of Jesus Christ is preached and the sacraments are delivered. And wherever the gospel is not preached and the sacraments are not given, there can be no church unity worth anything.

The problem remains, however, that the differently organized churches have lived their separate lives prior to the ecumenical movement, often doubting whether other churches do in fact preach the same gospel and administer the same sacraments according to the Scriptures. The ecumenical aim of the dialogues has been to remove such doubts where they do exist, and they most certainly have existed in spades, so as to prevent altar and pulpit fellowship. Lutherans have been at the forefront of insisting on a consensus of doctrine between churches for the sake of altar and pulpit fellowship. The Galesburg Rule of 1875 stipulated that "Lutheran pulpits are for Lutheran ministers only and Lutheran altars are for Lutheran communicants only." The Evangelical Lutheran Church does not adhere to such a rule, but it is still the official policy of some Lutheran Synods. The ecumenical dialogues have succeeded in bringing the Evangelical Lutheran Church in America into "full communion" with other Protestant denominations — The Episcopal Church, The Presbyterian Church (USA), The United Methodist Church, The Reformed Church in America, The United Church of Christ, and The Moravian Church. This would never have happened without the many inter-confessional dialogues in which the ELCA has been engaged.

Forde was not a member of Lutheran dialogues with other Protestant denominations. He served on the USA Lutheran/Catholic Dialogue, which has been incredibly more challenging. Forde's chief worry was that his fellow Lutheran dialoguers might violate the "*satis est*" clause, namely, that for church unity it is enough to agree on the Gospel of Christ and administering the

Sacraments. What does it mean to be faithful to the *satis est* clause? Forde answers: "What the *satis est* calls for is agreement not on a whole list of things or doctrines, but on the specific activity of teaching (preaching) the gospel and administering the sacraments according to the gospel."[64] Forde believes that the participating churches in dialogue have already "reached enough agreement simply to declare ourselves in fellowship, but that is not the end of theological conversation, but rather simply the beginning to it in earnest."[65] Most ecumenists, no matter from what denomination, are certainly not opposed to sharing theological ideas, but they are willing participants to repair the fractures — the divisions — brought about in the visible Church of Christ by the religious wars that occurred in previous centuries. What was so bad about that? Well, they anathematized each other, accused each other of numerous heresies; they could not worship together or break bread together. That is why the "*satis est*" clause could not serve as the be-all and end-all of the ecumenical drive to "visible church unity" and "full communion," goals which Forde derides as a waste of time, muddled, confusing, and romantic. "Romantic notions of the church have persisted and now take the form of the drive for visible unity, *koinonia*, 'full communion' and such grand things."[66]

What troubled Forde is that the dialogues delved into a ream of ecclesiological issues having to do with church orders, apostolic succession, magisterial authority, the historic episcopate, the papal office, and the like. All of these matters are written off as merely human ordinances, as *adiaphora*, all such "decadent ecclesiastical furniture."[67] Forde wanted the dialogues to engage

---

64. Gerhard Forde, "The Meaning of *Satis Est*," *A More Radical Gospel*, 169.

65. Gerhard Forde, "Lutheran Ecumenism: With Whom and How Much?" *A More Radical Gospel*, 177.

66. Gerhard Forde, "The Meaning of *Satis Est*," *A More Radical Gospel*, 167.

67. Gerhard Forde, "Lutheran Ecumenism: With Whom and How Much?" *A More Radical Gospel*, 188.

in serious dialogue about legitimate theological questions and concerns; unfortunately, the bundle of things having to do with ecclesiology were not among them. Forde even prided himself for being known as having no ecclesiology. "I can boast that I have a pin that says in red letters: 'Beware! This man has no ecclesiology.'"[68] Of course, that is a joke. His ecclesiology uses adjectives like "hidden," "invisible," "spiritual," and "revealed" to speak of the true church. "The church and its unity could itself be nothing other than an object of faith, not of sight. The 'invisibility' or better, 'hiddenness' of such unity was not, therefore, simply a counsel of last resort, a taking refuge in 'spiritualization' when all else failed. It would make no difference at all whether there were one physical church or several. The true unity would still be an object of faith and not sight. If the church and its unity is to be an object of that same faith that justifies, then it cannot be an object of sight."[69]

Ecumenical Lutheran theologians affirm the "*satis est*" principle that deals with the ultimate question of the righteousness that makes people right with God, certainly a higher level of concern than the best way to order the ministries of the church. However, the Lutheran Confessions do state: "We want to declare our willingness to keep the ecclesiastical and canonical polity, provided that the bishops stop raging against our churches."[70] These words were penned by Melanchthon, whom Forde frequently criticizes for being too irenic, worried that for the sake of peace, he might give away the store.

---

68. Gerhard Forde, "Lutheran Ecumenism: With Whom and How Much?" *A More Radical Gospel*, 179.

69. Gerhard Forde, "The Meaning of *Satis Est*," *A More Radical Gospel*, 164.

70. Article XIV, "Ecclesiastical Order," Apology of the Augsburg Confession, *The Book of Concord*, 215.

Rev. Dr. William H. Lazareth was born in New York in 1929 and died of cancer February 23, 2008 in Bar Harbor, Maine. William Lazareth earned his bachelor's degree in 1948 from Princeton University and a doctorate in theology from Union Theological Seminary in New York. He was awarded seven honorary doctorates that served to acknowledge his distinguished career as professor of systematic theology at the Lutheran Theological Seminary in Philadelphia, as Director of the Department for Church in Society of the Lutheran Church in America, as Director of the Secretariat on Faith and Order of the World Council of Churches, which produced the ecumenical document, *Baptism, Eucharist, and Ministry*, as pastor of Holy Trinity Lutheran Church in New York 1983-1987, and as bishop of the Metropolitan New York Synod from 1996-2007. From 1991 to 2002 he was co-president of the Lutheran-Eastern Orthodox International Doctrinal Dialogues, Lutheran World Federation, Geneva. At the time of his death, Lazareth was a faculty member at Carthage College, Kenosha, Wisconsin, serving as Jerald C. Brauer Distinguished Professor of Lutheran Studies. He was also founding co-director of the online Augustine Institute at Carthage.

Three

William H. Lazareth

Lutheran Social Ethics

W illiam H. Lazareth (1929-2008) was the most well known Lutheran churchman, theologian, and ecumenist of his (our) generation. He wore many hats, starting his highly acclaimed ministerial career as a professor of systematic theology at the Lutheran Theological Seminary at Philadelphia and served in that capacity for twenty years. In 1976 he left the Seminary and became the Director of the Department for Church in Society of the Lutheran Church in America (LCA). Lazareth used the Lutheran doctrine of the "two kingdoms" to rectify an imbalance in Lutheranism, which he acknowledged was strong in emphasizing the realm of redemption but has been too often weak on secular matters relating to social, political, and economic life in the realm of creation. From 1980-1983 Lazareth was the Director of the Secretariat on Faith and Order of the World Council of Churches. In his role as Director he oversaw the drafting of one of the most important ecumenical documents of the twentieth century, the Lima Text (1982), *Baptism, Eucharist and Ministry.* Whereas the churches historically have differed widely in both doctrine and practice on all three topics, this text represents a remarkable theological convergence, giving rise to hope that progress has been made toward the goal of visible unity. We will consider Lazareth's ecumenical experience and contributions later.

After completing his work with Faith and Order, Lazareth returned from Geneva to accept a call as pastor of Holy Trinity Lutheran Church, New York, serving from 1983 to 1987. Then he was elected Bishop of the Metropolitan New York Synod of the Evangelical Lutheran Church in America, and served for four years before retiring from active ministry at the age of sixty three. Lazareth, however, continued to serve in various part time positions: 1. Co-president of the Lutheran-Eastern Orthodox International Dialogues, representing the Lutheran World Federation; 2. Visiting professor at Union Theological Seminary, New York; 3. Staff member of the Center of Theological Inquiry, Princeton; 4. Visiting professor at Princeton Theological Seminary; 5. Faculty member of Carthage College, Kenosha, Wisconsin, serving as Jerald C. Brauer Distinguished Professor of Lutheran Studies, where he was serving at the time of his death in 2008. Lazareth authored thirteen books, wrote dozens of journal articles, and edited fifteen books.

I. The Christian Home

William Lazareth earned his theological doctorate from the joint faculties of Columbia University and Union Theological Seminary in 1958. The title of his dissertation is: *Luther on the Christian Home, An Application of the Social Ethics of the Reformation.* Wilhelm Pauck, a well known Luther-scholar in his own right, was the adviser of Lazareth's dissertation. A condensed adaptation of Lazareth's dissertation was published by Muhlenberg Press in 1960. Its basic thesis is that Luther inaugurated a social revolution deeply rooted in his theological convictions summarized in four popular slogans that appear repeatedly in his writings: *solus Christus, sola gratia, sola fide,* and *sola scriptura.* Luther used these slogans to voice his opposition to the theology and practices of the church of Rome, slogans he was trained to believe and observe as a faithful monk and student of theology. For Luther it was a clear choice between two ways of salvation set over against each other: either salvation by meritorious works that motivate God's gracious response of mercy and forgiveness of sins or salvation based solely on the steadfast mercy and love of God revealed in the cross and resurrection of Jesus Christ.

Lazareth's interpretation of Luther's theology conforms closely to the major theological contributors to the Luther-renaissance that began in Germany with Karl Holl's publication of a collection of his essays on Luther written between 1909 and 1921, and continued to flourish in Scandinavia after World War II to the present time. However, Lazareth's dissertation is based solely on his own original research into the German language edition of Luther's writings, Martin Luther, *Werke, Kritische Gesamtausgabe.* 58 volumes, Weimar: Böhlau, 1883ff. The American edition of *Luther's Works*, edited by Jaroslav Pelikan and Helmut T. Lehmann, had not yet been published when Lazareth wrote his dissertation. The method he used was to let Luther speak for himself, in his own words, ranging from his extremely brilliant and eloquent prose when expounding the Scriptures to the very unnerving vulgar and vituperative outbursts against his opponents and critics. All the way through he stayed close to the texts, by quoting, paraphrasing, and summarizing the material at hand.

Lazareth depicted the Luther parsonage as a model of what a Christian home should and can be like. Luther's life with his beloved and faithful wife, Katherine, has inspired many pastors and their wives down through the centuries to make the parsonage a blessing to their families and parishioners, as well as a welcoming hostel to strangers and persons in need. What Luther accomplished by his own marriage can be glimpsed by some words he wrote toward the end of his life.

When I was a boy, the wicked and impure practice of celibacy had made marriage so disreputable that I believed that I could not even think about the life of married people without sinning. Everyone was fully persuaded that anyone who intended to lead a holy life acceptable to God could not get married but had to live as a celibate and take the vow of celibacy. Thus many who had been husbands became either monks or priests after their wives had died. Therefore it was a work necessary and useful for the church

when men saw to it that through the Word of God mar-
riage again came to be respected and that it received the
praises that it deserved. As a result, by the grace of God
now everyone declares that it is something good and holy
to live with one's wife in harmony and peace.[71]

Lazareth identifies Luther's theology as Christ-centered Trinitarianism. The only God is the one revealed in Jesus Christ; there is none other. In the person and work of Christ God has reconciled the world from its bondage to Satan and exchanged his righteousness for our human sinfulness. Luther called this a "happy exchange" (*fröhliche Wechsel*); Bertram's phrase for it was "sweet swap." In plain English it's a "good deal," because we get something free of charge, namely salvation from sin, death, and the power of the devil, all because of Christ. Lazareth writes, "Luther's evangelical 'theology of the cross' condemns as idolatrous all human efforts to merit God's grace apart from Christ (*solus Christus*). It must further declare any church which does not acknowledge Christ as its sole head to be the body of the Antichrist. Sinful self-righteousness leads inevitably to religious defeat. 'But thanks be to God who gives us the victory through our Lord Jesus Christ.'"[72]

With their salvation assured on account of the atonement of Christ Christians are liberated to serve their neighbors' welfare. Christians are free from satanic bondage and their God-given faith looks for ways to serve their God-given neighbors. Lazareth writes, "In opposition to all unevangelical ethics of principles, 'blue laws,' ideals, or rules and regulations, Luther portrays the biblical pattern of a life of faith active in love. A Christian ethic based upon the 'divine indicative' of God's grace preserves the freedom of the believer under the guidance of the Holy Spirit through the Bible, the church, and prayer, to discover anew in

---

71. William H. Lazareth, *Luther on the Christian Home, An Application of the Social Ethics of the Reformation* (Muhlenberg Press, 1960), 33.

72. William H. Lazareth, *Luther on the Christian Home*, 66.

each concrete situation what the will of God permits or requires of him then and there."[73] One might ask, how is this different from the situation ethics popular in the 1960s proposed by the American Anglican theologian, Joseph F. Fletcher? Fletcher based his situation ethics on the Christian norm of neighborly love expressed in different ways depending on the situation. Within the context of the complexities of the situation, one should come to the most loving decision on how to act. This view is clearly opposed to moral absolutism as well as moral relativism.[74]

Lazareth presents Luther's theology of society in terms of his doctrine of the two kingdoms. There are two kingdoms in conflict, the kingdom God and the kingdom of Satan. The story of Jesus in the Gospels portrays a clash between the power of God and the demonic powers of evil at work throughout the whole creation. Jesus brings the rule of God into history, challenges the demons, and becomes victorious over death itself. Luther's theology cannot be understood without taking seriously his realistic sense of the cosmic antagonism between God and Satan. But there is another kind of dualism of equal importance, that is, the two ways of God acting in the world, symbolized by Luther as the "two hands of God." With his "left hand" God is universally at work within all the common structures of secular life, political, social, economic, and cultural, with the purpose of defending and promoting peace and justice and freedom for all peoples, races, and nations. As important as this work of God's "left hand" is, it does not bring about the one thing most needful, reconciliation with God by means of his redemptive work in Jesus Christ. This is the work of the "right hand" of God, the kerygma of the world's salvation recorded in the Scrip-

---

73. William H. Lazareth, *Luther on the Christian Home*, 100.

74. Basing Christian ethics on the New Testament concept of agapé-love was given impetus by Anders Nygren's book, *Agape and Eros*, which Lazareth cites as having influenced his interpretation of Luther's theology. Also Gene Outka's book, *Agape, An Ethical Analysis*, is supportive of the primacy of love in Christian ethics.

tures, proclaimed by the new community of Christ, and lived out in the world by those who believe. These two kingdoms function in distinctively different ways, but they must not be commingled or separated. The twofold activity of God within the world and by means of the church means that, on the one hand, God works creatively to promote the common good in all its personal and social dimensions and, on the other hand, God works redemptively to bring about the world's salvation by the gift of sheer grace.

Lazareth eloquently sums up Luther's doctrine of the two kingdoms: "Luther proclaimed the liberating message that society need not be run by the church in order to be ruled by God. In the kingdom of God, the Redeemer rules all believers religiously via Christ, the gospel, and personal faith. In the kingdom of men, the Creator rules all sinful creatures ethically via Caesar, the law and civil obedience. As both Creator and Redeemer, God is the Lord of both kingdoms; as both righteous and sinful the Christian is a subject of both kingdoms. Hence, for a biblical theology of society, the two kingdoms must always be properly distinguished, but never separated in secularism or equated in clericalism."[75]

Luther's social ethic sees God at work in the everyday affairs of ordinary people in their family life, vocation, and community. His doctrine of the priesthood of all believers dealt a blow to clericalism that elevated the religious callings at the expense of secular responsibilities. He judged the Roman divorce between sacred and secular vocations to be unbiblical. Luther taught that every believer engaged in socially productive work was in full-time Christian service. All Christians are called to serve their neighbors as faithful stewards of the gifts God has entrusted to them. The child of a Christian family called to preach in the pulpit and administer at the altar does not have a higher calling from God than one behind a plow or in front of a stove. "Luther

---

75. William H. Lazareth, *Luther on the Christian Home*, 131.

began to see clearly that the biblical doctrine of vocation, or calling, was the only adequate corrective for the Roman notion that the true Christian life demanded severance from the normal and natural communal responsibilities of everyday life."[76] This was a social revolutionary insight that included all situations in the common life — domestic, social, economic, political, and ecclesiastical — as God's divinely ordained instruments to work order out of chaos and good out of evil, for the sake of the common welfare.

The Christian household is for Luther where it all begins. "Luther's evangelical theology of society compelled him quite naturally to rebuild the walls of social order upon the solid biblical foundation of the family and home under God."[77] The home is a mini-community with all the problems and opportunities of the wider human society. "For its closely knit members, it is a society in embryo: a combination church, state, court, hospital, schoolroom, and playground all in one. It provides the young with a safe place for moulding character and gaining experience. Here they can learn to love and be loved, to trust and be trusted, to obey and be obeyed, to forgive and be forgiven. Consequently, although it dare never end there, the home is truly the right place for Christian charity to begin."[78] Luther seemed to enjoy family life. For him the highest calling on earth is being a wise and loving homemaker. Luther honored Katie for her exceptional role in administering the affairs of their household. He opined that "without women the household and everything else that belongs to it would quickly fall apart. The collapse of the civil government, the towns, and the police would soon follow. In short, the world couldn't do without women even if men were capable of bearing children themselves.... A woman can do more with a child with one little finger than a man can with both

---

76. William H. Lazareth, *Luther on the Christian Home*, 134.

77. William H. Lazareth, *Luther on the Christian Home*, 138.

78. William H. Lazareth, *Luther on the Christian Home*, 144.

fists."[79] It might be a stretch to call Luther a feminist ahead of his time, but he minced no words in praising and honoring the role of women as wives and mothers within the household. Luther seemed to have been content to yield to Katie the greater responsibility in overseeing the needs of the family with loving care. And what was Luther's role? Lazareth put it this way: "Luther's faith was simple enough to trust that after a conscientious day's labor, a Christian father could come home and eat his sausage, drink his beer, play his flute, sing with his children, and make love to his wife — all to the glory of God!"[80] Many a Lutheran parsonage would be a happier place for the entire family, spouse and children, would the parsons emulate Luther's example.

Luther was accused of leaving the Roman Church in order to get married. Luther championed the right of priests to marry if they so chose, and even proposed that they had a duty to renounce their ordination vows of celibacy as unscriptural and anti-Christian. He did not advocate that priests must get married. They should have a choice to remain celibate, but they need not remain celibate if they should decide to get married. As for monks, Luther came to believe and teach that there are no biblical grounds for requiring them to take a vow of celibacy. "Vows are in opposition to evangelical freedom."[81] Gradually Luther realized he had to revise the Roman doctrine of marriage as a sacrament. First of all, marriage is grounded in the realm of creation and not redemption, so unlike the sacraments of Baptism and the Lord's Supper, marriage is not a channel of salvific grace. This means that the marriage of a Christian couple is no more a real marriage than the marriage of an unbelieving man and woman. Marriage belongs to the "left hand" rule of God in the civil domain, and is not privy to the church acting as a means of God's "right hand" rule in the order of salvation.

---

79. William H. Lazareth, *Luther on the Christian Home*, 147.
80. William H. Lazareth, *Luther on the Christian Home*, 145.
81. William H. Lazareth, *Luther on the Christian Home*, 177.

Marriage as ordained by God going back to the creation of Adam and Eve is meant for life, but Luther stipulated that there are legitimate grounds for divorce, namely three, impotence, adultery, and the refusal of sexual relations from either party. Yet, Luther found himself in an ambiguous situation when he permitted Philip of Hesse to remain in a bigamous marriage rather than face the scandal of annulment. He advised Philip to tell a "good, strong, white lie" to clear himself of public scandal, giving Luther's critics plenty of fodder for their malicious attacks against him.

We conclude this section of Lazareth's dissertation on *Luther on the Christian Home* in his own final words: "Luther married as a public testimony of faith in witness to his restoration of the biblical view of marriage and home life under God. This assertion must be made boldly in the face of two common but erroneous myths in this area. First, it must be maintained against the contention in some Roman Catholic circles that Luther left the Church of Rome in order to marry. Our historical analysis proves this charge to be untrue. Second, it must be maintained against the contention in certain Protestant circles that Luther had no consistent theology of marriage and the home life to guide the social ethic of the church that bears his name. Our theological analysis proves this charge to be equally groundless. Hence, despite the scorn suffered for its daring, Luther's marriage provides evangelical Christianity with a very vivid and valid symbol of what it means to live responsibly in a Christian home under God."[82]

2. Christians in Society

William Lazareth published his *magnum opus* in the waning years of his life, at the age of seventy one. The title of the book is *Christians in Society. Luther, the Bible, and Social Ethics* (Augs-

---

82. William H. Lazareth, *Luther on the Christian Home*, 234.

burg Fortress, 2001). It is at once a comprehensive presentation of Luther's biblically grounded theological ethics and a defense against some of his severest critics. In his "Preface" the author acknowledges that "This book is written to serve as a basic text or reference work for those American seminaries or universities that still offer course work in the history and theology of Christian ethics. It offers to guide interested theological students (along with pastors, priests, and lay persons) through the rather formidable primary and secondary sources involved in the comprehension of a central theme in serious Luther research today."[83]

The first chapter is a survey of literature on Luther in the twentieth century, entitled "The Post-Nazi Recovery of Lutheran Public Responsibility." Lazareth writes: "Deplorably, it took the horrors and suffering of a major economic depression and two World Wars to tear most of Lutheranism, especially post-Nazi German Lutheranism, out of its ecclesiastical ghetto into the full exercise of its public responsibility."[84] Twentieth century Luther-scholars faced four devastating attacks on Luther's theological ethics, the first from Ernst Troeltsch (1865-1923) who blamed the "social quietism" of the Lutheran Church in Germany on Luther's teaching. Ernst Troeltsch wrote an important book translated into English that cast Luther's theology in a very negative light, which accounts for why American scholars, Protestant and Roman Catholic, viewed him as a social conservative. The book is entitled, *The Social Teachings of the Christian Churches*. Lazareth points out that Troeltsch did his research on Luther before the publication of the Weimar edition of Luther's many volumes, and thus tended to interpret Luther through the lens of the reactionary ethics of nineteenth century German Lutheranism. Troeltsch claimed that Luther's doctrine of the two kingdoms involved the separation of *private* Christian morality from *public* social

83. William H. Lazareth, *Christians in Society. Luther, the Bible, and Social Ethics* (AugsburgFortress, 2001), ix.
84. William H. Lazareth, *Christians in Society*, 3.

responsibility. All credit is due to Karl Holl, the outstanding Luther scholar, who contended that Troeltsch's view of Luther was not based on his own independent research into Luther's writings. Instead, Troeltsch wrongly equated the dichotomous view of the two kingdoms of German Lutheranism with Luther's dialectical understanding of how the two kingdoms are inter-related in real life. Karl Holl refers to Christian Luthardt who spoke for nineteenth century German Lutheranism when he said: "The Gospel has nothing to do with outward existence but only with eternal life. Christianity wants to change a person's heart, not the external situation."[85]

This dualistic scheme which separated the two kingdoms in twentieth century German Lutheranism — the kingdom of God's gospel and the church and the kingdom of God's law and society — helped to pave the way for the rise of Nazism in Germany in the 1930s. A number of prominent Lutheran theologians, namely, Paul Althaus, Werner Elert, Friedrich Gogarten, and Emanuel Hirsch, were attracted to Hitler's National Socialist Party and drafted a statement expressing their loyalty, the *Ansbacher Ratschlag* (Ansbach Counsel), which reads: "The will of God binds us to a particular moment in the history of the family, nation, and race,.... We as believing Christians thank the Lord God that in this hour of need he has given our people the *Führer* as a 'good and faithful sovereign,' and that in the National Socialist State, God is endeavoring to provide us with disciplined and honorable 'good government.' Therefore we acknowledge our responsibility before God to assist the work of the *Führer* in our vocations and callings." On the other hand, it must not be forgotten that there were courageous pastors and theologians who voiced their opposition to the Pro-Nazi German Christians (*Deutsche Christen*), namely, Hermann Sasse, Franz Lau, Edmund Schlink, Walther Künneth, Martin Niemöller, Hans Lilje, and Dietrich Bonhoeffer.

---

85. William H. Lazareth, *Christians in Society*, 5.

Troeltsch's distorted view of Luther's social ethics contributed to the sensational claims of some authors that Luther's theology was instrumental in the rise of Hitler's National Socialism. One was by Peter Wiener, *Martin Luther: Hitler's Spiritual Ancestor* (1944) and another was by William Montgomery McGovern, *From Luther to Hitler: The History of the Fascist-Nazi Political Philosophy* (1947). Such ill-founded interpretations of Luther were answered by Gordon Rupp's book, *Martin Luther: Hitler's Cause or Cure?*

The second devastating attack on Luther's social and political ethics was launched by the great Swiss Reformed theologian, Karl Barth, who called it "Law-Gospel Quietism." He applied this criticism against both Luther and German Lutheranism without seeing any notable difference. He charged that they both separate law from gospel, creation from redemption, and society from church. This means that the gospel of salvation confessed by the church deals with the private and personal lives of Christians and has nothing relevant to say about what goes on in the public realm of law and order in society. Such a view makes straight the road that leads from Wittenberg to Buchenwald. In an open letter to French Christians Barth charged, "The German people suffer from the heritage of the greatest German Christian, from the error of Martin Luther with respect to the relationship of law and gospel, or worldly and spiritual order and power, by which its natural paganism has not been so much limited and restricted, as rather ideologically transfigured, confirmed, and strengthened."[86] In another letter to the Dutch Christians Barth wrote, "To a certain extent, Lutheranism has provided a breathing space for German paganism, and has allotted it — with its separation of creation and law from the Gospel — something like a sacred precinct. It is possible for the German pagan to use the doctrine of the authority of the state as a Christian justification for National Socialism and for the German Christian to feel himself invited by the same

---

86. William H. Lazareth, *Christians in Society*, 11.

doctrine to a recognition of National Socialism. Both have in fact occurred."[87]

Lazareth proceeds to dismantle Barth's criticism by showing that, like Troeltsch, he read Luther through the lens of the German Lutheranism that bore his name. After the war German Lutheran theologians who had been imprisoned by the Nazis issued the *Stuttgart Declaration*, a public confession of guilt on behalf of their people. "With great pain do we say: through us endless suffering has been brought to many peoples and countries. What we have often borne witness to before our congregations, that we now declare in the name of the whole church. True, we have struggled for many years in the name of Jesus Christ against a spirit which found its terrible expression in the National Socialist regime of violence, but we accuse ourselves for not witnessing more courageously, for not praying more faithfully, for not believing more joyously and for not loving more ardently. Now a new beginning is to be made in our churches."[88] The signatories were well known leaders in post-war German Lutheranism — Otto Dibelius, Martin Niemöller, and Hans Lilje. Their repentance and confession made it clear that their German Lutheran history had not been true to the theology and ethics of Martin Luther. Speaking as the president of the Lutheran World Federation, Hans Lilje wrote in an editorial, "Our systematic theologians must show us how the theology of justification by faith is completed in the practical sphere by a theology of stewardship.... It is not true that the Lutheran doctrine of justification of the sinner must as a matter of principle result in a program of other-worldliness."[89]

A good number of systematic theologians from Scandinavia answered the call from Bishop Hans Lilje to demonstrate that Luther's teaching on justification by faith and the two kingdoms

---

87. William H. Lazareth, *Christians in Society*, 11-12.

88. William H. Lazareth, *Christians in Society*, 13.

89. William H. Lazareth, *Christians in Society*, 13-14.

of God does not lead to either of the faults that Troeltsch and Barth ascribed to him. The leaders of this Scandinavian group were Gustaf Aulén, Anders Nygren, Ragnar Bring, Lennart Pinomaa, Arne Siirala, Gustaf Wingren, and Regin Prenter, many of whose monographs were published and translated into English. They all showed that Luther did not affirm a separation of God's twofold rule of the world by law and gospel. Rather, Luther taught that the temporal life of persons in society cannot be ruled by the particular *gospel* of Christ but by the universal *law* of God. The two ways of God ruling in the world are thus distinctly different but not separable.

Closer to home Reinhold Niebuhr accepted Troeltsch's criticism of Luther's social ethics, asserting that Luther was guilty of "a complete severance between the final experience of grace and all the proximate possibilities of liberty and justice which must be achieved in history."[90] Lazareth rejects Niebuhr's interpretation of Luther as a caricature, quoting the Reformation scholar Wilhelm Pauck whom he calls the "dean" of postwar Luther researchers. "Precisely because Niebuhr is widely regarded as one who is bringing 'classical Protestantism' to life among us, it is very important to recognize that he fails to understand the whole of the faith of the Reformers and particularly that of Luther. First of all, it is to be noted that his thinking appears to be conditioned by a strange animosity against Luther which is all the more surprising in view of the fact that he is more closely related to Luther's faith than to any other. He takes frequent occasions to suggest inadequacies in Luther's teaching, but these criticisms do not seem to be founded on a careful study of Luther's work. They also seem to rise from a disregard of modern Luther research. It seems that Niebuhr's interpretation of Luther is still primarily determined by that of Ernst Troeltsch, who made the mistake of seeing the Reformation too much in the light of the spirit of modern (nineteenth-century) Germany

---

90. Reinhold Niebuhr, *The Nature and Destiny of Man*, vol. 2 (Charles Scribner's Sons, 1941), 193.

Lutheranism. Thus it is understandable that he can attribute a 'cultural defeatism' to Luther's Reformation as if it were true that Luther failed to articulate the ethical, and particularly the social-ethical, implications of his faith.... I say all this in full awareness of the fact that while this charge does not apply to Luther, it may justly be leveled against certain features of Lutheranism as they developed after the Reformation as a result of historical conditions and in disregard of what could have been learned from Luther himself."[91]

After having cleared the deck of such negative assessments of Luther by such scholarly giants as Ernst Troeltsch, Karl Barth, and Reinhold Niebuhr, Lazareth proceeds to unpack Luther's theological and social ethics in seven chapters with copious documentation from Luther's voluminous works. He introduces Luther as an evangelical catholic expositor of Holy Scripture. He identifies three principles of biblical interpretation. 1. For Luther the Word of God is the final authority for the church and its theology. There are three forms of the Word of God: a. the *personal* Word of God, the second person of the Holy Trinity, incarnate in Jesus of Nazareth; b. the *proclaimed* Word of God, functioning as both law and gospel; c. The *written* Word of God, the Bible. 2. The second principle that guides Luther's exposition of Scripture is the inseparable relation of Scripture to church tradition. The reason for this is that both Scripture and tradition function to proclaim Christ. Luther's thoroughgoing Christ-centered interpretation of Scripture is not something he imposed on Scripture from the outside; rather, it was derived from Scripture itself. He wrote, "All the genuine sacred books agree in this, that all of them preach and inculcate Christ. And this is the true test by which to judge all books when we see whether or not they inculcate Christ."[92] 3. Luther's third hermeneutical principle is reading the Bible as the history of the people of God in the Old and the New Testament. Luther's

---

91. William H. Lazareth, *Christians in Society*, 27.
92. Cited by William H. Lazareth, *Christians in Society*, 35.

radical Christocentric interpretation of the Bible meant that for him the true church of God did not start first with Pentecost but already in Paradise, "through Adam and Eve, who believed God's promise."[93]

Lazareth does not swallow everything Luther claimed to have found in Scripture hook, line, and sinker. He makes allowances for the fact that Luther knew nothing about the modern historical-critical principles of biblical exegesis. "After all, Luther was a pre-Enlightenment biblical theologian, not a postmodern, technical, exegetical specialist.... It cannot be denied that Luther's strained efforts to find historical allusions to Christ, the church, and the gospel of justification by grace through faith in the most remote chapters of the Old Testament frequently strike the modern biblical students overly contrived."[94]

Chapters three and four deal with how Luther saw the world as the arena of a cosmic struggle between God and Satan for power and dominion. No theologian since biblical times was more aware of Satan's presence and rule in the world than Luther. At the same time he was even more keenly aware that Satan had more than met his match in the encounter with Christ. No matter how fierce Satan is in threatening to devour us, "one little word can fell him," a phrase from Luther's famous hymn, "A Mighty Fortress is Our God." When Luther was struck by demons of depression, he would defiantly say, "I am baptized!" God is on his side with weapons of the Spirit, the Word and the Sacraments.

The following chapters, five through eight, present the core doctrines of Luther's social ethics — the two kingdoms, the orders of creation, the bondage of will, the theological and political functions of the law, justification by faith alone apart from the works of the law, the sanctifying work of the Holy Spirit, and the priesthood of all believers. Lazareth's book is a

---

93. Cited by William H. Lazareth, *Christians in Society*, 37.

94. William H. Lazareth, *Christians in Society*, 33, 39.

reliable systematic construction of Luther's theological and social ethics and in my estimation is the best available textbook on the subject. However, truth be told there are some highly controversial problems in Luther-interpretation among theologians, and Lazareth concludes his work by showing where he stands. In history and today there are virtually none of Luther's doctrines that enjoys a broad consensus among those who wish to claim him as their spiritual founder and leader. Lutheran Pietists did not agree with seventeenth century Lutheran Scholastics on the order of salvation (*ordo salutis*), on the relation of justification and sanctification, on the relation between the two kingdoms of God, and they could all justifiably find support for their convictions in Luther's own words. Lazareth frankly explains the reason for this ambivalence in the Lutheran tradition; Luther did not always agree with himself. The early Luther could be quoted contradicting the later Luther. Luther's views evolved from before and after the mid-1520s; he had a paradoxical way of expressing his ideas; and he was terminologically inconsistent; for example, referring to the *basileia* of God synonymously as kingdom (*Reich*) and as rule (*Regiment*). Key biblical words such as "world," "flesh," "spirit," "gospel," "law," and "justification," are frequently used with different meanings, depending on the context. For example, "world" can mean the whole of God's good creation, but it can also mean the sinful realm of Satan. "Flesh" can refer to the nature of being human, as in "the Word became flesh." But "flesh" can also mean the waywardness of the sinner at enmity with the "spirit." The "gospel" can refer specifically to the good news of God's grace over against the "law," but it can also refer to the whole of the Christian faith. "Justification" can refer to the exclusive forensic act of God imputing the righteousness of Christ to the sinner, but it can also mean both the initial act of regeneration and the consequent life-long process of sanctification empowered by the Holy Spirit. Lutheran theologians who stress the forensic aspect of justification tend to minimize the new obedience of sanctification that includes doing good works.

Lazareth summarizes his assessment of the problems inherent in Luther-interpretation in this way: "To attempt to systematize the views of so creative, profound and volcanic a thinker as Luther is to be tested sorely. Perhaps its final excuse lies only in its exasperating exhilaration. Wrestling with the proper distinction between God's law and gospel remains for him 'the essential task of Christian doctrine.' Yet even Luther confessed, 'There is no man living on earth who knows how to distinguish between the law and the gospel. We may think we understand it when we are listening to a sermon, but we're far from it. Only the Holy Spirit knows this.'"[95]

Lazareth ends his book on Luther treating the most controversial area in Lutheran theology. We saw in our presentation of the "Law-Gospel" theology of Robert Bertram, Edward Schroeder, and Gerhard Forde that they rejected the "third use of the law" taught by Article VI of the "Formula of Concord," in the Lutheran *Book of Concord*. The third use of the law is there confessed as a guide to assist Christians to live holy lives in accordance with God's will as expressed in the Ten Commandments. This is in addition to the two uses of the law which pertain to all persons, first, the political function of the law to command obedience and enforce discipline and second, the soteriological function of the law to accuse persons of their sin and their need of a Savior, which pertains to all persons, believers and unbelievers alike. Lazareth agrees with the majority of scholars that Luther taught only two uses of the law (*duplex usus legis*). It was primarily due to Philip Melanchthon's influence after Luther's death that he and his followers (so-called Philippists) were politically successful in settling controversies among Lutherans about the role of good works in the Christian life. The Majoristic Controversy, named after the teaching of Georg Major, held that good works are necessary for salvation. What did he mean by that? It could mean that good works are

---

95. William H. Lazareth, *Christians in Society*, 238.

necessary to obtain salvation or it good mean that good works are necessary as the result of salvation. Polar opposite was the Antinomian Controversy, named after the teaching of Johann Agricola and Nicholaus von Amsdorf, that good works are an impediment to salvation.

Lazareth's final word is that what Article VI of the "Formula of Concord" states on the third use of the law is incompatible with Luther's understanding of the Apostle Paul's teaching on the law in his Letters to the Galatians and Romans. Lazareth claims that "Article VI vacillates on whether the law's third use is needed by the regenerate (*renati*) as already righteous (*iustus*) or as still sinful (*peccator*). At stake: Is sanctification in Christian theological ethics finally governed by the law or the Spirit of God?"[96] When I read this I wrote in the margin: "Is this possibly a false alternative? Is not the Holy Spirit free and able to use the law of God summarized in the Ten Commandments in such a positive didactic way that it neither negates Christian freedom in the gospel nor does it conduce to legalism?" Yet, Lazareth does not leave the Christian life to fetch for itself as an autonomous law unto itself. In place of the third use of the law he proposes a second use of the gospel. "Therefore it is not by an alleged third use of the law (*tertius usus legis*), but through what we have earlier proposed to call the second or paranetic use of the gospel, that is, justifying faith in sanctifying love and justice, that the Holy Spirit calls and empowers us with new gifts to fulfill our new obedience to God's primal command of love (*mandatum*)."[97]

As Director of the Department for Church in Society Lazareth was in the position to translate his acquired knowledge of Lutheran Social Ethics into numerous social statements and study documents officially adopted by the biennial assemblies of the Lutheran Church in America. They dealt with such critical issues as marriage and family, race relations, poverty, economic

---

96. William H. Lazareth, *Christians in Society*, 240.
97. William H. Lazareth, *Christians in Society*, 244.

justice, criminal justice, capital punishment, social welfare, ecology, human rights, death and dying, religious liberty, church and state, conscientious objection, and others. In a book evaluating this achievement of the Lutheran Church in America, largely under Lazareth's leadership, Christa R. Klein and Christian von Dehsen wrote: "In its quarter century, the Lutheran Church in America developed an admirably coherent tradition in theological ethics. Taken as a body, the social statements exhibit an approach to social issues that is identifiable and that reflects Lutheranism's confessional heritage. This 'evangelical ethic,' as it was called, was present from the onset."[98] In a similar vein Robert Benne justifiably wrote, "It would not be brash to conclude that the Lutheran Church in America produced the most important array of official Lutheran public theology up to this point in American history."[99]

3. Lazareth's Ecumenical Experience

William Lazareth served as Director of the Secretariat on Faith and Order of the World Council of Churches from 1980-1983. In 1982 the Faith and Order Commission published a document entitled *Baptism, Eucharist, and Ministry*, also called the "Lima Text," because the Commission held its plenary meeting in Lima, Peru. Lazareth co-authored a Preface to the Text, with the Greek Orthodox theologian, Nikos Nissiotis, the Moderator of the Commission on Faith and Order. The Lima Text is the fruit of a fifty year process of studying issues of doctrine, especially having to do with the two sacraments, Baptism and the Lord's Supper, and the ministry of the church, ordained and non-ordained, that have divided the churches and still stand in the way of inter-communion and church unity. The Lima statement

---

98. Christa R. Klein and Christian von Dehsen, *Politics and Policy: The Genesis and Theology of Social Statements in the Lutheran Church in America* (Fortress, 1989), 173.

affirms that it strives for visible church unity, not only for its own sake, which is essential in itself, but also for the sake of the world it seeks to serve. The authors write, "We live in a crucial moment in the history of humankind. As the churches grow in unity, they are asking how their understandings and practices of baptism, eucharist and ministry relate to the mission in and for the renewal of human community as they seek to promote justice, peace and reconciliation. Therefore our understanding of these cannot be divorced from the redemptive and liberating mission of Christ through the churches in the modern world."[100]

The Preface affirms that "we have already achieved a remarkable degree of agreement. Certainly we have not yet fully reached 'consensus' (*consentire*), understood here as that experience of life and articulation of faith necessary to realize and maintain the Church's visible unity."[101] Though the churches have not yet reached consensus, they have discovered many convergences in how they understand the faith they believe and confess. All the major confessional traditions were involved in voting unanimously to approve the Lima Text — Anglican, Lutheran, Orthodox, Roman Catholic, Pentecostal, and all the major Protestant denominations, Presbyterian, Reformed, Methodist, United Church of Christ, etc. In closing the Preface sounds a very optimistic note: "We have become increasingly aware of our unity in the body of Christ. We have found reason to rejoice in the rediscovery of the richness of our common heritage in the Gospel. We believe the Holy Spirit has led us to this time, a *kairos* of the ecumenical movement when sadly divided churches have been enabled to arrive at substantial theological agreements. We believe that many significant advances are possible if in

---

99. Robert Benne, *The Paradoxical Vision: A Public Theology for the Twenty-first Century* (Fortress, 1995), 120.

100. William H. Lazareth and Nikos Nissiotis, "Preface," *Baptism, Eucharist and Ministry* (World Council of Churches, 1982), viii-ix.

101. "Preface," *Baptism, Eucharist and Ministry*, ix.

our churches we are sufficiently courageous and imaginative to embrace God's gift of Church unity."[102]

Lazareth put his ecumenical experience to good effect in contributing his support to the "full communion" agreements between the Evangelical Lutheran Church in America and six Protestant denominations — The Presbyterian Church (USA), Reformed Church in America, United Church of Christ, The Episcopal Church, The Moravian Church, and The United Methodist Church. Full Communion agreement means a common confession of the Christian faith, mutual recognition of Baptism and a sharing of the Lord's Supper, allowing for joint worship and an exchangeability of members, mutual recognition and availability of ordained ministers to the service of all, common commitment to evangelism, witness and service, and mutual lifting of any condemnations that exist between denominations.

Upon Lazareth's death in 2008 the Rev. Mark S. Hanson, the presiding Bishop of the Evangelical Lutheran Church in America, issued this fitting eulogy: "Dr. Lazareth was a teacher of the Church. The ecclesial, theological and ecumenical legacy that he leaves will bless the people of the Church for generations to come."[103]

---

102. "Preface," *Baptism, Eucharist and Ministry*, x.
103. https://www.elca.org/News-and-Events/6116

**Dr. Robert D. Benne** was born on May 24, 1937 in West Point, Nebraska. He was Professor of Religion and Chair of the Religion and Philosophy Department at Roanoke College for eighteen years before he left full-time teaching in 2000. Benne founded the Roanoke College Center for Religion and Society in 1982 and was its director until 2012. Before going to teach at Roanoke College in 1982, he was Professor of Church and Society at the Lutheran School of Theology at Chicago (1967-82). In 1959 he received a B.A. from Midland Lutheran College, Fremont, Nebraska and the following year he studied at Erlangen University in Germany on a Fulbright Scholarship. Upon returning to the United States he attended the University of Chicago Divinity School, earning a Ph.D. in the area of Ethics and Society in 1963. He began his teaching career as Professor of Church and Society at Augustana Seminary in Rock Island, Illinois (1965-67). Upon Benne's retirement Roanoke College renamed the center which he directed for thirty years in his honor as the Robert D. Benne Center for Religion and Society. He continues at Roanoke College as a research associate in its Religion and Philosophy Department. Benne is also a faculty member in the Institute of Lutheran Theology, Brookings, South Dakota.

Four

Robert Benne

Lutheran Public Theology

Robert Benne (1937-) was born and baptized in West Point, Nebraska; his parents were of German Lutheran background. Benne tells the story of an experience he had as a twelve year old lad. During the summer he worked as a gardener for Mrs. Hasebroock, the wife of the city's mayor who belonged to the same congregation as the Benne family. In his own words Benne wrote in his memoirs: "One lovely morning I was weeding her flower bed right below her open kitchen window. I heard this eminent lady talking on the phone with a friend. I listened even more closely when it seemed they were talking about me. Toward the end of the conversation she said quite clearly and authoritatively: 'That Bobby Benne would make a good minister.... That was the last thing I wanted to be. I wanted to be a jock, first an athlete and then a coach. But *she* said that about me, a gangly near teen-ager with no real record of accomplishment. What was happening?"[104] That experience stayed with Benne the rest of his life. While he never became an ordained minister, he embarked on a trajectory of church service his entire career as a Lutheran theologian specializing in ethics.

In his "Memoirs" Robert (Bob) Benne presented himself as a practical theologian. I have never liked the term "practical theology." Is not all theology intended to be practical? As seminary

---

104. Robert Benne, *Thanks Be To God! Memoirs of a Practical Theologian* (Delhi, New York, ALPB Books, 2019), 9.

students we poked fun at what was taught in the department of practical theology — we called it "practically theology." So I prefer a term that Benne himself used in the title of his most important theological work, *The Paradoxical Vision, A Public Theology for the Twenty-first Century.* Virtually all of Benne's writings deal with the social, political, and economic ethical implications of what the church believes and teaches on the basis of the Holy Scriptures and the classical Christian tradition, its creeds and confessions. Benne did not write theology for theologians but mostly for those he called "ordinary saints," the rank and file of lay Christians who work and witness in the real world beyond the walls of the church.

Bob Benne's roots are deeply embedded in the culture of Nebraska during his growing up years — robust family values, conservative Lutheranism, solid educational grounding in the three R's — reading, writing, 'rithmetic — and respect for hard work — everything it takes to pursue the American Dream! Sports was a major factor in Benne's formative years. He played quarterback for his high school football team and also did well in basketball (all conference) and track. He went on to excel in four sports at Midland College, football, basketball, track, and baseball, and was honored to be elected to the Midland Athletic Hall of Fame. As we quoted Benne above, he always wanted to be a jock and thereafter a coach. But Benne did not let sports diminish his intellectual development. Of his high school experience Benne wrote: "I was valedictorian of the class in 1955, along with other honors. It was a small pond. But what a wonderful start in life. Participation in instrumental and choral music, journalism, drama, sports, as well as excellent instruction in several subjects, especially English and Science."[105] That pace continued through his college years, as he recalled, "Over the four years I rose to the top of my class and gave the valedictory address upon graduation. But more important than

---

105. Robert Benne, *Thanks Be To God!*, 76-77.

that was winning two major fellowships: a Woodrow Wilson and a Fulbright."[106]

It was at Midland College that seeds were sown for Benne's eventual decision to concentrate on the ethical foci of theology, rather than the core themes of systematic theology. In his senior year he took courses on Christian Doctrine and Ethics, in which he read Reinhold Niebuhr's *An Interpretation of Christian Ethics*, which he recalled was "a life-changing book.... I was blown away.... It was a genuine intellectual awakening."[107] When Benne started his graduate studies at the Divinity School of the University of Chicago, he "came to the conclusion that my interests and gifts drew me to 'practical theology,' the application of theological ethics to societal issues: politics, economics, and culture. What excited me was the study of the role of religion in various sectors of public life. The courses I took in "Ethics and Society" stirred me more than those in theology. Moreover, as I listened to the many debates featuring systematic theologians, I often thought they got too tied up in highly subtle — and frankly, irrelevant — topics and distinctions. I knew, of course, that reliable theology was extremely important, but doubted that it meant delving into so many esoteric subtleties. Such efforts certainly were not my cup of tea. So I steered toward what I thought were far more relevant pursuits. That meant that I would be applying a given theology — Lutheran/Niebuhrian — to the public works rather than trying to construct one of my own."[108] That is truly a self-revealing reflection by a kid from Nebraska who went on to become America's most prominent and prolific Lutheran public theologian.

This account of Bob Benne's early life in Nebraska would be seriously lacking without mention that as a sophomore he "met Joanna Carson, who, I was told by a roommate, liked me.

106. Robert Benne, *Thanks Be To God!*, 79.

107. Robert Benne, *Thanks Be To God!*, 46.

108. Robert Benne, *Thanks Be To God!*, 104.

That intelligence emboldened me to ask her for a date. When we found we had so much in common — we seemed to be meant for each other — we began dating, 'went steady,' were 'pinned,' became engaged on New Year's Eve of 1958, and married in the summer of 1959, right before we embarked in September for a year on a Fulbright Scholarship to Erlangen University in Germany."[109] After sixty years of their life together, Benne dedicated his Memoirs to Joanna —"Wife, Friend, Lover, Co-Parent, and Companion along Life's Way." Those who know and love the Bennes would chime in and say in Luther's words, "This is most certainly true!"

1. Benne's Early Years as a "Liberal Idealist"

Bob Benne left Nebraska to spend one year as a Fulbright scholar at the University of Erlangen, Germany, not only to get caught up on the then current theological situation but also to learn about his German heritage and imbibing its culture. About this experience Benne wrote: "What an opportunity for a lower-middle class boy from a small town in Nebraska!"[110] The next year Benne used his Woodrow Wilson Fellowship to enroll in the graduate program of the University of Chicago Divinity School. At Erlangen he was inspired by the theological ethics of Walter Künneth which, added to what he had learned from the ethical writings of Reinhold Niebuhr, prepared him to do his graduate studies in the field of "Ethics and Society." It was a propitious moment at the Divinity School; there were two prominent theologians in that field, Alvin Pitcher and Gibson Winter. Chicago was at the center of the social movements for civil rights, anti-poverty, and community organization. This is what Benne recalled of that time: "The most influential professor I had in Ethics and Society was Al Pitcher, who was deeply

---

109. Robert Benne, *Thanks Be To God!*, 26.
110. Robert Benne, *Thanks Be To God!*, 82.

involved in all three movements and reported on them vividly in our classes with him. He was stirring; we were stirred. The American Dream that most of us students had experienced in our lives — and in that of our parents' — had the chance to be extended to the black and the poor. And the church could be an effective participant in that heady opportunity. Indeed, for us the church was viewed mainly as an instrument of social transformation."[111] Gibson Winter, Benne's doctor father, had published a widely read and influential book, *The Suburban Captivity of the Churches,* in which he argued that churches need to broaden their ministry to embrace the struggle for racial justice and urban renewal. Benne became an enthusiastic disciple of this view of the church to be the vanguard of the movement for social transformation. "Without denying my newly formulated Lutheranism, I put that on the back burner for the sake of a Niebuhrian-fueled involvement in social transformation. The traditional functions of the church — preaching, teaching, worship, personal formation — came in second to the great need for the church to participate in the movements.... I became a 'social justice warrior' before the term had been coined."[112]

After passing his doctoral exams Benne accepted a teaching position in Christian Ethics at Augustana Seminary in Rock Island, Illinois, a perfect fit for what the Divinity School had prepared him to do. About this good fortune Benne wrote, "I was so excited by my 'liberal idealism' that I hit the seminary like a storm. The seminary had been pretty insulated from the excitement of the early '60s and I was ready to inspire it about the church as a transforming agent in society, especially among the poor and black people of the inner city. I taught vividly about civil rights, community organization, and anti-poverty movements that I had been a part of. By the end of the year I had convinced the majority of the senior men (all the ministe-

---

111. Robert Benne, *Thanks Be To God!,* 83.
112. Robert Benne, *Thanks Be To God!,* 106.

rial students were men at that time) to commit themselves to ministry in the inner city.[113]

When in 1967 the Augustana Seminary merged with the Lutheran Theological School in Maywood, Illinois, to become the Lutheran School of Theology at Chicago (LSTC), Benne accepted a position as Assistant Professor of Church and Society. "I began teaching at LSTC from a liberal idealist perspective — that America had a good chance to overcome its problems by positive action by government, community organizations, and the church. Such teaching inspired only for a short while. Liberal idealism was soon outflanked by a far more critical — even revolutionary — interpretation of the challenges before America. The civil rights movement became Black Power; the student anti-war movement became an anti-American movement fueled by revolutionary expectations; the beginnings of radical feminism, gay rights, and environmental alarm made their appearance. An apocalyptic hue enveloped the country, especially in its urban university centers such as the University of Chicago, the nearby neighbor of the new LSTC."[114]

Benne's first two books were written during his early teaching years at LSTC, *Wandering in the Wilderness. Christians and the New Culture* (1972), and *Defining America: A Christian Critique of the American Dream* (co-authored with Philip Hefner). One can see that in both of these books Benne began to emerge from his dyed-in-the-wool self-understanding as a "social justice warrior," moving toward what he called "a much more dialectical view of America."

2. From Liberal Idealism to Neo-Conservatism

Shortly thereafter — in the early '70s — Benne made a decisive turn to the right, leaving his left-leaning years behind. He had

---

113. Robert Benne, *Thanks Be To God!*, 85.
114. Robert Benne, *Thanks Be To God!*, 87.

heard enough of the revolutionary anti-American rhetoric that filled the air during the Vietnam War years. In a self-reflective mood Benne wrote, "I was having grave doubts whether I could continue in the radical role I was trying to play.... I had come to the conclusion that the revolution was not for me. It was time to be honest with myself. These changes in political and economic opinion ... were accompanied by a return to a classical view of the church as the bearer of the Gospel. I finally came to the conclusion that the church as a vehicle of social transformation instrumentalized it and reduced its transcendent message to purely human efforts. In Lutheran lingo, my view of the church changed from a purveyor of the law — a human work — to the bearer of the Gospel, the divine work of God in Christ.... I did experience remorse that I had so fully accepted my earlier view of the church and its mission, and have often wondered how many students I influenced who never returned to a more orthodox view of the church."[115]

The upshot of this conversion of mind was to read some of the leading neo-conservative writers who presented a positive assessment of America and a strong defense of the market economic system — among them Irving Kristol, Norman Podhoretz, Daniel Bell, Michael Novak, and Richard John Neuhaus. He identified himself with Kristol's definition of a neo-conservative — "'A liberal who had been mugged by reality.' Or better for me, 'a wanna-be radical who had been mugged by reality.'"[116] At the same time Benne read the writings of University of Chicago economists, among them Milton Friedman, who was awarded the Nobel Prize for Economics in 1976, and Eugene Fama, who won the same Nobel Prize in 2013. Both of them were tennis players at the University Quadrangle Club, where Benne and I both got to know them as fellow tennis enthusiasts. Benne was taken by their writings. That led Benne to write a book that

---

115. Robert Benne, *Thanks Be To God!*, 89-90.
116. Robert Benne, *Thanks Be To God!*, 90.

thrust him into unwanted controversy: *The Ethic of Democratic Capitalism — A Moral Reassessment* (1981). The ensuing year was a miserable time for Benne; he felt increasingly isolated and out of sync with the prevailing ethos of the seminary and Hyde Park. Benne remembered the response to his book this way: "The activist students were appalled. I was on the wrong side of history, politically, economically, and culturally. A small discontented group showed their displeasure by organizing a successful boycott of a class I was offering on capitalism and justice. I no longer felt as welcomed in the coffee shop of the seminary. Further, I had taught by then seventeen years at LSTC and wondered whether that would be my only job. We also were getting weary of urban living. Hyde Park was not a family-friendly section of town."[117]

What was all the big fuss about? Benne was affirming what the majority of Americans believed at that time and still do; politically they (we) favor a democracy that really works and not one in name only, mixed with an economy that works from the bottom up rather from the top down. Only a dinky minority would prefer Marxist communism which is supposedly a class-less society in which the workers own and control the means of production and goods are owned in common and distributed according to need, or even democratic socialism in which the government owns and administers the means of production and distribution of goods, but still allows for private property and private enterprise. The United States of America presently has a mixed economy of democratic capitalism and democratic socialism. The Social Security Act was passed in 1935 as part of President Franklin D. Roosevelt's New Deal, dealing with a number of social problems — old age, poverty, unemployment, the plight of widows and fatherless children. Almost all the Congressional Republicans opposed the Social Security Act. After all, it was a government program they accused of undercutting

---

117. Robert Benne, *Thanks Be To God!*, 91.

individual freedom and personal responsibility. Republicans also opposed the adoption of Medicare and Medicaid in 1965 as part of President Lyndon B. Johnson's "War on Poverty" as a federal and state government health care program, dubbing it as a "Soviet-style kind of health care system." Republican leaders — Ronald Reagan, George H. W. Bush, Barry Goldwater, and Bob Dole — continued to oppose such programs as "socialism" and the elimination of freedom. Reagan said, "If you don't stop Medicare, one of these days you and I are going to spend our sunset years telling our children and children's children what it was once like in America when men were free." And Goldwater echoed the same sentiment; "Having given our pensioners free medical care, why not food baskets, why not public housing, why not vacation resorts, why not a ration of cigarettes for those who smoke and of beer for those who drink?" Now in 2020 the same old story is repeating itself. Republicans in office are continuing their diatribe against "socialism," sometimes even equating it with communism and Marxism.

I have digressed in order to support the claim I am about to make that Benne's, *The Ethic of Democratic Capitalism*, is not a radical departure from what the majority of Americans have supported since the Great Depression by Republicans, Democrats, and Independents alike in every presidential election going back to Franklin D. Roosevelt. The high-pitched revolutionary rhetoric in the 1960s of those who opposed the Vietnam War was primarily criticism of the imperialistic war that America had no business fighting — with 58,000 Americans killed, 150,000 wounded, at a cost of over 1 trillion dollars. Richard John Neuhaus, Benne's friend and cohort in their embrace of neo-conservativism, was one of the leaders of Clergy and Laity Concerned — along with Rabbi Abraham Heschel, William Sloane Coffin, and John C. Bennett — calling for opposition to United States' involvement in the Vietnam War. They were not anti-American revolutionaries; they loved America and for its sake they protested. However, Benne became convinced that the anti-war movement with all its rallies and marches and slogans and rhetoric spelled revolution. Benne wrote, "I had come to the conclusion that the revolution was not for me. It was time to be honest with myself. My own assessment of America was far more positive than what I heard from the revolutionaries."[118]

Benne's apologia for democratic capitalism is well-researched; he educated himself on subjects most theologians know little about, especially the world of economics and social justice. The two most important interlocutors who helped to buttress the theological and philosophical perspective Benne brings to his analysis of democratic capitalism are Reinhold Niebuhr and John Rawls, especially Niebuhr's *The Nature and Destiny of Man* and Rawl's *A Theory of Justice*. The seminary students at LSTC were shortsighted and misinformed when they boycotted Benne's offering of a class on "Capitalism and Justice." They would have learned that Benne provides a critique of democratic capitalism from a Christian ethical standpoint. He asserts that without legitimate criticism democratic capitalism "will become an unguided monster."[119]

So, the question is: what kinds of criticism does Benne offer, and are they valid? Lest I be inclined to substitute my predilections for Benne's judicious ethical critique of democratic capitalism, assessing its strengths and failures, I will stick to Benne's own words. "Without democracy, capitalism would degenerate into a social Darwinism of the survival of the fittest — the fittest being those with the most economic power.... There is no question of the need for state intervention in the achievement of a more just society."[120] Benne does support government intervention in providing assistance to the most disadvantaged members of society. "From a Christian point of view, this is the way that the democratic polity distributes care for the hungry, unemployed,

---

118. Robert Benne, *Thanks Bè To God!*, 89.
119. Robert Benne, *The Ethic of Democratic Capitalism, A Moral Reassessment* (Fortress, 1981), 16.
120. Robert Benne, *The Ethic of Democratic Capitalism*, 156.

defenseless, sick, and handicapped members of society. Basic minima must be provided whether the least advantaged are deserving or not."[121] Benne identifies the current government programs that provide such assistance, such as Social Security, Medicare, Medicare, Aid to Dependent Children, Food Stamps, and Head Start. "All of these programs are ways in which the democratic polity transfers wealth from those who can afford it to those who need more support.... Political intervention has ensured that the inequalities of the marketplace will work to the benefit of the least advantaged. These benefits increase as the overall wealth of the society increases.... There is little doubt that many in the lowest group are in a miserable state, but there is also little doubt that many have received benefits that have enabled them to lead lives of significantly more comfort and dignity."[122] But there is still room for improvement, Benne admits. "There are serious flaws with the system when people do not have enough economic wherewithal to register their preferences. But redistribution of enough wealth to do so is not inconsistent with democratic capitalism and is in fact being done."[123] Yes, true indeed, but there are always politicians with monied interests who scream "socialism" whenever government intervenes in creating social programs that provide benefits to those most in need.

For Benne the modern trend to expand the role of government in guaranteeing a decent floor to support human flourishing does not spell socialism, but instead is the principle of *agapé* at work, and he asks churches to play their part. "From a moral point of view, we are summoned to universalize the possibilities of human fulfillment to all beings. This is the burden of Christian *agapé* and, for that matter, of Rawlsian justice."[124] Benne

---

121. Robert Benne, *The Ethic of Democratic Capitalism*, 165-166.
122. Robert Benne, *The Ethic of Democratic Capitalism*, 168, 169.
123. Robert Benne, *The Ethic of Democratic Capitalism*, 212.
124. Robert Benne, *The Ethic of Democratic Capitalism*, 203.

believes that the private sector — religious and philanthropic institutions — should continue to play an important role in advancing justice in society, rather than counting on centralized government to do almost everything. "Efforts to extend justice to the disadvantaged and to provide needed social services ought to use the private sector as much as is feasible. Moving in these directions will allow for an important intentional role of the state without making it omni-competent, and at the same time it will protect and extend the functions of the mediating structures which transmit the cultural meaning systems of the people."[125]

The thesis of Benne's book is "that the combination of democracy as a polity and capitalism as an economy is morally viable and that democratic capitalism as practiced in the United States is pressing toward an approximation of the just society."[126] It successfully teaches those with an open mind to celebrate the values we citizens share in our democratic political system as well as how to work together to remedy the flaws endemic to our capitalistic economic system.

3. Benne's Move from LSTC to Roanoke College

In 1982 Bob Benne left the Lutheran School of Theology at Chicago (LSTC) to embark on a new venture to teach in the Department of Religion and Philosophy at Roanoke College, Salem, Virginia. The president, Norman Fintel, called upon Benne to "Lutheranize" Roanoke College which, like most church-related colleges, was becoming secularized, losing its Christian heritage. Benne wrote a major theological book every sabbatical year with no exception while at Roanoke College. In 1985 he returned to Cambridge, where he had written his book on democratic capitalism on a previous sabbatical. During that year Benne wrote a book on the Lutheran doctrine of vocation,

---

125. Robert Benne, *The Ethic of Democratic Capitalism*, 259.
126. Robert Benne, *The Ethic of Democratic Capitalism*, 179.

entitled, *Ordinary Saints: An Introduction to the Christian Life*, adding to a number of significant books on the subject by Lutheran theologians, most notably Einar Billing's, *Our Calling,* George Forell's, *Faith Active in Love*, and Gustaf Wingren's, *Luther on Vocation.* Benne said he entitled this book "ordinary saints" to underscore the Lutheran view that all Christians are saints, not because they are particularly saintly, but because of the wonderful exchange of Christ's righteousness for their sinfulness. All Christians are saints and sinners at the same time (*simul justus et peccator*). He was motivated to write this book to teach college students who are dismally ignorant of the basics of the Christian faith and morals. He added that in his latter years of teaching at the Lutheran School of Theology at Chicago he discovered that students preparing for the Christian ministry lacked a basic knowledge of the core teachings of Christianity.[127]

The theological foundation of Benne's understanding of the Christian life is the Pauline-Augustinian-Lutheran message of God's justifying grace received through faith on account of the life, death, and resurrection of Jesus Christ. The saving power of God's grace incarnate in Jesus Christ is mediated to Christians by the inspirational work of the Holy Spirit by means of the church's ministry of Word and Sacraments, empowering them to live lives of service to others. "This movement of the Spirit *through* us in obedient love for others is given concreteness in our particular responsibilities in the world.... Every ordinary Christian has been sought out by God's Word. Likewise, every Christian is called to responsible service in the world. We do not have to look far for the locations of our service to one another. These locations are very close-at-hand."[128] Lutheran theology calls such places of responsibility "orders of creation," such as family, government, economy, and education. These are universal

---

127. Robert Benne, *Ordinary Saints: An Introduction to the Christian Life* (Fortress Press, 1988), ix.

128. Robert Benne, *Ordinary Saints: An Introduction to the Christian Life* (Fortress Press, 1988), 64, 67.

structures inescapably applicable to all societies, and the means by which God governs and preserves the world.

I am not writing a biographical sketch of Benne's professional career, so I cannot do justice to his various accomplishments other than those strictly theological and ethical. However, several things should not go unmentioned. Benne established "The Center for Religion and Society" at the college "to foster a lively dialog between Christian intellectual and moral perspectives and the pressing issues of church and society."[129] Its record of achievement is truly impressive. It brought many world-renowned speakers to its many programs and conferences to dinky-town Salem, for example, Helmut Schmidt, Chancellor of West Germany, Michael Naumann, editor of *Der Spiegel*, Wolfhart Pannenberg, premier German systematic theologian, Martin Marty, church historian, Bishop N. T. Wright, and Richard John Neuhaus.

Benne had also been invited by Norman Fintell to revive the church-relatedness of Roanoke College. He became interested in the question why a few colleges have retained the religious heritage of their founding church while most others have drifted away into secular indifference. For his research project he chose six institutions that were academically strong and yet serious about fostering their Christian identity. The six he chose were Wheaton College, an evangelical liberal arts school, Valparaiso University, founded by ministers of the Lutheran Church, Missouri Synod, St. Olaf College, founded by Lutheran pastors of Norwegian descent, the University of Notre Dame, a Roman Catholic research university, Baylor University, carrying on the Southern Baptist tradition, and Calvin College, maintaining the Reformed Tradition. The policy of Wheaton and Calvin was to hire administrators, faculty, and staff who are members of their particular denominational background. The policy of Valparaiso, St. Olaf, Notre Dame, and Baylor was to hire a "critical mass" of such folks. "Those two types, I thought, 'kept the

---

129. Robert Benne, *Thanks Be To God!*, 127-128.

soul' publicly relevant in every facet of the life of the school.... Essentially, it came to having a robust theological vision for the school that was taken seriously in hiring and in cultivating practices that embodied the vision. For that you needed people who unabashedly knew and expressed the tradition."[130] Benne published a book of his findings with the title, *Quality with Soul: How Six Premier Colleges and Universities Keep Faith with Their Religious Traditions.*

Benne hoped to apply what he learned from his research for that book to strengthen Roanoke College's relation to its Lutheran heritage. This is what Norman Fintel had in mind when he hired Benne. In his Memoirs Benne tells the sad story of his disappointment that for all his efforts to bring the college closer to its Lutheran heritage the majority of the faculty had brought the college to the point of no return. The secular wing of the faculty, buttressed by many of its department heads, was not on board with the Fintel-Benne project to strengthen the religious heritage of the college. Benne concludes with a sigh of finality, "I'm afraid the 'game is over.'"

Yet, Benne's love affair with the college he served for thirty years was not over. After his retirement he wrote a history of the college, focusing on its relation to its Christian heritage. "I worked through the eras of each of the ten presidents of the college, examining their vision of the college in relation to its identity and mission. I also researched the curricula, the ethos, and faculty profile for each presidential era.[131] The title of his book is, *Keeping the Soul in Christian Higher Education: A History of Roanoke College.* Benne read the handwriting on the wall — its religious heritage would gradually continue to be marginalized until it it becomes irrelevant in any discernible way, mimicking the fate of many colleges and universities founded by Christians who believed in higher education for their youth.

---

130. Robert Benne, *Thanks Be To God!*, 143, 144.
131. Robert Benne, *Thanks Be To God!*, 156.

4. Robert Benne's *Magnum Opus* on Lutheran Public Theology

Benne wrote a dozen books, but the greatest of them is *The Paradoxical Vision: A Public Theology for the Twenty-first Century*. Benne wrote this book in 1992 when he and family went again to Cambridge on another sabbatical. This time he was responding to an article that Mark Noll published in *First Things* with the intriguing title, "The Lutheran Difference." Mark Noll was a well-known evangelical church historian from the Reformed tradition. Noll's article called for a Lutheran perspective on American public theology in preference to the predominant Calvinist version that has held sway since the founding of the nation. The Calvinist idea attempts to extend the saving acts of God in the experience of individual Christians and churches to the national public sectors of life. In this view America is a place where the kingdom of God can come in its power and glory by means of the interventions of born again believers. America can become a Christian nation; there can be such a thing as Christian politics and Christian economics. Noll described the Calvinist view of the church's involvement in society this way: "The dominant pattern of political involvement in America has always been one of direct, aggressive action modeled on Reformed theories of life in the world…. Americans have moved in a straight line from personal belief to social reform, from private experience to political activity. It has assumed the necessity of moving directly from passion for God and the Bible to passion for the renovation of society."[132] Noll suggests that the Lutheran approach would be a welcome difference, and Benne seized on the opportunity to prove him right, and that is what he did with *The Paradoxical Vision*.

Readers might reasonably ask, What is paradoxical about the Lutheran view? "Paradox" is an interesting word. My Webster's Dictionary defines paradox as a self-contradictory statement or

---

132. Quoted in Robert Benne, *The Paradoxical Vision: A Public Theology for the Twenty-first Century* (Fortress, 1995), 98-99.

a proposition opposed to common sense. Benne's precedent is H. Richard Niebuhr's use of the word in his book, *Christ and Culture*, in which he typologically portrays the Lutheran view as "Christ and Culture in Paradox." Paradox is a word used in many contexts. Sören Kierkegaard claimed that Jesus of Nazareth is the "absolute paradox" because he is truly God and truly man at the same time. God and man are as different as can be; one is eternal, the other is temporal; one is infinite, the other is finite; one is omniscient, the other is not. That is paradoxical, because they are ontologically totally other, and yet in Jesus Christ the divine and human natures are one person.

Benne makes good use of the word "paradox" in his exposition of the Lutheran view of public theology. He begins with the basic proposition of Christian soteriology: "The central paradox of the Christian faith is that God's salvation of the rebellious world is wrought through the life, death, and resurrection of an obscure Jewish figure, Jesus of Nazareth. That central paradox is built upon other paradoxes: the election of the Jews, a little-known people of the Near East, to be the vessel for bringing forth a Savior; the enfleshment in a Jewish boy of the all-powerful Creator God himself."[133] One of Ogden Nash's pithy poems expresses this paradox: "How odd of God to choose the Jews, but odder still are those who choose the Jewish God and reject the Jews." The core of the gospel is paradoxical, contrary to all human expectation, that God would reconcile the world to himself by the death of one innocent man on a cross. The apostle Paul expressed this paradox by asserting that "we preach Christ crucified, a stumbling block to the Jews and folly to Gentiles.... For the foolishness of God is wiser than men, and the weakness of God is stronger than men."[134]

What Luther called the "happy exchange" is a paradox. Christ exchanges his divine righteousness for our human sin-

---

133. Robert Benne, *The Paradoxical Vision*, 64.
134. I Corinthians 1:23,25.

fulness. The Lutheran doctrine of "justification by faith apart from the works of the law" expresses the same paradox of God's extravagant love to those who instead deserve his wrath. These formulations of the paradoxical vision are certainly not exclusive to Lutherans, but they are a major Lutheran emphasis. Luther was a master in finding fresh ways to speak of the paradox of the evangelical vision of the Christian life: "A Christian is a perfectly free lord of all, subject to none. A Christian is a perfectly dutiful servant of all, subject to all."[135] The Lutheran view of human nature is also expressed in the paradoxical phrase that Christians are simultaneously saints and sinners (*simul justi et peccatores*), a teaching which is perhaps exclusive to the Lutheran tradition. The USA Dialogue on Justification by Faith revealed that Roman Catholics object to the concept of "*simul*" in that they "hold that the sanctifying action of the Holy Spirit removes the guilt of sin and renders the justified pleasing in God's sight. The concupiscence that remains is not truly and properly sin in those born again."[136] Some Protestants teach the delusional belief in sinless perfectionism, believing they are fully sanctified by the Holy Spirit. Luther encountered some of them in his time; there were sectarian radicals he called "enthusiasts" (*Schwärmer*). Of them Luther lamented, "They have swallowed the Holy Spirit, feathers and all."

Benne proceeds to construct a framework for doing public theology in a Lutheran way. The first point to make clear is that the gospel of salvation is exclusively God's work and cannot be co-opted by humans to claim divine endorsement of any political, economic, or social schemes to make this a better world. This does not mean that Christians have no moral responsibility for what transpires in the world. Far from it: "Liberated from

---

135. Martin Luther, The Freedom of a Christian," *Luther's Works*, 31, eds. Jaroslav Pelikan and Helmut Lehmann (Fortress and Concordia), 343.

136. *Justification by Faith: Lutherans and Catholics in Dialogue VII*, eds. H. George Anderson, T. Austin Murphy, and Joseph A. Burgess (Augsburg, 1985), 51-52.

worry about our salvation, we can turn unobsessively to the human task of building a better world, not by prideful claims of transformation, but by determined and yet humble attempts to take small steps for the better."[137] Thus, Christians are spared the illusion that they or any other party can build a paradise on earth. Those who have tried it have created the opposite, a veritable hell on earth. The German Nazis under Hitler tried it with their promise of a "*tausendjähriges Reich*," which turned out to be a murderous totalitarian police state. Many Christians were complicit in this holocaust, Lutherans among them, including theologians, because they completely misinterpreted their own Lutheran doctrine of the two kingdoms.

Benne takes great pains to correct such a misinterpretation of the two-kingdoms doctrine. He quotes a well-known nineteenth century Lutheran theologian, Christian Luthardt, who wrote, "The gospel has absolutely nothing to do with outward existence but only with eternal life.... It is not the vocation of Jesus Christ or the gospel to change the orders of secular life and establish them anew.... Christianity wants to change the person's heart, not his external situation."[138] Benne minces no words; he calls this complete separation of what God does in a person's life from what he does in society "a Lutheran heresy." The effect of such a dualistic misinterpretation of God's two ways of working in the world is to clear the space for tyrants and dictators to do what they want in the social order without worrying about just criticism from the church. Properly understood the two-kingdoms doctrine draws a distinction between two strategies that God uses to rule in the world. One is the rule of God's" left hand" which administers the affairs of the secular word by means of the law to seek justice and preserve order. The other is the rule of God's "right hand" by means of the special revelation in the biblical history of salvation that culminates in the Christ-event,

---

137. Robert Benne, *The Paradoxical Vision*, 72.
138. Robert Benne, *The Paradoxical Vision*, 79.

and is proclaimed by the apostolic gospel throughout the world by the church, through Word and Sacraments, mediating an ultimate and everlasting salvation. This is a paradoxical way of God at work in the world, because what God does through the law is utterly different from what is done through the gospel. Lutherans are extremely alert to the danger of confusing the law and the gospel. Benne sums it up this way: "In the paradox tradition Christians live in two realms at the same time. Each reality is under the governance of God but in sharply different ways. God governs the 'kingdom on the left' with his law and the 'kingdom on the right' with his gospel. God's aim in both modes of rule is the same, to overcome evil and recall disobedient creation to himself, but God uses very different means in each 'kingdom.'"[139] The law of God is not redemptive, but it is politically necessary to sustain and judge all of human life and to make the world a better place in which to live. Christians have a calling to accept their share of responsibility in this realm.

Benne clearly contrasts the Lutheran paradoxical vision from both Roman Catholics and Reformed Protestants under the caption "The Law Becomes Gospel." "The error of Reformed views opens history to the possibility of salvation through political or social transformation.... The Reformed attitude expects too much from this worldly process, and it moves too easily toward a crusading mentality."[140] This is an instance of legalizing the gospel; the earthly city becomes the city of God. "The Catholic attitude leads to similar problems through a different route. Catholics believe that the duality in history can be overcome by humankind, directed by the synthesizing capacities of the church. The church in its wisdom and power aims at a synthesis of culture."[141] In H. Richard Niebuhr's typology in his classic, *Christ and Culture*, he calls the Roman Catholic tradition,

---

139. Robert Benne, *The Paradoxical Vision*, 82.

140. Robert Benne, *The Paradoxical Vision*, 91.

141. Robert Benne, *The Paradoxical Vision*, 92.

"Christ above Culture." The aim is to Christianize culture into a grand synthesis presided over by the church, in which the Pope has greater secular authority than the Emperor, symbolized by the medieval practice of him crowning the emperor.

Concerning the Lutheran doctrine of the law, Benne agrees with those who claim that Lutherans teach a twofold use of the law, the political or civil use and the theological or spiritual use, whereas the Reformed affirm a third didactic use of the law. The third use of the law — the Ten Commandments, the ethical teachings of Jesus, and the paranetic injunctions of Paul, "pray without ceasing," "in everything give thanks" — is meant to guide the behavior of Christians. Benne writes, "Reformed traditions have generally affirmed a third use of the law in addition to the two uses that Lutheranism accepts. The third use is meant to guide the life of the redeemed."[142] This assertion needs to be qualified. It is true that many Lutheran theologians, convinced by modern Luther-research, do reject the third use of the law. But to do that they have to discount the fact that the Lutheran Confessional Writings make a strong case for the third use of the law. The Formula of Concord, Article VI, teaches that there are three uses of the law; the third use of the law is addressed to those who have been born anew through the Holy Spirit to give them "a definite rule according to which they should pattern and regulate their entire life."[143] Admittedly, the first generation of Lutheran theologians were not unanimously in agreement on the matter. The same article concedes that "concerning the third function of the law a controversy has arisen among a few theologians. The question therefore is whether or not the law is to be urged upon reborn Christians. One party said Yes, the other says No."[144] The controversy remains unsettled among

142. Robert Benne, *The Paradoxical Vision*, 97.

143. Formula of Concord, Article VI, Epitome, *The Book of Concord* (Tappert Edition), 479-480.

144. Formula of Concord, Article VI, 480.

contemporary Lutheran theologians. A reasonable case can be made for either side. Confessional Lutherans who say Yes are loathe to quote Luther to contradict one of the articles in the Formula of Concord.

Benne shows how the paradoxical vision has been effective in guiding the social statements written and adopted by the various Lutheran churches in America. He gives high marks especially to the Lutheran Church in America for the many social statements it produced and gives credit to William Lazareth "whose influence can be traced in almost every committee, commission, or document having to do with social issues.... Lazareth labored effectively to shape a public theology informed by the paradoxical vision."[145] Benne laments, however, that the social statements produced by official Lutheranism have had no wide public impact beyond itself. On the other hand, Benne shows that the Lutheran public theology did acquire wider influence beyond official Lutheranism by the contributions of three theologians, none of whom happens to be Lutheran, whose thought was structured by the paradoxical vision — Reinhold Niebuhr (Evangelical and Reformed Church), Glenn Tinder (Episcopal Church USA), and Richard J. Neuhaus (Roman Catholic). Benne writes, "So we have three individual practitioners of the paradoxical vision. A theological professor and liberal reformer, a political philosopher and hesitant radical, and a freelance writer and neoconservative activist make up our varied sample. They hold in common, however, the crucial themes of the paradoxical vision.... They have had more effect on public discourse in our nation than has official Lutheranism."[146]

Benne has succeeded in explicating the Lutheran paradoxical vision that provides a valuable framework for a public theology that engages the complexities of American society today, its political, economic, and cultural configurations. But he does

---

145. Robert Benne, *The Paradoxical Vision*, 109.
146. Robert Benne, *The Paradoxical Vision*, 179.

not claim too much for it. "The paradoxical vision itself does not provide a substantive public theology, i.e., one that leads to specific policy positions.... Within this framework provided by the paradoxical vision, Christian public theology can move in liberal or conservative directions.... The framework itself does not move necessarily toward specific public-political ideologies, though it sets a general direction for such ideologies."[147] Lutheran practitioners of the paradoxical vision run the gamut from the liberal socialist left to the middle of the road centrists or to the conservative far right. That may be the beauty of it, or maybe its fatal flaw. *Chacun à son goût!*

5. On Relating Religion and Politics

In 2010 Benne published a book on political ethics, *Good and Bad Ways to Think about Religion and Politics*, which is more timely in 2020 than when he wrote it. He continued to apply the Lutheran paradoxical vision to avoid two bad ways of relating religion and politics. One bad way is to completely separate them. Militant voices call for religion to be silent about what goes on in the public square. They confuse the "separation of church and state" with the separation of religion from politics. Are persons of faith expected to denude themselves of their religious beliefs when they take a stand on public policy issues? Those who worship the God of the Bible confess that he not only created the whole world but is actively engaged in every facet of its history going forward. They pray every day, "Thy will be done, on earth as it is in heaven!" Their faith in Jesus Christ drives them to side with those who struggle for peace and non-violence and against torture of prisoners, for example. Thus, Christians do not believe their faith is a private matter of no relevance for the public life they share with others of different persuasions. On the other hand, Benne warns of too

---

147. Robert Benne, *The Paradoxical Vision*, 62.

tight a connection between religion and politics, as in the case of theocratic societies. "Neither the church — nor individual Christians *qua* Christians — are given the mandate by God to govern the world."[148]

The other bad way Benne calls fusionism. This happens when religion is recruited to support political parties or regimes. Benne offers as examples both the Nazis under Hitler and the Communists under Stalin who managed to co-opt churches and their leadership to pursue their horrendous political ends. Benne faults churches both from the left and the right that draw a straight line from their religious beliefs to a political party or ideology. It is simply wrong to believe that to be a Christian necessarily means to support the political agenda of the left-wing liberals or the right-wing conservatives. That is fusionism and it is not a rare phenomenon in present-day America. Political leaders foster it to bolster their political ambitions.

Benne's proposal of how religion and politics should be related is called "critical engagement." There are indeed constructive ways to move from the core beliefs of Christianity to the mundane realities of political life. The first important thing is to be utterly clear about the essentials of the Christian faith, what matters and what doesn't. "Christianity comes to politics with the freight of the whole Trinitarian faith."[149] The next important step "in moving from core to periphery is to distill principles from that core that are relevant to politics.... Christians of good will and intelligence, as well as Christians from differing traditions, would perhaps derive different principles — though perhaps not radically different — from the core."[150] Benne has written a book full of wisdom and common sense, on sound theological ground from a Lutheran perspective, and

---

148. Robert Benne, *Good and Bad Ways to Think about Religion and Politics* (Eerdmans, 2010), 17.

149. Robert Benne, *Good and Bad Ways to Think about Religion and Politics*, 42.

150. Robert Benne, *Good and Bad Ways to Think about Religion and Politics*, 45.

knowledgable about the political lay of the land in the United States in these early decades of the twenty-first century. I close this discussion of Benne's writings on public theology with an example of his wisdom tinged with humility. "There are many facets of the Christian moral and intellectual tradition upon which persons of differing political persuasions draw. There may indeed be a straight line from the core to the public policy in God's unerring mind, but we sinful and finite human beings cannot enjoy such certainty. We can only grope for the best connections we can discover."[151]

---

151. Robert Benne, *Good and Bad Ways to Think about Religion and Politics*, 113.

Rev. Dr. Paul R. Sponheim was born in Thief River Falls, Minnesota in 1930. He received his B.A. degree from Concordia College, Moorhead, Minnesota. He earned an M.Div. from Luther Seminary in 1957, and a Ph.D. from the University of Chicago Divinity School in 1961. He also attended the University of Copenhagen on a Fulbright Scholarship (1953-1954) to study Sören Kierkegaard. He wrote a thesis on Kierkegaard and Schleiermacher on Christology, which eventually became his doctoral dissertation at Chicago. At the Chicago Divinity School he latched on to the philosophy of Alfred North Whitehead. From graduate school he went on to become professor and chair of the Department of Religion at Concordia College, Moorhead, Minnesota, joining its faculty in 1961. He was visiting professor of systematic theology at Lutheran Seminary in Gettysburg in 1966-67. Paul Sponheim was ordained in 1962 and served in various parishes in Wisconsin. He joined the faculty of Luther Seminary in 1969 as associate professor and was named Professor of Systematic Theology in 1974. Sponheim served as dean of academic affairs at Luther Seminary from 1974-1976. He retired from Luther Seminary in 2000, but continued to serve eight more years as senior lecturer, forty years of service in all.

Five

Paul R. Sponheim

Lutheran Process Theology

P aul Sponheim was a professor of systematic theology who taught at Luther Seminary in St. Paul for forty years. During most of that time he was a colleague of Gerhard Forde who labelled his own theology "radical Lutheranism." As we present Sponheim's type of theology readers will understand how appropriate for him to refer to Forde as "my opposite number on many issues. I've wondered if I harbored a little envy toward Gerhard, who carried the mantle of our denominational name so masterfully.... I settled in somewhat on the left edge of the faculty, or at least walked through most of my days feeling that's the place I best fit."[152]

1. From Thief River Falls to the University of Chicago

Sponheim was born in Thief River Falls, Minnesota, in 1930. His mother was a devout Christian who taught her children the basics of faith and told them Bible stories. His father was an agnostic who never went to church. Paul was one of six children. The family was split right down the middle. One brother and two sisters chose to go their father's way, he and two other brothers chose their mother's path into the faith of the church. Paul and his brother Don became ordained Lutheran ministers.

---

152. Paul R. Sponheim, *Learning on Life's Way. Remembering and Reflecting by a Teller of Tall Tales* (Wipf and Stock, 2018), 75.

However, the factor of honest doubt and sincere disbelief which he encountered in his family life haunted Sponheim throughout his struggle to understand how humans stand before God and what difference it makes in the end. The matter was compounded later in life when Paul recounts that although he and his wife Nell raised their three children in the church, none of their eight grandchildren have been baptized. These stories of faith and unbelief in the Sponheim family became interwoven in Paul's personal search for an open theological stance of inclusion and listening to disagreeing others in a non-judgmental way.

After graduating from High School Paul Sponheim enrolled at the University of Minnesota, but after one month he discovered that it was not a good fit for him. So he transferred to Concordia College in Moorhead, Minnesota, from which he graduated four years later with an outstanding academic record. At Concordia he encountered the writings of the great Danish philosopher, Sören Kierkegaard (1813-1855), introduced to him by Professor Reidar Thomte, himself a Kierkegaard scholar. Kierkegaard wrote volumes on faith, God, church, and morality in a style that in the twentieth century became known as "existentialism." His love affair with the Danish genius led to a Fulbright grant to study in Copenhagen, Denmark, where he met leading Kierkegaard scholars. About this significant year as a Fulbright scholar Sponheim reminisced, "I've been reading and teaching Sören Kierkegaard ever since…. I'll just say that each time I turn to this poet of paradox and master of dialectic, I go through a two-stage reaction: 1) 'This guy is crazy; this can't be right'; and 2) 'He's hit the nail on the head; this is how things are with God and the creature.'"[153]

From Concordia College Sponheim entered Luther Seminary to prepare for ordination as a Lutheran pastor, four years of study including one year of internship. There we met for the first time in a class of eighty students, all male in those years.

---

153. Paul R. Sponheim, *Learning on Life's Way*, 18.

Robert Jenson, nicknamed "Billy-Bob," and Gerhard Forde, nicknamed "Bish," were also classmates of ours in those early '50s. The three of them lived in the student dormitory; I lived off campus, married with one child, and working twenty hours a week at a Nabisco plant loading delivery trucks at night. How could it happen that the four of us contemporaries would head off to graduate school to earn doctorates in theology soon after graduating from Luther Seminary? At the time I said I had to do it to get a real theological education. It is no exaggeration to say that none of our professors had an earned theological doctorate in the field in which they were teaching. Paul Sponheim went to the University of Chicago Divinity School, Robert Jenson went to the University of Heidelberg, which at the time had the best Lutheran theological faculty in the world, Gerhard Forde and I went to the Harvard University Divinity School, which was enjoying a theological renaissance under President Nathan Pusey. Almost overnight he built a new prestigious faculty with the advent of Paul Tillich, Georges Florovsky, Richard R. Niebuhr, John Dillenberger, Frank Cross, Krister Stendahl, John Wild, George Buttrick, and others.

In 1957 Paul Sponheim entered the doctoral program in systematic theology at the Chicago Divinity School. He had already spent a year in Denmark as a Fulbright scholar, writing a thesis comparing the Christology of Sören Kierkegaard, a child of Danish Lutheran pietism, and Friedrich Daniel Ernst Schleiermacher, the father of German liberal Protestant theology. The seeds of this study later blossomed into the first book he published, *Kierkegaard on Christ and Christian Coherence* (Harper & Row, 1968), a revised version of his doctoral dissertation advised by Jaroslav Pelikan. Sponheim's four years at the Chicago Divinity School resulted in a radical intellectual transformation from the warm religious categories of Reformation theology to the cold metaphysical abstractions of process philosophy. It would have meant for me an inoperable intellectual hernia. But Sponheim revelled in his newly found wellspring of ideas that he discovered in the process thought of Alfred North Whitehead (1861-1947) and Charles Hartshorne (1897-2000). A summary of what this meant for Sponheim's grasp of Christian theology is available in one of the ten books he wrote, *Faith and Process: The Significance of Process Thought for Christian Faith* (Augsburg, 1979).

2. Sponheim's "Two Big Guys": Kierkegaard and Whitehead

Sponheim left Chicago deeply immersed in the thought of two great philosophical minds, Kierkegaard and Whitehead. Looking back decades later Sponheim wrote, "In 2011 I made an effort in *Love's Availing Power* to bring together the two 'big guys' in my half century of professional activity, Kierkegaard and Whitehead. These two figures seem a strange pair to conventional scholarship. Whitehead was born six years after Kierkegaard died, but I argue that we need them together.... I suggest their mutual need in the terms of the first article, which had come to function so prominently in my theology. I argue that Kierkegaard's deficient cosmology needs the Englishman's help, but the Dane contributes a richer anthropology that Whitehead's cosmological scheme needs. The Danish genius luminously describes what it is to be a human being, but he needs his English brother to help him fathom the teeming life beyond the border of human skin. The Cambridge mathematician brilliantly sketches the most general cosmological principles, never failing of exemplification, but falls short in figuring out what distinguishes human reality in particular. So, I pondered Kierkegaard in writing how we are called to image God's love in freedom and Whitehead in discussing how that freedom enables us to imagine the relatedness of the world."[154]

It is significant that Sponheim chose two philosophers to be his guiding lights to illuminate a professional career of more

---

154. Paul R. Sponheim, *Learning on Life's Way*, 90.

than fifty years teaching and writing as a Lutheran systematic theologian. Not that there is anything wrong for a theologian to make use of philosophy in doing constructive Christian theology. Augustine used Plato, Aquinas used Aristotle, Luther used Ockham, Barth used Kant, Tillich used Schelling, Pannenberg used Habermas, and so forth. It is necessary for Christian theologians to engage the history of philosophy, since they inescapably share the realm of ideas — e.g., logic, epistemology, and ontology. As Sponheim's thought evolved and was disclosed in his numerous reviews, articles, and books, he professed that it was his intention to respect the great tradition of granting the ultimate word to God's self-revelation in the history of salvation, and not to be trumped by the penultimate insights of philosophy.

Whitehead's influence on Sponheim's theology is most pronounced in his concentration on the first article of the Creed. Sponheim was critical of the tendency of Christian pastors and theologians who reduce their speaking of God to speaking of Jesus. He quoted H. Richard Niebuhr approvingly who characterized this as "a Unitarianism of the second article."[155] This does not mean that Sponheim totally neglected the second article of the Creed which speaks about the life, death, and resurrection of Jesus. He would frequently say "the first article is the *first* article," by which he means that we can already know a lot about God and the works of God before his incarnate presence in Jesus. This should be obvious by the sheer fact that the Old Testament comes before the New Testament. Sponheim is in good company when he stresses that it is simply bad theology to overload the second article at the expense of the first article. Even when it comes to soteriology, the doctrine of salvation, the God of the Hebrew Scriptures did not only create the world as an exercise of power, but he elected the people of Israel as an expression of his saving love. Sponheim's emphasis on the foundational role

---

155. Paul R. Sponheim, *Speaking of God: Relational Theology* (Chalice Press, 2006), 1.

of the first article of the Creed is most clearly developed in his book, *The Pulse of Creation: God and the Transformation of the World* (Augsburg Fortress, 1999).

3. The Knowledge of God

Inasmuch as all of Sponheim's writings are centered on God, he considers the different dimensions of the relationship of human creatures to their Creator — speaking *to* God in prayer, speaking *for* God in evangelism, and speaking *of* God in theological reflection. He also warns against the pretentious tendency of some evangelistic crusaders to act as though they are speaking *as* God. Sponheim joined the team of Lutheran systematic theologians who produced the two-volume work of *Christian Dogmatics*.[156] He was selected to write on the Third Locus, "The Knowledge of God." He acknowledges that it is the function of dogmatics to give a truthful account of what Christians believe and know about God based on both his general revelation through nature and his special revelation in the biblical history of salvation. He writes, "Our task is confessional; it is to overhear, albeit somewhat analytically, Christians speaking of their knowledge of God. It is not essentially apologetic. We are not trying to persuade non-Christians that they can or do know God."[157]

What do Christians claim they know of God, according to Sponheim? First of all, they know that God exists; God is real. He calls into question Paul Tillich's assertion that "The being of God is being-itself. The being of God cannot be understood as the existence of a being alongside others or above others.... Grave difficulties attend the attempt to speak of God as existing.... It is as atheistic to affirm the existence of God as it is to

---

156. *Christian Dogmatics*, Vols. I & II, eds. Carl E. Braaten and Robert W. Jenson (Fortress, 1984).

157. Paul R. Sponheim, "The Knowledge of God," *Christian Dogmatics*, Vol. 1, 213.

deny it. God is being-itself, not a being."[158] For Sponheim such a way of speaking of God seems to border on pantheism. God and the world are ontologically other. Adopting the language of process philosophy Sponheim affirms the "categorical supremacy of God." He writes, "Some theologians suggest that 'existence' is inappropriately applied to God. I disagree."[159] Christians also know that what they know of God is because God reveals his will to be in relationship with those who are not God. Then comes the whopper: "Christians find their clearest access to the knowledge of God in the gospel concerning what God has done in the person and work of Jesus for the salvation of all."[160] This Christological proposition is important because in the end it is Sponheim's ticket to be one of the authors of a textbook on Christian dogmatics. Actually, however, among the ten books Sponheim wrote, not one was on the Second Article of the Creed, on Christology, treating the personal identity or Jesus Christ or on his atoning work, though occasional comments can be found here and there that indicate his leaning toward what is known as a "low" rather than a "high" Christology. Nor did he write anything of substantial length on the Third Article of the Creed, on the Holy Spirit, the Church and Sacraments, and Eschatology.[161]

Sponheim's profound and detailed exposition of the reality and revelation of the categorically supreme God and on its recep-

---

158. Paul Tillich, *Systematic Theology*, Vol. 1 (The University of Chicago Press, 1951), 235, 236, 237.

159. Paul R. Sponheim, "The Knowledge of God," *Christian Dogmatics*, Vol. 1, 200.

160. Paul R. Sponheim, "The Knowledge of God," *Christian Dogmatics*, Vol. 1, 200.

161. In a self-revealing comment Sponheim confessed that he asked to write the locus on "The Knowledge of God" for *Christian Dogmatics* "because I didn't want to get stuck with something like 'The Church and the Sacraments.' This aversion to an assignment on the third article of the creed was part sensing I would have to work very hard to get the important things said and part fear that what I would find interesting would place me outside the pale of presumed orthodoxy." Paul R. Sponheim, *Learning on Life's Way*, 61.

tion in human experience and language is perhaps unmatched by any other American Lutheran systematic theologians. Yet, for Sponheim the revelation and knowledge of God are not subjects to be kept within the walls of the church. Sponheim is passionate about entering into dialogue with those outside, with adherents of other religions as well as those with no religion at all, agnostics and atheists. This passion was fueled early on by his unsettling encounter with atheism in his own family. In particular the sincere atheism of his sister Carol continued to haunt him throughout his life. His brother Irwin and sister Marion also expressed no feeling or belief in the God of religion. The theological question Sponheim mulled over was how would unbelievers like them be included within the orbit of God's universal love? Wouldn't God honor their freedom to reject the offer of his boundless love? On the other hand, might not their sincerity and honesty count for something in their standing *coram deo*? Sponheim writes about his sister Carol: "Before God she did not believe in God. From my viewpoint I seek to believe God somehow recognizes and welcomes that honesty. She and I needed to talk together about what at bottom mattered to each of us. We failed to do that, failed to be *fully* honest with each other."[162]

4. Christianity and Other Religions

Sponheim fully respected the Christian claim that its message is true. "The truth question matters to us for, as humans, meaning is essential to our salvation. Thus the truth question matters to the Christian. It matters that the Christian faith is claiming to be true."[163] According to the Holy Scriptures the apostolic faith claims that the gospel of God which Christ commissioned his

---

162. Paul R. Sponheim, *Learning on Life's Way*, 94.
163. Paul R. Sponheim, "The Truth Will Make You Free," *Lutherans and the Challenge of Religious Pluralism*, eds. Frank W. Klos, C. Lynn Nakamura, and Daniel F. Martensen (Augsburg, 1990), 141.

church to tell to the nations bears the good news of salvation for all. That message is particular and universal at the same time. C. S. Lewis coined the phrase "the scandal of particularity." Acts 4:12 states it most sharply: "There is salvation in no one else, for there is no other name under heaven given among mortals by which we must be saved." This verse coupled with I Timothy 2:4 underscores the dilemma, "God desires all to be saved and to come to the knowledge of truth." Sponheim captured the problem the "scandal of particularity" poses for Christian theology in his book, *Faith and the Other*: "A God who would not desire all is not good enough to be God.... A God who desires all but is capable of reaching only some is not great enough to be God."[164] Sponheim sees the problem: "Is it not problematic that the Christian God, the true God, has no more than a minority following after all these centuries? We are told that God wants all. But is not this God strangely ineffective? Ironically, thus to protect the uniqueness of the Christian God seems to undercut the very credentials of that God. Moreover, the Christian text itself refuses the simplification involved in this response, for it speaks of God's witness and word well beyond the boundaries of Christendom: God has not left any people without some witness (Acts 14:17). Thus, given the actual plurality of faiths and given the Christian faith's own claim on the others, simply to say only Christianity is true is not to engage the truth question adequately."[165]

In a number of his writings Sponheim wrestles with the engagement of the Christian faith with other religions, especially Judaism, Islam, Buddhism, and Hinduism. "Pluralism is in the air we breathe," he noted. He would clearly endorse the call of Nicholas of Cusa (1401-1464) in *De Pace Fidei* for religious tolerance and peace between the religions, for they all have a share

---

164. Paul R. Sponheim, *Faith and the Other: A Relational Theology* (Fortress Press, 1993), 151.

165. Paul R. Sponheim, "The Truth Will Make You Free," *Lutherans and the Challenge of Religious Pluralism*, 145.

in the truth revealed by God. Even Paul, Christ's apostle to the Gentiles, declared that the living God "allowed all the nations to walk in their own ways; yet he did not leave himself without witness" (Acts 14:16-17). All the religions somehow bear witness to religious truth to some degree. But is that enough? The same apostle thought not, because he gave himself unstintingly on his three missionary journeys to preach the gospel of salvation to Jews, Greeks, and Romans alike. Like so many world missionaries following in his footsteps he experienced imprisonment, beatings, stoning, shipwreck, sleepless nights, and all kinds of danger (II Corinthians 11:23-27). It is good and useful for professors of religion to engage in dialogue with persons of other faiths, seeking as much common ground as possible for the sake of world peace, usually conducted at room temperature. Sponheim quotes many of them — John Cobb, John Hick, Fritjof Capra, Mohandas K. Ghandi, Sarvepalli Radhakrishnan, D. T. Suzuki, and Masao Abe. But academic dialogues (apologetics) and missionary proclamation (evangelism) have very different objectives. As important as inter-religious dialogue certainly is to cool down the temperature of over-heated religious passions, it is to the credit of the Christian world missionary movement that the center of Christianity has shifted from Europe to the Global South. There are more Anglicans worshiping every Sunday in Nigeria than in England, more Lutherans attending church in Ethiopia than in Norway.

Sponheim does express his thoughts and concerns about Christian evangelism which merit serious consideration. What he says may be true and wise even though one might wish he would say more that needs to be said. But every theologian without exception writes from a particular situation and limited experience and not from a universal outlook above the fray. Sponheim reminds us that God had a mission in mind that began before the foundation of the world. The first outward act of God in creating the world is continued through an ongoing creative evolutionary forward movement toward the end, the goal of promised fulfillment. At some time in the middle of things (the history of *Homo sapiens*) God revealed that he "is seeking a relationship of loving intimacy with all God's creatures."[166] Christians learn of God's love in the story of Jesus in perhaps their favorite Bible verse: "For God so loved the world that he gave his only Son, that whoever believes in him should not perish but have eternal life." (John 3:16). But Sponheim avers that this gracious movement of God to his creatures did not begin with Jesus. "It is rooted way 'back' in the will of the Creator. Indeed, it is rooted even further back in the very reality of the inner life of God."[167] Love is the essence of the inner life of God; it is what Sponheim calls "'the category proper,' that central character of God that is present wherever God is present."[168] Sponheim is in good company when he makes this assertion, appealing to Eberhard Jüngel and Robert W. Jenson who defined the Trinity as God's being as love in the perichoretic[169] relations of the Father, the Son, and the Holy Spirit. Sponheim quotes Jenson as saying "to be God is to be related."[170] Then he adds, "The doctrine of the Trinity assures us that God has relationships within God's own reality."[171]

God expresses his eternal love to all creatures in a way that can be experienced and known. "The idea of a God of love is hardly the private property of Christians.... Similarly, the notion of incarnation has not been successfully patented by Christianity."[172] The classical Christian tradition has always affirmed that there is knowledge of God in other religions through what is called "general revelation." A rather large pool of religious ideas is shared to a great extent by the major religions. However, for Christian

---

166. Paul R. Sponheim, *Speaking of God*, 126.

167. Paul R. Sponheim, *Speaking of God*, 126.

168. Paul R. Sponheim, *Speaking of God*, 9.

169. "*Perichoresis*" is a Greek term referring to the relationship of the three persons of the Triune God to one another.

170. Robert W. Jenson, "The Triune God," *Christian Dogmatics*, Vol. 2, 127.

171. Paul R. Sponheim, *Speaking of God*, 43.

172. Paul R. Sponheim, "The Knowledge of God," *Christian Dogmatics*, 256.

faith the incarnation of God in Jesus is not merely an idea but an actual historical event that happened once for all (*ephapax*). Sponheim takes account of this difference in many different locutions. The omnipresent God who is everywhere present in all moments of time is "newly present in Jesus."[173] "In this Jew from Nazareth Christian faith finds God decisively present 'in the flesh'.... The decisiveness of God's commitment in the coming of Jesus is why Paul in Romans can so boldly declare that nothing can 'separate us from the love of God in Christ Jesus our Lord.' (Romans 8:39b) ... I have tried to capture this decisiveness by telling people, 'If you want God not to love you, good luck!'[174]

5. God's Big Operation in the World

Sponheim frequently spoke about the scope of what God is doing in the world. He liked to use the phrase, "God's big operation in the world." As we have indicated, Sponheim's account of God's work certainly included the story of Jesus of Nazareth, most of what is recited in the second article of the Creed, his death on the cross and resurrection from the tomb. But then the narrative seems to stop all too abruptly. What about the third article of the Creed? Lutherans are famous for being allergic to talk about the Holy Spirit. The allergy goes back to Martin Luther's attack on the Zwickau Prophets who claimed they had received direct revelations from the Holy Spirit and possessed all the Pentecostal gifts. Luther dismissed them as "*Schwärmer*," which means "enthusiasts." Luther's criticism of what he saw as their abuse of the Spirit's power does not mean he himself had a low appreciation for the work of the Holy Spirit. Luther wrote these beautiful words in his *Small Catechism:*

> *I believe that by my own reason or strength I cannot believe in Jesus Christ my Lord or come to him. But the Holy*

---

173. Paul R. Sponheim, *Speaking of God*, 22.
174. Paul R. Sponheim, *Speaking of God*, 23, 24.

Spirit has called me through the gospel, enlightened me with his gifts, and sanctified and preserved me in the true faith, just as he calls, gathers, enlightens, and sanctifies the whole Christian church on earth and preserves it in union with Jesus Christ in the one true faith. In this Christian church, the Holy Spirit daily and abundantly forgives all my sins, and the sins of all believers, and on the last day he will raise me and all the dead and will grant eternal life to me and to all who believe in Christ. This is most certainly true.

The Danish Lutheran theologian, Regin Prenter (1907-1990), set the record straight concerning Luther's doctrine of the Holy Spirit in his book, *Spiritus Creator.*[175] Prenter showed that in Luther's view the Holy Spirit dominates every aspect of his vast theological output in his sermons and commentaries. It is no exaggeration to say that without the creative work of the Holy Spirit all talk about the Father and the Son falls on deaf ears. Without the Holy Spirit Christ is really absent from the church's proclamation of the Word, really absent from the water of Baptism, really absent from the bread and the wine in the Sacrament of the Altar, as well as absent from the church's ministry and mission to the world. What Paul states in I Corinthians 12:3, "No one can say 'Jesus is Lord' except by the Holy Spirit," should be a sobering reminder that a full presentation of the Christian faith and hope requires due attention to the person and work of the Holy Spirit. Sponheim was right to quote H. Richard Niebhur's lament about "a unitarianism of the second article," reducing all God-talk to Jesus-talk, as in much of Protestant Evangelicalism. What is needed is a full-orbed treatment of the works of all three persons of the Holy Trinity.

Sponheim wrote the Fifth Locus on "Sin and Evil" in the two-volume work of *Christian Dogmatics* in a very thorough manner, covering in depth all the relevant issues — creation

---

175. Regin Prenter, *Spiritus Creator* (Muhlenberg Press, 1953).

and the fall, the nature, origin, and effects of sin, evil and suffering. In the final section that deals with "The Work of God Against Evil" Sponheim's lead sentence states: "God responds decisively to sin in Jesus and the sacramental life of the church, and God draws human beings to faith, obedience, and hope in a kingdom which is beyond Eden." Sponheim explains that this happens on account of the work of Christ in response to the human predicament in bondage to sin and evil — and death. The dogmatic locus on the work of Christ deals with various soteriological theories of atonement. In his little classic, *Christus Victor*, Gustaf Aulén discussed three types of theory, the subjective view (Abelard), the Latin penal theory (Anselm), and the classic patristic view revived by Luther. Sponheim shows that each of them has a valid insight into the salvific work of Christ, each accenting in distinctively different ways the role played by his incarnation, life, death, and resurrection in the triumph of God over sin, death, and the devil. He continues by explaining how God uses the sacramental life of the church to respond to the human predicament, especially in baptism. He is silent about the other sacraments, absolution and the Lord's Supper, nor does he treat the work of the Holy Spirit in applying the benefits of Christ in the Christian life, in his acts of justification, regeneration, and sanctification.

6. The Future of Life Beyond Death

The third article of the Creed confesses Christian belief in "the forgiveness of sins, the resurrection of the body, and the life everlasting." In closing his treatment of "Sin and Evil," Sponheim looks ahead to the future of Christian hope and offers, in his words, "some emphatically indicative sentences."[176] This is Sponheim at his best, in my estimation. He asks, "How does it end? Of that we will say only three things. First, it will be a

---

176. Paul R. Sponheim, *Learning on Life's Way*, 105.

time of consequence; the direction of our pilgrimage will reach its consummation in a new ontological state.... God's faithful will be clearly beyond Eden, for they will be "not able to sin. Second, in the main Christians have held that God does indeed will that all shall be saved and come to the knowledge of truth.... Third, that new life perfects the pilgrimage which is our present life.... Surely that new condition will entail an intensification of life, of living.... But all that hinders us in our relationship to God will not remain."[177] Sponheim was right in saying that these are "emphatically indicative sentences." Decades later he reaffirms what he believes about the future of life beyond death. "Speaking of God, perhaps we do best to settle for saying that at death we go to God who cannot die. That is the God in whom we — and all — live, move, and have our being even now. That God is a continuing Creator, who has shown a penchant for 'doing a new thing.'... The 'life now' of which we have spoken looks ahead to a life 'beyond Eden,' where one is 'beyond freedom' and yet more fully alive.... The moral change sought can only be secured through an ontological change.... For human beings not to be able (to want to) sin would be such an ontological change."[178]

In his Memoirs, *Learning on Life's Way*, Sponheim returns to the topic of eschatology, quoting "mind-blowing" Bible passages that speak of "a new heaven and a new earth" (Rev. 21:1), of death being "swallowed up in victory" (I Cor. 15:54), of God who "will wipe away every tear" (Rev. 7:17), and when "we will see God face to face" (I Cor. 13:12). He writes here with a bit more tentativeness. He asks, "Is it true?" He asks about the evidence, what constitutes evidence and how much evidence is enough. He claims to find help from his two big mentors, Kierkegaard and Whitehead, in answering these questions, rather than seeking wisdom from the "Great Tradition," starting with the Scriptures, which has much to say about the Christian hope.

---

177. Paul R. Sponheim, "Sin and Evil," *Christian Dogmatics*, 461-462.
178. Paul R. Sponheim, *Speaking of God*, 159, 162.

He strikes the refrain, "There is so much we do not know."[179] So what can we know? What is there to know? We can know what God has revealed. Christians can have, according to Robert W. Jenson, "The Knowledge of Things Hoped For."[180] Such knowledge is given where alone it can be found, in the substance of God's revelation in the biblical story of Jesus the Christ. Sponheim ends his account somewhat wistfully, "Funny thing, it may be true. As my colleague Gerhard Forde used to say, 'We can hope so.' Actually, I'm not in a very good position to call this a slam dunk either way."[181]

Addendum

Paul Sponheim was a master wordsmith with a sense of humor. Here is brief sample of some of his quips that have delighted many readers, including me.

"If you have more than one God, you don't have any."

"God has a very big operation going on in the cosmos."

"The ommis do not stand or fall together."

"God has a pretty good left hand."

"I will never curse finitude. Only God is immortal."

"Lutherans only feel good when they feel bad."

"One does not praise the Creator by cursing the creatures."

"God gets up early and stays up late."

"If you want God not to love you, 'good luck' with that."

179. Paul R. Sponheim, *Learning on Life's Way*, 110.

180. Robert W. Jenson, *The Knowledge of Things Hoped For. The Sense of Theological Discourse* (Oxford University Press, 1969).

181. Paul R. Sponheim, *Learning on Life's Way*, 116.

Rev. Dr. Philip Hefner was born December 10, 1932 in Denver, Colorado. He is Professor Emeritus of Systematic Theology of the Lutheran School of Theology at Chicago. Philip Hefner received a B.A. in 1954 from Midland Lutheran College, Fremont, Nebraska, an M.Div. in 1959 from Chicago Lutheran Theological Seminary, Maywood, Illinois, and a Ph.D. in 1962 from the University of Chicago Divinity School. In 1988 Philip Hefner was instrumental in creating the Chicago Center for Religion and Science, which was later renamed the Zygon Center for Religion and Science. He was the first director of the Center and remained in that capacity from 1988 to 2003. Hefner is the former editor of *Zygon: Journal of Religion and Science*, the leading journal of religion and science in the world. Hefner was four times co-chair of the annual conference of the Institute on Religion in an Age of Science (IRAS), Hefner became a prominent leader in the paradigm of "religious naturalism," which rejects any reliance on a supernatural explanatory framework, theoretically espoused by traditional religion. He is a Senior Fellow at the Metaxus Institute. The major focus of Hefner's research career has been on the interaction of religion and science. The Publications Board of *Zygon* has established the "Philip Hefner Fund" to honor his twenty years of editorial leadership. He is an ordained minister of the Evangelical Lutheran Church in America.

Six

Philip Hefner

Lutheran Theological Anthropology

P hilip Hefner was born in in Denver, Colorado, in 1932. He received a B.A. from Midland Lutheran College, a B.D. from the Lutheran School of Theology at Chicago, and a Ph.D. from the the University of Chicago Divinity School. He is an ordained minister of the Evangelical Lutheran Church in America, and served as a professor of systematic theology at the Lutheran School of Theology at Chicago for his entire teaching career. His demonstrated a keen interest in the interaction of religion and science very early in his professional life. In 1988 Philip Hefner established the Chicago Center for Religion and Science, later renamed the *Zygon Center for Religion and Science*, which he served as director from 1988 until 2003. In 1989 Hefner became the editor for *Zygon: Journal of Religion and Science*, the most prestigious periodical dealing with religion and science in the world. Four times he co-chaired the annual conference of the Institute on Religion in an Age of Science (IRAS), and established his reputation as a leading proponent of "Religious Naturalism," a new paradigm for interpreting religion exclusively within a naturalistic framework. Philip Hefner was honored for his many contributions to the interface of religion and science by being elected as a Senior Fellow of the Metanexus Institute, founded in 1997 to promote advanced scientific and philosophical explorations of fundamental questions of worldwide significance, including those of interest to all faith traditions, academic and scientific disciplines. Hefner has written six books and more than 150 articles, half of which deal with religion and the natural sciences.

1. Hefner's Predecessors in the Study of Religion and Science

The systematic interaction between religion and science is a new discipline in the history of Christian theology, beginning in the early 1960s. About that time theologians and scientists began serious inquiry into the ways their disciplines impinge on each other. For many years Christian theologians were suspicious of and often even hostile to modern science, especially its practically universal adoption of the evolutionary theory of Charles Darwin. The study of science seemed to have a negative effect on religious belief and scientists, whether rightly or wrongly, got the reputation of being less interested in religious matters. The great showdown between religion and science was featured in the Scopes Monkey Trial in the 1920s when William Jennings Bryan, a three time Democratic nominee for President, debated the highly celebrated defense lawyer, Clarence Darrow. The trial highlighted the conflict between Fundamentalism and Modernism, one that still lingers on mostly in the South. This conflict was further magnified by the famous sermon delivered in 1922 by the Baptist preacher, Harry Emerson Fosdick, "Shall the Fundamentalists Win?", in which he repudiated the core beliefs of Fundamentalism and called for an open-minded, intellectual, and tolerant encounter with the issues at hand.

Within a generation later (1960s) some theologians took up the study of religion and science in an interdisciplinary way. One of the first was Thomas Torrance, a professor of Christian Dogmatics at the University of Edinburgh, who challenged the idea that religion and science are necessarily at odds with each other, but should rather be seen as allies in a common front to understand reality.[182] Another pioneer in the dialogue between the two disciplines was Ian Barbour, trained as a physicist with a Ph.D. from the University of Chicago and as a theologian from Yale University. He was Professor of Science, Technology and Society at Carleton College.[183] Wolfhart Pannenberg was a German Lutheran systematic theologian who wrote comprehensively on the methodological interconnections between theology, philosophy, and science.[184] Another early contributor to the religion and science dialogue was the British theologian, Arthur Peacocke, a prolific author of many lucidly written books.[185] The point of referencing these four theologians — Scottish, American, German, and English — is to show that Hefner followed in the footsteps of theologians who had already attempted to reconcile religious and scientific methodologies and perspectives.

2. The Doctrine of Creation

In the early 1980s I realized that I had been teaching dogmatics for fifteen years without an adequate textbook that explains the core doctrines for American Lutheran seminarians studying

---

182. See two influential books by Thomas F. Torrance, *Theological Science* (Oxford University Press, 1962) and *Theological and Natural Science* (Wipf and Stock, 2002).

183. Ian Barbour delivered the Gifford Lectures at the University of Aberdeen, published as *Religion in an Age of Science* (Harper and Row, 1990). Two other important books at the forefront of the dialogue between scientists and theologians are: *Issues in Science and Religion* (SCM Press, 1966) and *Myths, Models, and Paradigms: The Nature of Scientific and Religious Language* (SCM Press, 1974), which discuss in detail the relations of religious thought and the methods and theories of science.

184. Wolfhart Pannenberg's two important works on theology and science are: *Theology and the Philosophy of Science* (Westminster Press, 1976) and *Anthropology in Theological Perspective* (Westminster Press, 1985).

185. Arthur Peacocke was one of Hefner's most frequently cited interlocutor. Two titles are worthy of mention here: *Science and the Christian Experiment* (Oxford University Press, 1971); *Creation and the World of Science* (Clarendon Press, 1979).

for the ordained ministry. The only textbook available was a translation of Gustaf Aulén's *The Faith of the Christian Church* (Muhlenberg Press, 1948). I wondered, why don't we write one of our own? I presented this idea to Robert Jenson with whom I had collaborated on a number of projects. In 1961 we were the founding editors of *dialog — A Journal of Theology*, still going strong after sixty years, although under subsequent editors it has become a very different kind of publication. And we had co-authored *The Futurist Option* (Paulist Press, 1970) that dealt with the recovery of the future dimension of time in Christian eschatology. We agreed that such a dogmatics textbook is definitely needed, but also that it would work best if it were multi-authored, in order to respect the varieties of perspectives emerging among American Lutheran theologians. We invited four other theologians to join us — Gerhard Forde, Paul Sponheim, Hans Schwarz (a German theologian teaching at Lutheran Theological Southern Seminary), and Philip Hefner. Gerhard Forde, Paul Sponheim, Robert Jenson, and I came out of the Norwegian Lutheran Church in America, that changed its name to the Evangelical Lutheran Church, to delete its ethnic identification. Philip Hefner came out of the United Lutheran Church in America, mostly of German ethnic background. We issued the invitations and they all accepted. All of the authors had demonstrated in their early writings that they would be creative, productive, and prolific authors of serious books and articles on Christian theology. Hefner had co-authored with Robert Benne, *Defining America, A Christian Critique of the American Dream*. He also had written a number of scholarly articles published in *Zygon: Journal of Religion and Science* and various other periodicals. Our plan was to produce a dogmatics text book in two volumes with twelve loci. Each of us would write two of the chapters. Philip Hefner chose to write the Fourth Locus on "The Creation" and the Ninth Locus on "The Church."

Hefner's choice to write on the doctrine of creation turned out to be opportune. He produced as fine a treatise on the doctrine of creation as one could find in any text on dogmatics. We were pleased to have it. Hefner covered all the bases, starting with a well-researched survey and summary of current scholarship on the biblical witness to creation in both the Old and the New Testaments. The first basic statement is that God is the Creator of all that is. The second is that there is considerable diversity in the biblical witness, offering a rich fund for speculation and edification. Third, the biblical writers linked their witness to God's creation to the existential situation in which they lived. Fourth, the biblical writers related their belief in the original creation to the experience in the present and vision of the future. Fifth, the New Testament is unmistakably clear that Christ is central as the agent, goal, and power of creation.[186]

The confession that God created the world "out of nothing" (*ex nihilo*) is essential to underscore the world's total dependence on its Creator. The early church fathers distinguished the "*ex nihilo*" assertion from Plato's idea of the Demiurge who fashioned the world out of some preexistent material and imposed order on it. The doctrine insists that everything that is depends for its being on God the Creator. "*Creatio ex nihilo* is first and foremost a statement about who God is and what kind of a God that God is. It is because of their experience of God that the Hebrews, the Jews, and the Christians have asserted the Creator of the *creatio ex nihilo*."[187] The world is the creation of a God who ceaselessly cares about the world in an ongoing manner. Hefner writes, "The Lutheran tradition has emphasized the caring quality of God *vis-à-vis* the creation by referring to God as 'Father'."[188] Then he quotes Luther's explanation of the First Commandment which every confirmand should know by heart, "A god is that to which we look for all good and to which we find refuge in every time of need. To have a god is nothing else than to trust and believe him with all our heart.... The pur-

186. Philip Hefner, "The Creation," *Christian Dogmatics*, 293-294.
187. Philip Hefner, "The Creation," *Christian Dogmatics*, 310.
188. Philip Hefner, "The Creation," *Christian Dogmatics*, 302.

pose of this commandment, therefore, is to require true faith and confidence of the heart."[189] Confessing the caring motif is further elaborated in the dogmatic tradition by the concept of God's continuing creation (*creatio continua*) and providential governance (*conservatio* and *gubernatio*). The effect of the traditional Christian concept of God the creator of all things was to reject all dualistic ways of relating God and the world, such as the church encountered in Gnosticism, Manicheism, and Marcionitism, movements that separated the Old Testament God of creation from the New Testament God of redemption.

Philip Hefner received his Ph. D. from the University of Chicago Divinity School which was the hotbed of process theology, devoted to the metaphysics of Alfred North Whitehead and Charles Hartshorne. In the previous chapter we discussed the impact of this philosophy on the theology of Paul R. Sponheim for good or ill. Hefner provided a helpful evaluation of the contribution process thought made to the understanding of creation, and I quote at length, "The process theologians, by and large, present the concept of a God who does not *create* in the *ex nihilo* sense.... This concept of God is clearly not the same as the one that we have elaborated in our survey of biblical and later traditional sources. We have portrayed a God who is Creator *ex nihilo*, a God on whom all things depend for their being, as well as for meaning and purpose, goodness, and order. Process theologians object that such a picture of God is autocratic, 'imperial,' and conceptually impossible, since a being who has the power to control and determine other beings is not even thinkable to our minds. Our discussion has put the matter in such a way as to suggest that the process-theological objection is not precisely on target. The Christian concept of God intends to break away from an autocratic God and an imperial image of deity. It wishes to speak of the freedom and self-determination that the entities of this world possess. It insists, however, that

---

189. Philip Hefner, "The Creation," *Christian Dogmatics*, 302.

all this must be done without overlooking or dismissing the fact that God is Creator and source, while the entities of this world are created and sourced by God."[190]

3. The Human Being as Created Co-Creator

In writing on the Christian doctrine of creation Hefner indicates that he is aware of the new challenges posed by modern science. He writes, "Scientific discovery in the past 150 years has opened up breathtaking vistas for a new understanding of nature (physical, biological, and social). The concepts of the creator God and of creation must be related to this understanding of nature if they are to be credible. Scientific concepts provide the most persuasive interpretations of the natural world for the majority of people today. Those interpretations, however, cannot undergird the Christian affirmations that the world is dependent on God for its being and that it is a purposive order. But neither do scientific concepts, properly understood, disprove the ideas of dependency and purpose."[191]

Among the challenges to Christian theological reflection on creation is the concept of evolution, ever since Charles Darwin elaborated it in 1859. Even though some theologians continue to reject it altogether, Hefner is convinced that the theory of evolution is beyond denial by theologians who take science seriously. "It is now almost universally held among theologians that the stories and concepts we have of Adam and Eve in paradise are legends and myths. The idea of humans living in a blessed primeval stage before the fall is looked on as poetical speculation, not history.... To hold to the primeval condition in Eden as a matter of history would be an intellectual impossibility and to misunderstand faith.... Having said this about the myths of primeval conditions in Paradise, we must immediately add

---

190. Philip Hefner, "The Creation," *Christian Dogmatics*, 316, 317.

191. Philip Hefner, "The Creation," *Christian Dogmatics*, 318.

that these myths tell us a great deal that is essential to Christian anthropology."[192]

It was while writing the locus on "The Creation" for *Christian Dogmatics* that Hefner coined a new concept to define what a human being is. The term he chose was "created co-creator" that became the key descriptor of his theological anthropology. Hefner's novel idea took off like a rocket, becoming the subject of books and articles published in journals of religion and science in many languages. Was this idea original with Hefner? Something akin to it was floating around, for example, in something Nicolas Berdyaev wrote that Hefner quoted, "Christian anthropology should unfold the conception of man as a creator who bears the image and likeness of the Creator of the world."[193] The traditional theological concept of *imago dei* suggests that humans are made uniquely special by God. The natural and social sciences have methods that can disclose useful knowledge concerning human being, but it is the province of Christian theology to affirm that human beings have their origin and destiny in God their creator. "Unless we perceive the human being's divinely ordained destiny, we have failed, from the outset, to comprehend who and what *Homo sapiens* is.... Formally, human destiny is to bring to fulfillment the position the human was given at creation — placed by God the Creator in the preeminent position in the ecosystem."[194]

Hefner's idea of the human being as "created co-creator" has been criticized by some theologians who see a problem with the "co" aspect. Might not the "co" imply that humans creators are co-equal with the divine Creator? Hefner clearly rejects such an interpretation of "co-creator." He wrote, "God's creating is the norm for human co-creating, not in the sense that *Homo sapiens* is to equate its activity with God's, but rather in the sense that

192. Philip Hefner, "The Creation," *Christian Dogmatics*, 328.
193. Nicholas Berdyaev, *The Destiny of Man* (Geoffrey Bles, 1948), 49.
194. Philip Hefner, "The Creation," *Christian Dogmatics*, 324, 326.

human activity is perverse if it does not qualify as participation and extension of God's primordial will of creation.... The motif of created co-creator points clearly to the distinction of humans as creatures with a high destiny, a destiny that is essential to the world if it is to bear the mark of its creator God.... We suggest that this co-creatorhood is what it means to be 'in the *image of God.*'"[195] That's the good news. The bad news is the image of God in human beings has been terribly damaged, as conveyed by the Genesis story of the fall of Adam and Eve, the biblical basis for the doctrine of original and hereditary sin. The biblical story ends with the restoration that God brought about in Jesus Christ. The restoration is not a return to the primeval state in the Garden of Eden; rather, it represents something new, an ascent in history to the coming of the new Adam.

4. Hefner's Major Work, *The Human Factor: Evolution, Culture, and Religion*

Philip Hefner's concept of the created co-creator became the core of his theological anthropology, elaborated in his major work, *The Human Factor: Evolution, Culture, and Religion.* We cannot do justice to his massive description of human beings that has deservedly attracted widespread attention, a book so full of novel imagination and speculative theory, not only in the fields of science and religion, but also the arts, poetry, and technology. But we can summarize the basic ideas of his research program that he models on the work of Imre Lakatos, a philosopher of science, with this proviso, "I underscore that I follow Lakatos in principle, but that not all of the details of his philosophical proposal will fit my theological method perfectly."[196] At the heart of Lakatos' research program is the notion of a "hard core," the

---

195. Philip Hefner, "The Creation," *Christian Dogmatics*, 326, 327.

196. Philip Hefner, *The Human Factor: Evolution, Culture, and Religion* (Augsburg Fortress, 1993), 23.

basic insight that will be pursued and tested. The argument is developed by the use of auxiliary hypotheses that elaborate the program's significance and expanse. Hefner describes the "hard core" in the following paragraph:

> *Human beings are God's created co-creators whose purpose is to be the agency, acting in freedom, to birth the future that is most wholesome for the nature that has birthed us — the nature that is not only our own genetic heritage, but also the entire human community and the evolutionary and ecological reality in which and to which we belong. Exercising this agency is said to be God's will for humans.*[197]

The purpose of Hefner's theory is to develop a theological anthropology that offers new ways of thinking about human beings within creation that correlate with scientific perspectives. He sets forth three basic statements describing the "hard core" of this novel theory. "1. The human being is created by God to be a co-creator in the creation that God has brought into being and for which God has purposes. 2. The conditioning matrix that has produced the human being — the evolutionary process — is God's process of bringing into being a creature who represents the creation's zone of a new stage of freedom and who therefore is crucial for the emergence of a free creation. 3. The freedom that marks the created co-creator and its culture is an instrumentality of God for enabling the creation (consisting of the evolutionary past of genetic and cultural inheritance as well as the contemporary ecosystem) to participate in the intentional fulfillment of God's purposes."[198]

From this elaboration of the core of the theory Hefner spells out nine auxiliary hypotheses. To clarify the nature and purpose of these hypotheses Hefner writes that "whereas the core of the theory is an explicitly theological proposal, each of the

---

197. Philip Hefner, *The Human Factor: Evolution, Culture, and Religion*, 27.

198. Philip Hefner, *The Human Factor: Evolution, Culture, and Religion*, 32.

auxiliary hypotheses is stated in such a manner that theological presuppositions are not necessary for its discussion. These hypotheses can be subjected to scrutiny, energetically probed for their significance and fruitfulness, without necessarily adopting the theological stance of the author. Consequently, to the extent that the auxiliary hypotheses are fruitful and credible, to that same extent the status of the hard core is enhanced."[199]

Natural scientists may not consider themselves competent by profession to evaluate the "hard core" of Hefner's theological theory of human being, but they are invited to examine the auxiliary hypotheses in order to evaluate them in light of contemporary science. Scientists will want to weigh the evidences from science whether to corroborate or falsify the numerous assertions set forth in the hypotheses. Here we will quote the nine hypotheses and let the readers wrestle with their highly complex and intertwined propositions.

> *Hypothesis #1: Integral to* Homo sapiens *and its evolutionary history are certain structures and processes, the requirements for whose functioning may be said to constitute, at least in a tentative way, goals and purposes for human life.*
>
> *Hypothesis #2: The meaning and purpose of human beings are conceived in terms of their placement within natural processes and their contribution to those same processes.*
>
> *Hypothesis #3: A concept of 'wholesomeness' is both unavoidable and useful as criterion governing the behavior of human beings within their natural ambience, as they consider what their contribution to nature should be.*
>
> *Hypothesis #4: Nature is the medium through which the world, including human beings, receives knowledge, as well as grace. If God is brought into the discussion, then nature is the medium of divine knowledge and grace.*

---

199. Philip Hefner, *The Human Factor: Evolution, Culture, and Religion*, 27.

Hypothesis #5: Freedom characterizes human existence as the condition in which humans have no choice but to act and to construct the narratives and symbols that contextualize that action. Such contextualization provides justification, explanation, and norms for guiding and assessing the action. This condition is intrinsic to the evolutionary processes at the level of Homo sapiens.

Hypothesis #6: Homo sapiens *is a two-natured creature, a symbiosis of genes and culture.*

Hypothesis #7: The challenge that culture poses to human beings can be stated thus: Culture is a system of information that humans must construct so as to adequately serve the three tasks of interpreting the world in which humans live, guiding human behavior, and interfacing with the physico-biogenetic cultural systems that constitute the environment in which we live.

Hypothesis #8: We now live in a condition that may be termed technological civilization. This condition is characterized by the fact that human decision has conditioned virtually all of the planetary physico-biogenetic systems, so that human decision is the critical factor in the continued functioning of the planet's systems.

Hypothesis #9: Myth and ritual are critical components of the cultural system of information and guidance. They are marked in linguistic form by declarative or imperative discourse, and their concepts are vastly underdetermined by the data of evidence. In light of human evolutionary history, these marks were necessary if culture was to serve its evolutionary function.[200]

The "hard core" of Hefner's theological anthropology featuring human beings as created co-creators is fixed for the sake of the research program as proposed by Imre Lakatos, but

---

200. Philip Hefner, *The Human Factor: Evolution, Culture, and Religion*, 40-49.

the auxiliary hypothesis are open to discussion, evaluation, and modification. The reception of Hefner's work has already shown that there is much for theologians and scientists to discuss in earnest, especially those who care about the human future and the natural world threatened by ecological disaster and nuclear Armageddon. Meanwhile, theologians will want to ask what makes Hefner's theory theological. Theology has to do with *theos* — God. Hefner writes a great deal about God and the kind of God-talk in which he engages in this book. He borrows an idea from Paul Tillich. "When I use the term God, I refer to that which is ultimate, somewhat in the manner of Paul Tillich, who spoke of God as the 'name for that which concerns us ultimately.' ... In this book I most frequently speak, not of ultimate concern, but rather of *the way things really are* and *what really is*. God is the term men and women use to signify what they are talking about, what they have come upon in their experience, touches upon the way things really are."[201] He further explains what he means by God-talk. "God-talk should be viewed as expressing something about our experience of a world that is scientifically understood.... I can hardly overemphasize how significant our views of nature are for the possibilities of talking about God. Nor can I overemphasize how virtually all of the God-talk that is current in the plural cultures of the world today is the result of long, meticulous, rigorous effort — centuries in the process — to articulate human experience of the world under the impact of pictures of nature that no longer seem credible or even natural for us. We now view nature through eyes that have been fundamentally conditioned by the sciences, and the scientific study of nature, including human nature, does not corroborate the concepts that set the parameters for earlier centuries of God-talk. This obsolescence of our talk about nature seriously obstructs our sense of what the experience of God might be."[202]

---

201. Philip Hefner, *The Human Factor: Evolution, Culture, and Religion*, 32, 33.
202. Philip Hefner, *The Human Factor: Evolution, Culture, and Religion*, 81, 83.

Having tipped his hat to the importance of science for our contemporary understanding of the world of nature and how our human experience of nature impacts the way we speak of God today, Hefner concedes that he does not bring to the discussion any clearly developed concept of God. "I have no intention in this work of developing a philosophically sophisticated concept of God.... The reader will note that little or no effort is expended in this volume to fashioning or commenting upon a concept of God."[203]

Instead Hefner focusses on the information about God conveyed by myth and ritual. This means that the Bible and the traditional rituals of the church will be the chief sources of information available to the Christian theologian. "My own program starts ... from the actuality of myth and ritual as components of the cultural system of information that is essential to human being. Myth and ritual are rooted in the biological history of planet earth and also in the neurobiological equipment of *Homo sapiens*. They also have a record as adaptive behavior in human history. The question of whether religion is to be explained on grounds that are either naturalistic or transcendent is really not important. The central questions are whether, in some credible and effective manner, the information conveyed in myth and ritual is consonant with the ways things really are and capable of motivating and engendering behavior (praxis) that shares in that consonance. God-talk, in the Western traditions, is a way in which we have responded 'yes' to these questions."[204]

The reason I have expressed Hefner's thoughts at length in his own words, rather than in summaries and paraphrases, is to avoid every possible misinterpretation of his intention and meaning. Hefner states that myth and ritual provide the raw material for theological construction and reflection. The theological formation of doctrine and the church's solemn prom-

---

203. Philip Hefner, *The Human Factor: Evolution, Culture, and Religion*, 32, 215.
204. Philip Hefner, *The Human Factor: Evolution, Culture, and Religion*, 221.

ulgation of dogma such as at the 325 A.D. Council of Nicaea (Trinity) and the 451 A.D. Council of Chalcedon (Christology) are the next steps. The doctrine and dogmas do not replace the information gleaned from myth and ritual but rather provide new interpretation requisite for new situations and challenges. Hefner affirms both decisions of the ancient church regarding the doctrine of the Trinity and the Two Natures of Christ that reinforce his theology of the created co-creator. The dogma declares that the natural order is capable of receiving the divine grace incarnated in Jesus Christ. The Chalcedonian dogma rejected the heresy of Eutyches who believed that Christ's divine nature absorbed the human nature, denying thereby that nature is capable of being at one with God. This means that God can dwell in a person without that person ceasing to be a fully natural human being and without God ceasing to be God. "The understanding of Christ through the image of the incarnation has worked throughout Christian history as a hermeneutic for understanding nature as such. The incarnation demonstrates, as the Chalcedonian documents attest, that nature is fit to be a vessel for the presence and power of God. Martin Luther insisted that 'the finite is capable of the infinite' — a maxim that undergirded his sacramental theology derived from reflection on Christ."[205]

Hefner takes note of the fact that twentieth century theology witnessed a revival of interest in the doctrine of the Trinity (Robert Jenson, Wolfhart Pannenberg, Eberhard Jüngel, and Catherine LaCugna, among others). He disclaims interest in the fine points of speculation that each of these theologians created, such as the relation between the immanent and economic aspects of the Trinity. Of special interest to Hefner is the way in which "the Trinity represents an authentic attempt to engage in world-view construction on the basis of the Christian faith. It presents an all-encompassing picture of what really is, and no

---

205. Philip Hefner, *The Human Factor: Evolution, Culture, and Religion*, 233.

sector of nature is distanced from God. Each of the three persons of the Trinity represents an arche, a first principle."[206] The First Person is God the Creator, the principle on which everything depends. The Second Person is the principle of meaning in Jesus the Logos, who illuminates and redeems all things. The Third Person is the ground of all living things, present within all of nature. In the Trinity the theologians of the church (Gregory of Nyssa, Augustine of Hippo, Anselm of Canterbury, and Thomas Aquinas) created an all-encompassing world-view, grounded in God and centered in Jesus, the Logos made flesh.

5. Myth and Ritual

Hefner continues his exploration of the meaning of the mythic and ritual dimensions of the Christian faith with reflections and interpretation about the fall and sin, the image of God, the sacraments, the nature of grace, forgiveness of sin, justification by faith, Christ as the New Adam, as the Paradigm of what it means to be truly human, as the model of the godly life, his sacrificial life and death, in short, we might say a mini-dogmatic survey that pours new meanings into old symbols. Throughout Hefner's book he appeals to myth and ritual as the primal source for the second order reflections of constructive theology. Hefner speaks of myth in the sense that two of his professors at the Chicago Divinity School, Mircea Eliade and Paul Ricoeur, wrote about myth and ritual.[207] The story of Adam and Eve is an example of myth. The idea of a God who acts to create the world in the beginning and who redeems humankind in bondage to sin, death, and the devil is at the center of the Christian mythology. Obviously talk like this has nothing to do with the common usage of myth as an invented story, a fiction, fantasy, or tall

---

206. Philip Hefner, *The Human Factor: Evolution, Culture, and Religion*, 234.

207. Cf. Mircea Eliade, *Cosmos and History: The Myth of the Eternal Return* (Harper and Brothers, 1959) and Paul Ricoeur, *The Symbolism of Evil* (Beacon Press, 1967).

tale. Myth conveys meaning about life and the world. Hefner endorses Paul Tillich's term, ultimate concern, for speaking of God. Myth conveys information about the ultimate ground and meaning of ultimate reality. In Hefner's terminology, myth provides a picture of "the way things really are."

All religions have their mythologies. Concerning Christian mythology Hefner writes: "The essential Christian myth consists of the narrative that includes at least the following events: 1) God made the world, including humans in the image of the maker. 2) Human beings were created in the garden, in unity with their maker and with one another, but they came to be alienated from both, and the alienation manifests itself in their actions. 3) The man Jesus of Nazareth conveyed in word and deed the grace of God and its moral consequence, unqualified love for what God created: thus he embodies both the revelation of God's will and also the redeeming action of God. 4) Jesus broke the boundary of death in his resurrection: we shall be raised also in the context of God's bringing to perfection and consummation the entire created oder."[208]

In what sense can modern people in the age of science believe and accept as real and true the events that comprise the biblical mythology. This is the question that led Rudolf Bultmann to propose his program of demythologizing in his essay "New Testament and Mythology."[209] Long before Hefner Bultmann worried about what effect the natural sciences have on the substance of the Christian faith based on the Bible inasmuch as its gospel message is encased in a mythology that modern people no longer find acceptable. Bultmann wrote, "So far as the New Testament speaks mythologically, it is incredible to modern man,"[210] The New

---

208. Philip Hefner, *The Human Factor: Evolution, Culture, and Religion*, 189.

209. Rudolf Bultmann, "New Testament and Mythology," *Kerygma and Myth*, ed. H. W. Bartsch, tr. R. H. Fuller (London: S. P. C. K.,1954).

210. Rudolf Bultmann, "New Testament and Mythology," *Kerygma and Myth*, 3.

Testament presupposes a three-storied world, earth, heaven, and hell. The basic structure of the drama of salvation is mythical, with supernatural powers such as angels and demons playing their part. The idea of a pre-existing divine being becoming a human being is mythical. For the next half century theologians struggled hard and long to meet the challenge Bultmann posed to Christian theology. The voluminous theological *oeuvre* of Wolfhart Pannenberg was in essence a successful response to Bultmann's highly reductionistic existentialist interpretation of the biblical message. Hefner never quotes Bultmann when he writes about the Christian myths nor does he provide a hermeneutic that deals with Bultmann's kind of concern for the obvious discrepancy between the New Testament mythology and modern thought shaped by modern science.

Hefner does make clear that he does not swallow the biblical myths hook, line, and sinker, noting that "myth and ritual can be *wrong*; they can speak less than the full truth about life, or they can speak truth that was once viable but today is virtual untruth."[211] At another point he concedes that our modern relation to myth is "critical." "Today, we may recognize the wisdom in the myths, but we cannot believe them naively. We are critical; we can entertain the myths only as proposals, as hypotheses. We can believe only through what Ricoeur terms the second naiveté, which requires critical philosophical analysis and interpretation."[212]

The most neuralgic part of the Christian mythology has to do with what the New Testament says about Jesus Christ, the human person who is God incarnate. Apart from Christ there is no gospel, no church to preach the gospel to the world, and ergo no need for Christian theologians to give a hoot about any of this stuff. The first chapter of the Gospel of John asserts that the Word became flesh (John 1:14), and that this same Word was in the beginning with God and indeed was God, through

211. Philip Hefner, *The Human Factor: Evolution, Culture, and Religion*, 174.
212. Philip Hefner, *The Human Factor: Evolution, Culture, and Religion*, 187.

whom all things were made (John 1:1-3). Every Christian theology will want to be clear from the beginning about the identity of God and of Jesus.

In every epoch, ancient, medieval, modern, and postmodern, Christian theologians have had to ask and answer the same fundamental question, "Who is God, the one true God among all the putative deities in the religions of the world?" They spend a lifetime doing the three things that Martin Luther said make a theologian: *oratio, meditatio, tentatio.* Hefner's basic concept of the human being is "created co-creator." Both the adjective and the noun are quintessential. In this book Hefner's working definition of God is *"the way things really are* and *what really is."*[213] These twin locutions, *"the way things really are"* and *"what really is,"* appear scores of times throughout the book and function as the concept of God that Hefner brings to his theological anthropology. I would have thought that God is the Almighty One who created "the way things (plural) really are," namely, the world and everything in it. Or, are to think that God and the world are two expressions of the same reality? If so, how is that fundamentally different from Baruch Spinoza's metaphysical assertion, *Deus sive Natura,* that spells pantheism? The unambivalent consensus among Christian theologians who have responded to Spinoza concluded that such a naturalistic concept of god does not fit the God of the Bible.

And who is Jesus and what does he do, in Hefner's account? It is important to answer this question using his own words. "Jesus' life and death as the church interprets them serve as a model.... His life and death were not instrumental to his gaining any particular value for himself. They constituted his career trajectory, so to speak, and as the temptation stories tell us, his life and death were of intrinsic value. He lived and died for the benefit of those with whom he came in contact; he did what he did for the sake of benefiting the world by witnessing

---

213. Philip Hefner, *The Human Factor: Evolution, Culture, and Religion,* 33.

to and obeying what he believed was fundamental truth."[214] Jesus is a *model* of a life lived for others, even to the point of a self-sacrificial death. Sacrifice is the most common term employed in the New Testament to interpret the death of Jesus. "When we are concentrated on *what really is*, what we are and do is very important. We further recognize that Jesus Christ is the paradigm, the model of what it means to be humans in the image of God, of what it means to be the human beings that God intended."[215]

Jesus is also a teacher. The Sermon on the Mount includes some of Jesus' most memorable teachings, which include the Beatitudes, the Love Commandment, the Lord's Prayer, and the Golden Rule. The Beatitudes, for example, provide the key to Jesus' God-talk. "Jesus is here presenting a picture of what the wisest, most profoundly adequate human life would look like, the life that is most fully in accord with the fundamental nature of reality."[216] Recall that "what really is" is Hefner's coinage for speaking of God. Jesus' love commandment is the core of his ethical teaching. "You shall love the Lord your God with all your heart, and with all your soul, and with all your mind... and....you shall love your neighbor as yourself. On these two commandments hang all the law and the prophets" (Matthew 22:37-40). "Love for God translates into awe and regard for the central reality that is the ground of all finite existence that we observe.... Love for neighbor translates into unreserved action in behalf of our fellow human beings."[217]

Hefner's answer to the question, "Who is Jesus?" is that he is a *model* or *example* of the life God intends for human beings to live and also that he is a *teacher* of the great commandment to love God and to love our neighbors, even our enemies. In Hef-

---

214. Philip Hefner, *The Human Factor: Evolution, Culture, and Religion*, 73.

215. Philip Hefner, *The Human Factor: Evolution, Culture, and Religion*, 243.

216. Philip Hefner, *The Human Factor: Evolution, Culture, and Religion*, 86.

217. Philip Hefner, *The Human Factor: Evolution, Culture, and Religion*, 190.

ner's words, "Jesus Christ takes the role of revealer, an occasion of our coming to the awareness of our own acceptability in the face of what really is, as receivers and agents of gracious *shalom*, and as a paradigm of the behavior we must undertake if we are to be in harmony with *what really is*.... Jesus is the determinative instantiation of *what really is*; it is in terms of Jesus that we perceive and define *what really is*. As with all myth-ritual transactions, Jesus is teacher (revealer), example, and the one with whom we have communion, even though it is difficult to articulate what communion means and how it comes into existence."[218]

Hefner is surely right in stressing the significance of Jesus' exemplary sacrificial life and death and his teachings in sermons and parables. The story and picture of Jesus of Nazareth in the Gospels, conveyed in symbolic and figurative language associated with the literary genre of myth, soar to a level far exceeding that of moral example and prophetic teacher. Thomas, one of the twelve disciples, when he saw the risen Jesus, exclaimed, "My Lord and my God!" (John 20:28). Hefner favorably quotes the writings of Wolfhart Pannenberg that deal with science and religion, especially his large volume on *Theology and the Philosophy of Science* (Westminster Press, 1976). Pannenberg also wrote another large tome on Christology, *Jesus — God and Man* (Westminster Press, 1968), in which he made the historical event of Jesus' resurrection the key to understanding the Christian faith. Pannenberg used his tremendous learning to demonstrate that without the Easter event there would have been no gathered memories recorded in the Gospels that Jesus of Nazareth ever existed, the Christian Church would not have been born, and the apostles would not have propagated the name of the Triune God to the far corners of the universe.

The resurrection of Jesus is one of the things that disappears in Hefner's retrieval and interpretation of the Biblical-Christian narrative. As Hefner said, the myth can be *wrong*; it can be

---

218. Philip Hefner, *The Human Factor: Evolution, Culture, and Religion*, 251-252.

outdated, no longer believable in the light of modern scientific knowledge. Many modern theologians agree with that assessment with respect to the resurrection (Rudolf Bultmann, Fritz Buri, Paul van Buren, Schubert Ogden, David Griffin, Robert Funk, and John Dominic Crossan, to mention a few). The truth is that the resurrection of Jesus constitutes the core of the Christian gospel, because in this event God vindicated Jesus' claim to be God's eschatological representative. The cause of Jesus would have perished from the earth if his crucifixion would have been the end of the story.

Rev. Dr. Theodore F. Peters, known as Ted Peters, was born April 3, 1941. He is currently Distinguished Research Professor Emeritus of Systematic Theology and Ethics at Pacific Lutheran Theological Seminary and the Graduate Theological Union in Berkeley, California. Ted Peters received a B.A. in 1963 from Michigan State University, an M.Div. in 1967 from Trinity Lutheran Seminary in Columbus, Ohio, and a Ph.D. in 1973 from the University of Chicago Divinity School. He taught at Newberry College (1972-76) and at Loyola University in New Orleans (1976-78). Ted Peters was Professor of Systematic Theology at Pacific Lutheran Theological Seminary from 1978-2012. He received honorary doctorates from the Universities of Wittenberg and Lund, Sweden. Ted Peters was the editor-in-chief of *dialog — A Journal of Theology* from 1993 to 2007. He also served as "Science and Religion" editor for the German encyclopedia, *Religion in Geschichte und Gegenwart*, Volumes IV-VIII. Along with Robert Russell Ted Peters is the co-founder and co-editor of the journal, *Theology and Science*. He served as Principal Investigator for a research project funded by the National Institutes of Health on "Theological and Ethical Questions Raised by the Human Genome Initiative," hosted at the Center for Theology and the Natural Sciences, of the Graduate Theological Union. Ted Peters is an ordained minister of the Evangelical Lutheran Church in America and has served as pastor of parishes in Illinois and New York.

Seven

Ted Peters

Lutheran Theology in Dialogue with Science

Ted Peters (born 1941) is Distinguished Research Professor Emeritus of Systematic Theology and Ethics at Pacific Lutheran Theological Seminary (PLTS) and the Graduate Theological Union (GTU) in Berkeley, California. He is also an ordained Lutheran pastor in the Evangelical Lutheran Church in America (ELCA). He received a B.A. from Michigan State University, an M.Div. from Trinity Lutheran Seminary in Columbus, Ohio, and a Ph.D. from the University of Chicago. In 1978 he began teaching in Berkeley not only in a Lutheran seminary (PLTS) preparing students for ordination in the ELCA, but also at the Graduate Theological Union, an ecumenical and inter-religious setting with students from many church backgrounds, Protestant and Roman Catholic, as well as other religious traditions. In 1991 he succeeded me as editor-in-chief of *dialog — A Journal of Theology* and served in that capacity for more than a decade. Peters is also co-editor along with Robert John Russell of the journal, *Theology and Science*, a publication of GTU's Center for Theology and the Natural Sciences (CTNS).

Ted Peters is a prolific author and editor of books on a wide array of subjects on theology, science, and culture and he has co-authored and co-edited many more. His *magnum opus* is entitled, *God – The World's Future,* first published in 1992 with the subtitle, *Systematic Theology for a Postmodern Era.* A revised version was published in 2000 with a change of subtitle, *Systematic Theology for a New Era.* In less than a decade he believed the cultural situation had changed sufficiently to warrant the change. What had changed was the invasion of French deconstructionism. One might wonder about the wisdom of tying Christian theology so tightly to the shifting winds of culture from one decade to another. That puts the theologian on a roller coaster, as it were, of trying to keep up with the rapidly changing cultural fads and fashions. Peters himself is aware of the problem and balks at the prospect of having to pay homage to deconstructionism. He wrote in the Preface to the Second Edition, "I find I must simply depart from deconstructionist postmodernism, namely, I pursue construction of a universal vision of reality. I work with certain assumptions: theology seeks to be rooted in the truth. For the truth to be truth, it must be truth for all places and all times. For truth to be truth, it must be more than the subjective projection of an individual from his or her social location; it must be rooted in objective reality as well as subjective perspective. This means, finally, that the truth must be one, and it must be encompassing. Otherwise, it is less than the truth."[219] Well said. The gospel of Jesus Christ is the truth no matter what epistemology controls the thinking of modernists or postmodernists of any stripe. For the Christian theologian the truth that came out of dinky town Nazareth outmatched the truth of the greatest philosophers of ancient times, Plato and Aristotle. Ted Peters would agree with that. A revised third edition of Peters *magnum opus* was printed in 2015, with yet more alterations. More on this later.

---

219. Ted Peters, *God – The World's Future. Systematic Theology for a New Era* (Fortress Press, 2000), xvi.

Prolepsis: The Key Concept of Peter's Theology

I first met Ted Peters when he was a graduate student at the University of Chicago Divinity School and I was a professor of systematic theology at the Lutheran School of Theology at Chicago. One day he came to my office to introduce himself and to discuss the state of things theological. I recall that we talked about Wolfhart Pannenberg, who was a fledgling leader of a new school of thought in Germany, beckoning theology to go beyond the two competing alternatives, Barth and Bultmann. I had just written about Pannenberg's theology in my first two books, *History and Hermeneutics* (1966) and *The Future of God* (1969), recommending his thought as the best available path forward to break the perceived stalemate. Pannenberg introduced me to the concept of "prolepsis" which for him is the hinge on which eschatology swings in the midst of the historical process. I attempted to explain what it means in both books. I developed the concept further in my book *Eschatology and Ethics* (1974). To my surprise and delight I discovered that Ted Peters made "prolepsis" the key concept of his systematic theology.

What is the meaning of "prolepsis?" Webster's New Universal Unabridged Dictionary defines prolepsis as "the representation of something in the future as if it already existed or had occurred." Peters offers a good example of this meaning in writing, "In Christ we find the resurrection, the prolepsis of the new creation."[220] In the Preface of his systematic theology, *God – The World's Future*, Peters acknowledges the importance of this idea: "The central theme of this book is the concept of *prolepsis*, whereby the gospel is understood as announcing the preactualization of the future consummation of all things in Jesus Christ. The world has been given God's promise that in the future all things will be made whole. The promise comes to us through Jesus who died on Good Friday and rose from the

---

220. Ted Peters, *God as Trinity. Relationality and Temporality in the Divine Life* (Westminster/John Knox Press, 1993), 175.

dead on Easter Sunday. As prolepsis, he embodies the promise because he anticipates in his person the new life that we humans and all creation are destined to share."[221] Through faith in Christ believers already now proleptically participate in the future consummation in which they will be granted full and final salvation by the grace of God.

Genesis 1:27 says that "God created man in his own image." The phrase "*imago Dei*" is the backbone of Christian anthropology. Peters uses the concept of prolepsis to explicate this doctrine. "Hence the *imago Dei* is essentially future. But it has a proleptic quality as well. Our created humanity is our eschatological humanity. Who we are is determined by who we will be. To think of ourselves as created in the image of God is to think backward from the fulfillment to the present, from the final creation to the present process of creating. To the extent that the *imago Dei* is present now, it is present proleptically — that is, it is an anticipation of a reality yet to be fully realized."[222]

Likewise, Peters uses the concept of prolepsis to develop his Christology. The kingdom of God is the main theme in the teachings of Jesus according to the Synoptic Gospels. The time dimension of the future is essential in what Jesus' meant by the coming of the kingdom. "He was anticipating something, namely, the kingdom of God. This anticipation appeared not only in his announcement that the kingdom would be coming, but it appeared also quite concretely in his deeds, in his miracles, healing, in his passion, and in his resurrection. Jesus preactualized in his person what will ultimately become reality for all of us and for all creation.... The not yet has become an already in the preactualization of it in the person of Jesus. The future unity of all things with God is proleptically anticipated in the man from Nazareth."[223]

---

221. Ted Peters, *God – The World's Future*, xi.

222. Ted Peters, *God – The World's Future*, 157.

223. Ted Peters, *God – The World's Future*, 233.

In my book *Eschatology and Ethics* (1974) I developed the theory of "proleptic ethics," inspired by Wolfhart Pannenberg's chapter, "The Kingdom of God and the Foundation of Ethics," in his book, *Theology and the Kingdom of God* (Westminster Press, 1969). Some years later Ted Peters did the same, also acknowledging Pannenberg's influence. Chapter 12 of his systematic theology is entitled "Proleptic Ethics," an appropriate conclusion to his *magnum opus*. Peters calls "proleptic ethics" an evangelical ethic, as it makes the gospel of Jesus Christ its point of departure to meet the challenges emerging in our postmodern world. Love is the primary axiom of an evangelical ethic. Love frees persons to serve their neighbors, especially those most in need, the least and the lost. The dynamic movement of love is creative in making decisions and taking actions that foster what is most fruitful in any given situation. Such love cannot be hampered by a set of rules or commandments bequeathed to us from the past. "Creative love may require radical change, even revolution."[224] Peters cites as illustration the 1985 *Kairos Document* in post-apartheid South Africa which said, "The fact that the State is tyrannical and an enemy of God is no excuse for hatred. As Christians we are called upon to love our enemies (Matt. 5:44).... But then we must also remember that the most loving thing we can do for both the oppressed *and* for our enemies who are oppressors is to eliminate the oppression, remove the tyrants from power and establish a just government for the common good of *all the people*."[225]

Engaging in politics calls for attention to the norm of eschatological justice. Peters writes, "In terms of ethics this means that as citizens of the eschatological polis we are called to support just political structures in the present and to transform those structures when they fail to embody and enhance justice.... The proleptic dimension of this is that by choosing the future of God

---

224. Ted Peters, *God – The World's Future*, 374.
225. Quoted by Ted Peters, *God – The World's Future*, 374.

over the present existence of any given body politic we are in fact choosing what is best for that body politic.... What we want to endure are social and political institutions that better embody and anticipate the justice of God's eschatological community."[226]

Peters intends his theology to be ecumenical and ecumenic. "Ecumenical" refers to the unity of Christians and their communities within the one body of Jesus Christ, whereas "ecumenic" refers to openness toward the world beyond the church, concerned with religions other than Christian as well as the welfare of nature and culture. Peters writes, "We need an ecumenic scope, and I suggest here that we gain that ecumenic scope by founding ethical thinking on a vision of the eschatological kingdom of God. Beginning with the future of God's kingdom as the source and ground of value, I attempt to discern what we should do by developing principles based upon this vision. Our present world situation reveals how badly we need middle axioms, principles that mediate between our vision of ultimate harmony and the realistic appraisal of what we can actually do. We need some principles for guidance. Based on a proleptic ethic, in what follows I will try to develop a set of provolutionary principles."[227]

What are "provolutionary principles?" Ted Peters gives credit to Jürgen Moltmann for the concept of provolution. He suggests that we should use the future-oriented prefix of the *pro*, replacing *re*volution with *pro*volution. We should turn our attention forward to welcome new possibilities the future might have in store for us. Here I will list the seven pros that Peters suggessts for a Christian provolutionary program, each of which is accompanied with a shopping list of practical ideas, mixed with a few that seem more like utopian ideals. 1. Project a vision of the coming new order. 2. Promote a sense of global community. 3. Provide for posterity. 4. Protect human dignity.

---

226. Ted Peters, *God – The World's Future*, 376-377.
227. Ted Peters, *God – The World's Future*, 378.

5. Proffer the distinction between needs and wants. 6. Propose alliances. 7. Profess faith. The seventh is the most important; it gives vital hope and robust energy in support of the others. Peters here defines "faith as trust in the God of the future, trust in the God who raised Jesus to new life on Easter and who promises to transform the present world into a new creation.... Professing proleptic faith could make the faith itself contagious. Others might catch on and join the project of bringing the future reality of God's kingdom to bear on the present crisis."[228]

2. Recurrent Themes and Emphases

A. The Doctrine of the Trinity

Ted Peters has written extensively on the Christian doctrine of the Trinity, but not as a mere repristination of the standard treatments of trinitarian thought in Eastern and Western Christianity. The third chapter (42 pages) of his systematic theology, *God – The World's Future*, is entitled, "God the Trinity." In addition he has dealt with virtually every aspect of the doctrine in a monograph, *God as Trinity: Relationality and Temporality in Divine Life*. The book serves as a very readable and teachable textbook that covers the history of the doctrine of the Trinity — its origins in the Bible, its orthodox dogmatic definitions in the ancient church, its reaffirmation by the Reformers, its rejection in the Enlightenment, culminating in its revival in the last half of the twentieth century by both Protestant and Roman Catholic theologians. After analyzing the many controversies in trinitarian theology, Peters offers his readers a well considered resolution of each the issues in question.

If Christianity is one of the monotheistic religions, along with Judaism and Islam, why complicate it and threaten it by converting the oneness of God into three of something — three

---

228. Ted Peters, *God – The World's Future*, 391.

of what? Theologians have often thrown up their hands and cried "mystery." Peters asks, "What is the basic issue? I believe the real question has been, and still is, this: How do we understand the God of the gospel, the one creator of all things who raised Jesus on Easter and who is spiritually present in the believing community? ... Now, we must admit that the conception of three-in-one and one-in-three is a complicated conception. However, the complexity of the conception is no warrant for consigning the discussion to divine mystery or to redefine the question merely in terms of contradictory arithmetic."[229]

The theologians who deserve the most credit for reanimating the doctrine of the Trinity are the two Karls, Barth and Rahner. According to Barth's analysis of God's self-revelation, the God of the Bible is experienced in terms of Father, Son, and Holy Spirit.[230] According to Rahner, the economic Trinity (God as he appears in his temporal activity in the history of salvation) and the immanent Trinity (God as he is eternally within himself) are one and the same.[231] This is called "Rahner's Rule," accepted by virtually all the theologians engaged in the renewal of the doctrine of the Trinity. Ted Peters agrees with the reaffirmation of the Trinity in the wake of their combined influence. This means that he did not succumb to the process metaphysics of Alfred North Whitehead and Charles Hartshorn in full bloom when he attended the Divinity School of the University of Chicago. As we observed in our brief review of the theology of Paul Sponheim, his commitment to process thought seemed to create a roadblock to a full affirmation of orthodox Trinitarian and Christological doctrines. Not so with Ted Peters. With his knowledge of the relation of Process theology to Christian theology Peters concluded, "Process theology represents a detour

---

229. Ted Peters, *God as Trinity: Relationality and Temporality in Divine Life* (Westminster/John Knox Press, 1993), 18.

230. Karl Barth, *Church Dogmatics*, vol. 1/1 (T. & T. Clark, 1936-77).

231. Karl Rahner, *The Trinity* (Herder & Herder).

that leads to a dead end as far as Christian trinitarian thinking goes."[232] His explanation is that process theism "is based upon common human experience and human reflection, which leads to speculative metaphysics, which describes the phenomenal realm. It is constructive metaphysics based upon general revelation, not special revelation. It is synthesis, not analysis. The biblical symbols of Father, Son, and Holy Spirit play at best a minimal role. The result is that process theologians, for the most part, find they can no longer embrace the Christian doctrine of the Trinity. If they keep a version of the Trinity, it is so transformed that it is scarcely recognizable."[233]

Peters weighed in on the controversy stirred up by radical feminists who reject the trinitarian name of God as Father, Son, and Holy Spirit, because its two male nouns allegedly support the social oppression of women. Sallie McFague proposed instead to refer to the Trinity as "Mother, Lover, Friend." Some feminists suggest we should use nouns that refer to the specific function of each person of the Trinity, such as "Creator, Redeemer, and Sanctifier." Peters writes this about an exchange between a layperson and a theologian:

Layperson: "My pastor baptized my baby in the name of the Creator, Redeemer, and Sanctifier. Will my baby go to hell?"
Theologian: "No, but the pastor will."

Peters suggests the interchange was probably apocryphal. No it wasn't. That theologian happened to be me, except that in my recollection the layperson asked the question in a hypothetical mood. I was frequently asked such questions, and I always responded that for a baptism to be Christian, it will always be "in the name of the Father and of the Son and of the Holy Spirit." The command to baptize comes directly from the mouth of the risen Jesus, ""Go therefore and make disciples of all nations,

---

232. Ted Peters, *God as Trinity*, 110.
233. Ted Peters, *God as Trinity*, 33.

baptizing them *in the name* of the Father and of the Son and of the Holy Spirit" (Matt. 28:19). Peters also discusses an assertion on which Robert Jenson insisted, "Father, Son, and Holy Spirit is the proper name of God."[234] Jenson uses the term "proper name" not to suggest merely that it is proper to use the Trinitarian name, but in the sense that for biblical Christians "Father, Son, and Holy Spirit" is God's very own name non-interchangeable with any other, for example, some other triadic combination of metaphors. Peters opines, "I am reluctant to grant that 'Father, Son, and Holy Spirit' constitute the proper name of the divine.... In the New Testament we find many words by which we may address the divine, such as "God" or, of most importance, 'Lord.'"[235] Which is to miss Jenson's point. "God" is not the "proper name" of God. "Lord" is not the "proper name" of God. Peters "proper name" is Theodore Frank Peters, because that is his very own name, but he is better known as Ted Peters. "Proper name" in French is "*nom propre*," which means "one's very own name." No other God in the pantheon of deities is known as "Father, Son, and Holy Spirit," the very name of the God in whom we are baptized. This does not mean that Peters agrees with those who wish to substitute other nouns for the Triune name to avoid patriarchal oppression of women. He writes, "There is no way that an honest explication of the trinitarian symbols, including God as Father, can be used to justify the social oppression of women or any other group of people.... The problem of social oppression does not originate in the existence of Christian symbols. Nor is the solution to this problem to be found either in abandoning the symbols or in diluting them by inventing parallel symbols."[236]

Ted Peters writes a richly informative chapter on the renaissance of trinitarian theology in the last half of the twentieth

---

234. Robert W. Jenson, *The Triune Identity* (Fortress Press, 1982), 10-16.
235. Ted Peters, *God as Trinity*, 53.
236. Ted Peters, *God – The World's Future*, 127.

century, starting his discussion with Claude Welch's book, *In This Name,* which deals extensively with Karl Barth.[237] According to Welch Barth's basic thesis is that the trinitarian formula of threeness-in-oneness derives from an analysis of revelation. Welch argued that Barth overcame the influence of Schleiermacher who "made the doctrine of the Trinity an expendable appendix to monotheism."[238] Trinitarian theology continued to evolve under the impact of Barth's analytic revelational approach and "Rahner's Rule" in the theology of Eberhard Jüngel. Jüngel wrote two important books on the Trinity.[239] Like Barth before him Jüngel insists on starting with God's revelation in the person of Jesus Christ rather than with an idea of God that derives from natural theology based on general revelation. By doing this Jüngel claims that the marks of finitude, historicity, suffering and death experienced by Jesus are as such the very attributes of God. Jüngel states, "Jesus Christ is that man in whom God has defined himself as a human God."[240] Here Jüngel is borrowing an idea from a lecture Barth delivered to a Reformed Ministerial Association in 1956, "The Humanity of God." Jüngel also reached back to Luther's theology of the cross to affirm the death of God. In his treatise *Concerning the Councils and the Church* Luther stated, "If it is not true that God died for us, but only a man died, we are lost.... So it could be said: God dead, God's passion, God's blood, God's death. According to his nature God cannot die, but since God and man are united in one person, it is correct to talk about God's death when that man dies who is one thing or one person with God."[241] For Luther this was

---

237. Claude Welch, *In This Name: The Doctrine of the Trinity in Contemporary Theology* (Charles Scribner's Sons, 1952).

238. Ted Peters, *God as Trinity*, 89.

239. Eberhard Jüngel, *The Doctrine of the Trinity: God's Being is in Becoming* (Eerdmans, 1976) and *God as the Mystery of the World* (Eerdmans, 1983).

240. Quoted by Ted Peters, *God as Trinity*, 91.

241. "Formula of Concord, Solid Declaration," Article VIII. Person of Christ, *Book of Concord*, Tappert Edition, 599.

a paradoxical way of speaking. As Peters interprets Jüngel, the paradoxical aspect is removed because of "Rahner's Rule." What can be said about God in history (*ad extra*) can also be said about God within himself (*ad intra*).

Peters offers lengthy discussions, interspersed with critical observations, of the most important theologians who go down the path that places the temporal history of the incarnation within the eternal life of God. They are Jürgen Moltmann,[242] Leonardo Boff,[243] Catherine Mowry LaCugna,[244] Robert Jenson,[245] and Wolfhart Pannenberg.[246] Peters shows what each one contributes to further explication of "Rahner's Rule" — the economic Trinity is the immanent Trinity and vice versa. For Moltmann the history of Christ's suffering and death defines the very being of the triune God. For LaCugna the reason that the doctrine of the Trinity was virtually marginalized in both Catholic and Protestant theology is because the inner life of the eternal God was separated from the history of salvation, and so drifted off into unfathomable mystery. LaCugna's axiom is this: "Theology is inseparable from soteriology, and vice versa."[247] Peters then discusses Robert Jenson's revision of the doctrine of the Trinity that begins with his rejection of the traditional idea of eternity as timelessness. For Jenson the God of the Bible is not bound by some timeless and immutable essence. Peters applauds Jenson's use of the concept of "identity" so as to be able to say that the being of God is one but has three identities

---

242. Jürgen Moltmann, *The Trinity and the Kingdom* (Harper & Row, 1981).

243. Leonardo Boff, *Trinity and Society* (Orbis Books, 1988).

244. Catherine Mowry LaCugna, *God for Us: The Trinity and Christian Life* (HarperSanFrancisco, 1993).

245. Robert W. Jenson, *The Triune Identity. God According to the Gospel* (Fortress Press, 1982).

246. Wolfhart Pannenberg, "The Trinitarian God," *Systematic Theology* (Eerdmans, 1991), vol. 1, 259-336. Also, "Problems of a Trinitarian Doctrine of God," *dialog – A Journal of Theology*, 26 (1987), 250-257.

247. Ted Peters, *God as Trinity*, 124.

— one *ousia* and three *hypostases* — to use the terminology of the Cappadocian Fathers (Gregory of Nazianzus, Gregory of Nyssa, and Basil of Caesarea). Jenson's main work on the Trinity is entitled, *The Triune Identity*, and he also wrote the second locus of *Christian Dogmatics*, "The Triune God." We will discuss both of these in greater detail in the ninth chapter of this book that deals explicitly with Jenson's theology. Lastly Peters takes up Wolfhart Pannenberg's theology of the Trinity, which uses the same starting point as Barth, the method of revelational analysis. Pannenberg says that trinitarian theology "simply states explicitly what is implicit already in God's revelation in Jesus Christ."[248] To follow Pannenberg's stratospheric cogitations on all conceivable aspects of the doctrine of the Trinity is truly a high wire act of theological gymnastics. Pannenberg has been Ted Peters leading mentor as he was mine since I first met him at the University of Heidelberg in 1957. He was then a *Privatdocent*, a beginning instructor of theology who was already conceptualizing a new direction in theology, published in 1961 as *Offenbarung als Geschichte*.[249]

B. The Resurrection of Jesus Christ

The resurrection of Jesus is the linch pin of Ted Peters' theology, holding its various parts together; it plays the pivotal role in his proleptic theory of reality in history and nature. The centrality of belief in the resurrection appears throughout the corpus of Peters writings, not only those that deal with theology but those that engage in dialogue with science on many fronts. In his systematic theology he acknowledges the importance of Pannenberg's theology of the resurrection. He summarizes Pannenberg's analysis of the significance of Jesus rising from death on Easter Day. First, if Jesus has been raised, that signals the end of the

---

248. Quoted by Ted Peters in *God as Trinity*, 135.

249. Wolfhart Pannenberg, with Rolf Rendtorff, Trutz Rendtorff, and Ulrich Wilkens, *Revelation as History* (Macmillan, 1968).

world has dawned. The general resurrection of the dead has begun. Jesus leads the way and the rest will follow. Second, in raising Jesus from the dead, God has confirmed the authority of Jesus' life and ministry. In this event the Father has ratified the claims of his Son. Apart from Easter Jesus would have gone down in history as an impostor and blasphemer, proving that his accusers were right after all. Third, the resurrection legitimates the titles ascribed to Jesus, such as Messiah, Lord, Savior, Son of Man and Son of God. Fourth, the resurrection validates the apostolic assertion that God is definitively revealed in Jesus. Fifth, the eschatological aspect of the resurrection establishes the universal significance of the event, reaching far beyond the people of Israel to include all the Gentiles.

Some theologians find it possible to talk about the resurrection as a symbol without affirming its historicity. Bultmann said the resurrection does not refer to something that happened to Jesus; it refers to the rise of faith in his disciples after his death. It didn't happen but yet the symbol has some meaning. Pannenberg does not believe that, neither does Peters. Such happy talk is nonsense and self-delusion, if it is not true. The resurrection is an actual event that Jesus experienced. Peters writes, "It seems to me that the weight of the evidence and strength of the argument falls in favor of the objectivists.... It seems much more reasonable to think that the rise of the resurrection faith was a response to just what those who experienced it said it was, namely, the resurrection of Jesus.... The resurrection of Jesus is eschatological in character. This is essential to the concept of prolepsis with which I am working: the future consummation of all things has appeared ahead of time in the Christ-event.... If it were not for Easter the church would not have come into existence, and the cultural history of the last twenty centuries would be very different."[250]

---

250. Ted Peters, *God – The World's Future*, 202, 203.

C. Creatio Continua

The concept of *creatio continua* is important in Ted Peters' constructive engagement with modern natural science. God did not only create the whole cosmos out of nothing (*ex nihilo*) but God's creative work in the world continues. Peters says, "We need both."[251] I will leave it to others to explain what the theory of thermodynamics and the theory of evolution have to do with a theological understanding God's creative work in nature and history. These are hypotheses in current scientific thinking which Peters thinks are important in advancing consonance between natural science and the Christian doctrine of creation. Peters introduces his concept of prolepsis to expedite this consonance. "If we are to understand God's creation in light of the gospel promise of a new creation, there must be an eschatological component. My hypothesis, then, is the following principle of proleptic creation: God creates from the future, not from the past."[252] Peters admits that this idea of causality goes against common sense. The ordinary view is linear; causes come from the past and produce effects in the present, with implications for the future. This view is not suitable for thinking about the process of divine creativity. "The first thing God did for the world was to give it a future. Without a future it would be nothing. Referring to the finite beginning with the phrase *creatio ex nihilo,* then, means referring to God's first gift of futurity.... God bestows the future by opening up the possibility of its becoming something it never has been before and by supplying it with the

---

251. Ted Peters, *God – The World's Future*, 142.

252. Ted Peters, *God – The World's Future*, 142. In a footnote Peters references something I wrote in my book, *The Future of God. The Revolutionary Dynamics of Hope.* "Here I am led by the early work of Carl Braaten, who said, 'The new place to start in theology is at the end — eschatology. Braaten's eschatological approach to ontology and ethics influenced the title of this present work.'"

power to change.... Hence, I suggest we think of God's creative activity as a pull from the future rather than a push from the past."[253] This thumbnail sketch of Peter's proleptic view of divine causality cannot do justice to his full description of how it works in all its details.

D. Sin and Evil

Ted Peters relates that he became intensely interested in the subject of sin and evil by encountering the phenomenon of Satanism. Once he was asked to give a theological evaluation of the Satanic cult for which he was not prepared to do. So along with another colleague he began to teach a course simply called "Evil" at the Graduate Theological Union. In doing research for the course he asked why it is that "mainline Protestant and Roman Catholic theologians of our present generation seem to have lost the ability to talk about such topics as sin. For the last quarter century or so, the theological establishment has consigned the human predicament to structures of political and economic oppression or to such systemic evils as race and gender discrimination. In the process, theologians lost interest in the internal workings of the human soul. The evils of our world have been consigned to social forces beyond the scope of our own personal responsibility."[254] In 327 pages of his book, *Sin: Radical Evil in Soul and Society,* he creates his own list of seven deadly sins which he calls "Seven Steps to Radical Evil." The steps are: anxiety, unfaith, pride, concupiscence, self-justification, cruelty, and blasphemy. He goes into such great depth and detail that one marvels that he learned all this from reading books and personal experience, if not his own, that of others via interviews. The footnotes and bibliography indicate that no mention was made of Karl Menninger's popular book,

---

253. Ted Peters, *God – The World's Future,* 143, 144.
254. Ted Peters, *Sin: Radical Evil in Soul and Society* (Eerdmans, 1994), 2.

Whatever Became of Sin?, which gives support to his thesis by a leading psychologist.

Ted Peters' interest in the subject of sin and evil is connected to his greater concern to develop a theological understanding of human being. Christian anthropology deals with the story of the creation of Adam and Eve in the state of perfection in the image of God (*imago dei*) and their fall into sin. Then follows the story of the restoration of the *imago dei in* Christ, the new Adam, the resurrection of the dead in a "spiritual body" (*soma pneumatikos*), and the final consummation. Again Peters pours all of these notions into the framework of his theory of prolepsis. "Hence the *imago dei* is essentially future. But it has a proleptic quality as well. Our created humanity is our eschatological humanity. Who we are is determined by who we will be. To think of ourselves as created in the image of God is to think backward from the fulfillment to the present, from the final creation to the present process of creating. To the extent that the *imago dei* is present now, it is present proleptically — that is, it is an anticipation of a reality yet to be fully realized... the power of the eschatological whole is effective in the present. It is effective proleptically. It is the power of God's grace calling us forward and empowering us to center our existence through trust in the future that will be God's."[255]

3. Seeking Consonance between Theology and Science

Ted Peters makes the surprising claim that contemporary scientific research into the natural world is raising again the question about God. Does God exist? Does God have anything to do with what is going on in the world of nature, history, and human experience? Natural science deals with the cosmos, the whole world. Theology affirms the doctrine of creation; the cosmos is

---

255. Ted Peters, *God – The World's Future*, 157, 178.

the creation of God. Peters asks, "How can we understand our cosmos as God's creation? ... What should be the relationship between theological knowledge and scientific knowledge about the world in which we live?"[256] For theologians like me who have not specialized in the interface between theology and science Ted Peters proves to be a master teacher. His numerous writings help us neophytes to understand a bit more about the most complicated scientific theories and discoveries and their possible relevance for theological reflection. Peters is pursuing what he calls "hypothetical consonance." Consonance suggests rapprochement, correspondence, points of contact, and possible harmony between the disciplines. He offers as an example the Big Bang theory of the origin of the universe (cosmogony) which suggests that both scientists and theologians might reasonably ask about the possible role that God might have played in creating the world.

There are other perhaps more popular ways to understand how theology and science are related. Peters calls them "blind alleys." The first one he calls "scientism," which dogmatically claims that scientific method is the only way to acquire knowledge about reality. Religion is myth in the negative sense of the word — pseudo-knowledge. Bertrand Russell, the British philosopher, said, "What science cannot tell us, mankind cannot know."[257] A second blind alley is exactly the opposite, ecclesiastical authoritarianism, which assumes that if there is a conflict between modern science and church authority, science must be wrong. This approach was asserted by the infamous Papal document of 1864, the *Syllabus of Errors.* The church has by divine authority the right to set limits to what science can know. Vatican II thankfully reversed this judgment in favor of academic freedom from church authority. The third blind alley

---

256. *Cosmos as Creation: Theology and Science in Consonance*, ed. Ted Peters (Abingdon Press, 1989), 12, 13.
257. *Cosmos as Creation*, ed. Ted Peters, 14.

is scientific creationism. The *Book of Genesis* is interpreted literally; it delivers scientific truth. Creationists believe the Bible tells us how the world came into existence, so the scientific theory of evolution must be denied. They fail to take into account the hermeneutical difference between the ancient view of the world from that of modern times. The fourth blind alley is highly respected by both scientists and theologians, called the two-language theory. This view maintains that science and religion each has its own way of thinking and speaking. Hence, scientific theory and religious faith each has its own validity. Peters asserts, "The problem with the two-language theory is that it prevents any rapprochement from the outset. We could not explore the possibility that the language of one might serve to illumine the other. We could not develop the assumption that both are speaking about the same reality.... I like the theory of hypothetical consonance better."[258]

The search for consonance means to reflect theologically on the data provided by the natural sciences, seeking answers to the question how to understand God's relation to the world. Science tells us that the world of nature is dynamic, always changing, bringing forth new things. The Big Bang theory might lend support to the theological idea of *creatio ex nihilo*. Yet, not everything was created all at once. Creation is ongoing, which looks a lot like the traditional theological idea of *creatio continua*. The ongoing creative activity of God brought about the human race, creatures endowed with freedom and responsibility, which has far-reaching ethical implications, the first being that humans ought to care for the world in which they live.

Ted Peters has assembled a group of theologians, some of them scientists as well, at the forefront of seeking consonance between theology and science. The names are generally familiar because most of them are well known for their works beyond theology and science: Arthur R. Peacocke, Ian G. Barbour,

258. *Cosmos as Creation*, 16, 17.

Wolfhart Pannenberg, Robert J. Russell, Philip Hefner, Nancey C. Murphy, Roger E. Timm, and H. Paul Santmire. Here we are interested in taking account of Peters' contribution to the dialogue in his essay, "Cosmos as Creation."

Peters starts his reflections on the proper relationship between scientific cosmogony and the Christian doctrine of creation with a description of the Big Bang Cosmology. The world-famous English theoretical physicist, Stephen Hawking, suggested at one time that the Big Bang model implies the existence of God. The Big Bang theory avers that the cosmos had a beginning, leading to the question as to what was before the beginning. Yet, Hawking, a convinced atheist, would not take the bait. Peters concludes his discussion of atheists like Stephen Hawking and Carl Sagan by saying that the God they are rejecting is the God of deism, who created the world in the beginning with fixed natural laws and let it run on its own. This is not the God of biblical-Christian theism. "What is at stake for the theist is to understand God as a contemporary factor in world events. This means that God's creative work is not limited to a one-time event in the ancient past; but it continues now and we can expect more things yet in the future.[259]

After the many interesting points of contact that theologians and scientists are contemplating, Peters concludes by acknowledging that the Christian doctrine of creation stands on its own feet and is not dependent on the hypotheses and conclusions of science. Peters writes, "The question regarding the origin of the universe simply cannot be answered within the scientific method.... Our religious commitment is of a different order. It begins with the experience of the Beyond, with that which transcends the cosmos. What is relevant about the Beyond is that it is the source and Lord of all that is.... The scientific method cannot deny the relevance of the Beyond; but it cannot affirm it either.

---

259. Ted Peters, *Cosmos as Creation*, 56.

The Beyond is just what the word implies, namely, something beyond the domain of human inquiry. The Beyond lies outside the perimeter of scientific knowing, and always will."[260] The Beyond refers to God. Then Peters returns to his favorite idea of the best way for theology to seek consonance (not proofs) with science, namely, the proleptic power of the God of the future at work in the course of history and human events. The *cantus firmus* of the Christian faith is the promise of the new reality that God has in store for humanity and the world, the resurrection of the dead and life everlasting, based on what God has already done in raising Jesus from the dead. "God's future action is not just one more expression of natural laws first formed during the Big Bang of the past. God acts independently, and it is this independence that is the ground of our hope.... Our hope is a response to a revelation from the Beyond, from God whose plans for the future are not only governed by principles or processes produced in the past. Our hope, in short, is the result of our faith."[261]

Who says so? At this point Peters takes recourse to a chorus of church theologians who heed the precedence of the biblical prophets and apostles who affirm that our knowledge of the world as the creation of God derives from faith. "By faith we understand that the world was created by the word of God, so that what is seen was made out of things which do not appear" (Hebrews 11:3). Bultmann says so, "To every eye than the eye of faith the action of God is hidden." Thomas Aquinas says so, "We hold by faith alone and it cannot be proved by demonstration, that the world did not always exist." Karl Barth says so, "The doctrine of the creation no less than the whole remaining content of Christian confession is an article of faith, i.e., the rendering of a knowledge that no man has procured for himself or ever will, which is neither native to him nor

---

260. Ted Peters, *Cosmos as Creation*, 107.
261. Ted Peters, *Cosmos as Creation*, 108.

accessible by way of observation and logical thinking."[262] Yet, it is not quite true to say that Peters is merely reaffirming the good old Lutheran slogan, "*sola fide.*" He says, "I would not want to set aside completely the powers of natural reason or knowledge gained through observation and logical thinking.... The awareness of the Beyond is a matter of faith. Thinking about the Beyond is an intellectual activity, the structure of which we share with all other thinking activities. The Christian doctrine of creation as we have it, then, is a product of both revelation and reason, of both faith and science. It is the result of evangelical explication."[263]

4. Controversial Issues, Ethical and Cultural

Ted Peters has ben actively involved in addressing a variety of ethical and cultural issues that have arisen with the advancement of modern science. The first one involves issues surrounding the evolution controversy. Peters advocates "theistic evolution." He co-authored with Martinez Hewlett *Evolution From Creation to New Creation* (Abingdon Press, 2003). He authored *Can You Believe in God and Evolution?* (Abingdon Press, 2006) and soon thereafter *A Scientific Commentary on Darwin's "Origin of Species"* (Abingdon Press, 2008). Peters was the Principal Investigator for a research project on theological and ethical questions raised by the "Human Genome Project" undertaken by the Center for Theology and the Natural Sciences. That led to a book Peters wrote entitled *Playing God? Genetic Determinism and Human Freedom* (Routledge, 2003). In this book Ted Peters mounts a strong case against the "Gene Myth" because it favors genetic determinism. Peters argues, rather, that a human being is an interaction of three things, genetics, environment, and free will. The genes do not determine human behavior *tout court.*

---

262. Ted Peters, *Cosmos as Creation*, 109, 110.
263. Ted Peters, *Cosmos as Creation*, 110.

Another ethical issue that Peters tackles is the Stem Cell Controversy. He advertises his position in the title of a book he co-authored with Karen Lebacqz and Gaymon Bennett, *Sacred Cells? Why Christians Should Support Stem Cell Research* (Roman and Littlefiled, 2008). "Stem cell research is a step to be taken toward the improvement of transplantation therapy and toward lengthening a person's life."[264] There are forceful criticisms of stem cell research from Catholic Bishops in the United Kingdom and the USA as well as from the Southern Baptist Convention. In spite of the fact that there is no slam dunk moral position on either side of the argument, Peters says, "It is my own judgment that stem cell research deserves public and private support on the grounds of the beneficence principle. This bioethical principle is supported in the Christian tradition by the concept of *agapé*, self-sacrificing love. The investment and even sacrifice of present-day resources on behalf of medical research that could yield such a benefit in health and well-being to our great grandchildren is an opportunity to love our neighbor, as Jesus commanded and as compassion suggests. By no means does this grant blessing to crass commercialization and unbridled profiteering; yet it asks our society to be stewards of present resources on behalf of the welfare of future generations."[265]

Cloning is another controversial topic brought about by genetic research. Dolly is the name of the first cloned sheep, named by *Time* Magazine "the world's most famous sheep." It happened at the Roslin Institute of the University of Edinburgh, Scotland, in 1996. This proved that a cell taken from one body could recreate another individual like it. The ethics of cloning became the controversial topic of the day and Peters joined in the fray. Cloning sheep is one thing; cloning human beings is quite another. A *Time* magazine poll asked,"Is it against God's will to clone human beings?" 74 % answered yes; 19% answered no. A preponderance of responses from church officials and theologians

---

264. Ted Peters, *Playing God? Genetic Determinism and Human Freedom*, 176.
265. Ted Peters, *Playing God?*, 192.

was negative, fearing the commodification and selling of cloned children, in violation of their dignity. Peters writes, "Warning sirens should sound to alert us of potential harm to the dignity of children. Ethical thinking leading to public policy should be the order of the day. Rather than a green light or a permanent red light, I endorse the amber light of a temporary ban until safety and ethical issues can be sorted out."[266]

Another chapter in *Playing God?* deals with the hot topic whether science has discovered a "gay gene." Having examined the evidence Peters concludes that "science is in doubt."[267] The gene myth seems to blame one's sexual preference and conduct on one's genes. To the question, "Why do you do it?", the answer would be, "the genes make me do it." Would that mean that science can resolve the ethical question whether homosexual activity is moral or immoral? Peters does not reach a conclusive answer that any of the positions in the controversy can cite in its favor. "What does seem clear to me is that the point of departure given us by current genetic science does not in itself determine our ethical destination. What the genes tell us leaves us immediately between the path of self-proclaimed innocence, on the one hand, or acceptance of responsibility for what we have inherited, on the other.... For those looking for a scientific justification of their existing position on gay rights or even for a red line on the map marking the best road to the land of ethical correctness, this chapter may be disappointing."[268]

Ted Peters wears many hats. He writes on the UFO phenomenon,[269] on astrotheology[270] that deals with space explora-

---

266. Ted Peters, *Playing God?*, 171.

267. Ted Peters, *Playing God?*, 104.

268. Ted Peters, *Playing God?*, 115.

269. Ted Peters, *UFOs – God's Chariots? Flying Saucers in Politics, Science, and Religion* (John Knox Press, 1977).

270. Ted Peters along with his colleagues at the Center for Theology and the Natural Sciences wrote, *Astrotheology: Science and Theology Meet Extraterrestrial Life* (Cascade Books, 2018).

tion, on extraterrestrial life, and the like. Peters explores UFOs to understand that part of contemporary culture that incorporates them in their religious worldview. He also writes fictional espionage thrillers that mix science and faith. One is entitled, *For God and Country* and another is *Cyrus Twelve* (Apocryphile Press, 2018). Ted Peters also has a blog that features his interests on a wide variety of topics involving theology, ethics, science, and culture.

Dr. George A. Lindbeck was born in China in 1923, the son of Lutheran missionaries of the Augustana Synod. Lindbeck came to American after finishing high school in Korea. He enrolled at Gustavus Adolphus College in St. Peter, Minnesota and in 1943 received a B.A. From college he attended Yale Divinity School and received a B.D. in 1946. In 1955 he received a Ph.D. from Yale University. He was also trained at the University of Toronto and the University of Paris to study medieval thought with Étienne Gilson and Paul Vignaux. Lindbeck spent his entire teaching career at Yale Divinity School, appointed to the theological faculty in 1952 where he remained until his retirement in 1993. Inasmuch as he was a medievalist, he was invited to serve as a "Delegated Observer" to the Second Vatican Council, representing the Lutheran World Federation. Lindbeck devoted his career to ecumenical dialogue, especially the national and international dialogues between Lutherans and Roman Catholics. Together with his colleague Hans Frei, Lindbeck became a prominent leader of postliberal theology, also known as the "New Yale School of Theology." Lindbeck was the recipient of five honorary doctorates, from the University of Notre Dame, Augustana College, University of Munich, Upsala College, and Gustavus Adolphus College. In 2009 Lindbeck was afflicted by a brain aneurism; he died in 2018 in an assisted living center in Florida in 2018.

Eight

George A. Lindbeck

Lutheran Postliberal Theology

George A. Lindbeck (1923-2018) was born in China, the son of Lutheran missionaries of the Augustana Synod, of Swedish ethnic background. He attended school in China and Korea through his high school years. He attended Gustavus Adolphus College in St. Peter, Minnesota, earning a B.A. in 1943. The following year he attended the seminary of his church, Augustana Lutheran Seminary in Rock Island, Illinois. The next year he transferred to study at a non-denominational divinity school in New Haven, Connecticut, Yale University, where he earned both a B.D. (1946) and a Ph.D. (1955). This decision was an omen of what lay in his future, as he embarked on an ecclesially independent career unmatched by any other Lutheran theologian of our generation. While studying for his doctorate at Yale he took a two year detour to study at the University of Paris and at the Pontifical Institute of Medieval Studies in Toronto, Canada, mentored by two of the most eminent scholars of medieval thought, Étienne Gilson and Paul Vignaux. Having been trained as a medievalist he was equipped to write a doctoral dissertation on John Duns Scotus (1265-1308), focussing on the issues of essence and existence. In 1952, still as a graduate student, he was appointed to the faculty at Yale, where he remained until his retirement in 1993.

1. Redefining Lutheranism

As a self-avowed Lutheran theologian George Lindbeck was *sui generis*, one of a kind. He once described himself as a "Wittgensteinian Thomistic Lutheran." He was better known among his fellow Lutheran theologians as an "evangelical catholic," his usual definition of what it means to be a Lutheran today. He was not alone in suggesting that "evangelical" does not mean "Protestant" and "catholic" does not mean "Roman." As an historical theologian Lindbeck wanted to recover the original intention of Martin Luther's reforming movement. He would often speak of Lutheranism as "a reform movement within the Catholic Church of the West." Such a self-understanding of global Lutheranism was shared by many of Lindbeck's confrères engaged in the international Lutheran-Roman Catholic Dialogues, such as, Edmund Schlink, Kristin Skydsgaard, Peter Brunner, Harding Meyer, among others.

"*Ressourcement*" was a key concept in the theological debates at the Second Vatican Council. It means "back to the sources." This was also Lindbeck's approach to reconceptualizing Lutheranism. He called Lutherans to return to the sources, to mine the ore of the great Lutheran confessional tradition, rather than to ride piggy back on this or that ethnic tradition, whether German, Danish, Swedish, Norwegian, or Finnish. The unifying core of essential Lutheranism must be what is shared by all, and not one peculiar to any of the ethnic branches. It is not surprising, therefore, that the *sola*s of the Lutheran Reformation are the bread and butter of what Lindbeck brought to the table of ecumenical dialogue. *Sola gratia*, *sola fide*, and *sola scriptura* are three *sola*s that help to flesh out the full meaning of the *solus Christus*. These *sola*s have been used as polemical slogans in the history of controversial theology that has characterized centuries of inter-confessional relations since the sixteenth century. This is all the more reason to return to the sources to scrub away all the barnacles that have accrued in the meantime. Lindbeck had the historical knowledge and hermeneutical skill to do this in such a way as to buttress his argument that evangelical Lutheranism is a reform movement within the church catholic.

Lindbeck's early writings taught many Lutherans in America to think of their ecclesial identity in new ways. Lindbeck observed that there are two different ways of evaluating the Lutheran Reformation, corrective versus constitutive. The constitutive view maintains that Luther broke away from the Catholic Church to found a Protestant Church repristinating the church of the first five centuries. Protestantism understands itself to be essentially anti-Catholic. On the other hand, the corrective approach underscores Luther's fundamental continuity with the Catholic Church that baptized, confirmed, educated, and confirmed him, intending only to correct (reform) the things that he believed were corrupting the church he loved.

Lindbeck wrote an especially influential article entitled, "A Protestant View of the Ecclesiological Status of the Roman Catholic Church," in which he penned these words: "The Catholic Church was for the early Protestants the one and only church. It was their home church, it was their ecclesiastical homeland — but it was under enemy occupation. The government had become tyrannical. It drove out not only those who would reform it, but even those who wished for nothing more than the freedom to preach the gospel. There was nothing to do except to form a government, an ecclesiastical order, in exile. But the Reformers at first no more thought of this as a new, a second church than de Gaulle thought of his war-time regime as a replacement, a substitute for France."[271] This image of the Reformers as protesters in exile seemed to capture the provisional character of Lutheranism and of the mission of the ecumenical movement to work for the reunion of separated Christians and ecclesial communities in the one, holy, catholic, and apostolic church. The ecumenical impasse is that exiles are free to return

---

271. George Lindbeck, "A Protestant View of the Ecclesiological Status of the Roman Catholic Church," *Journal of Ecumenical Studies,* 1/2 (1964), 244.

to their homeland only when a radical change in government has taken place. The exiles talk about justification by faith and the excommunicators talk about papal infallibility. What are the prospects of reunion for those locked in such a church-dividing conflict? Lindbeck proceeded to exert an enormous amount of time and energy to reconcile the two alienated parties.

2. Delegated Observer at Vatican II

The Lutheran World Federation was invited by Rome to delegate three theologians to serve as observers at the Second Vatican Council. Inasmuch as the Lutheran Churches in America were major financial supporters of the LWF, the Geneva officials decided that one of the three should be an American. But who? Lindbeck was chosen because of his credentials — multilingual (Latin, German, French), a specialist in medieval thought and contemporary Roman Catholic theology, and free to take a leave of absence from his teaching position at Yale Divinity School. So Lindbeck packed his bags and went with his family to live in Rome for two years (1962-1964). The other two LWF observers were Vilmos Vajta, a Swede of Hungarian descent and Kristen Skydsgaard of Copenhagen, Denmark. In addition Edmund Schlink was an observer representing the Evangelical Church of Germany as well as Oscar Cullmann, a world famous New Testament theologian who had authored a book on the Apostle Peter. Lindbeck's responsibility for the Lutheran World Federation included worldwide travel to keep Lutheran churches informed of the conciliar discussions and decisions at the Vatican Council. Lindbeck remembered his role as an observer as "a truly heady experience."[272]

Lindbeck was at the center of a world-historical event that dominated the headlines for five years. Reporters from

---

272. George Lindbeck, "Reminiscences of Vatican II," *The Church in a Post-liberal Age*, edited by James J. Buckley (Eerdmans, 2002), 13.

newspapers, magazines, and TV networks were hungry for interviews which Lindbeck was happy to accommodate with his expertise. "Even a second stringer like myself was regularly interviewed (and quoted half a dozen times or more) by *Time* and *Newsweek*."[273] Of course, as a scholar Lindbeck had read the works of the most famous Roman Catholic theologians who were called *periti* (experts), consultants at the Council — Karl Rahner, Yves Congar, Jean Daniélou, Joseph Ratzinger, Henri de Lubac, and Eduard Schillebeeckx. Now he was able personally to hobnob with them. "There were the academic and governmental receptions, lectures arranged for and by the bishops for their instruction, and long Italian lunches and dinners. It was scarcely possible to avoid coming to know the already famous or about to be famous.... Trust developed, barriers disappeared, and a sense of common mission for the renewal of the Church, both Roman and non-Roman, came to be shared by the observers and most Council members. Solidarity was solidified by the existence of a common enemy, the Curia and its Tridentine supporters."[274] Cardinal Ottaviani and Cardinal Ruffini were the two notorious conservatives who tried to steer the Council back to the glory days of the Counter-Reformation. Lindbeck told of a joke circulating that says a lot about the attitudes and atmosphere at the Council. The two Cardinals got into taxi, asked the driver to take them to the Council, and fell into a deep conversation. Suddenly they realized they were heading in the wrong direction. They noticed they were outside the old city gate going north. Ruffini yelled, "But we told you to take us to the Council." To which the cabbie responded, "That's where we're going; we're on our way to Trent."

George Lindbeck edited a book of descriptions and evaluations of the sessions and its decisions of the Council written

---

273. George Lindbeck, "Reminiscences of Vatican II," *The Church in a Postliberal Age*, 13.

274. George Lindbeck, "Reminiscences of Vatican II," *The Church in a Postliberal Age*, 15.

by a group of Lutheran observers officially delegated by their churches. The essays are written by authors of five nationalities, American, German, Swedish, Danish, and Swiss. The book is entitled, *Dialogue on the Way*, covering the first three of four sessions. The authors speak for themselves and not for the churches that sent them. They dealt with the new principles promulgated by the Council on Scripture and Tradition, the Liturgy, the Church, the Virgin Mary, and Ecumenism. What is clear from the involvement of the delegated observers at Vatican II is that they did not only watch and listen; they spoke and they were heard and sometimes heeded. They played a crucial role and Lindbeck's voice was a persistent and eloquent expression of the new situation in which the standard pre-Vatican II stereotype of being "pro" or "anti" Catholic could now be relegated to a footnote of past history. John Paul II expressed the new ecumenical situation brought about by Vatican II when he said in *Ut Unum Sint*, "We all belong to Christ." That means we are all sisters and brothers in the one church of Jesus Christ, no matter what denominational differences remain unresolved on the ecumenical agenda.

3. Lutheran-Roman Catholic Dialogues

George Lindbeck was one of the chief architects in the construction of the highly successful international and national dialogues between Lutherans and Roman Catholics. It would require several volumes to document all of his contributions in his capacity both as author and editor. Here we will focus on only three major subjects, Justification by Faith, Papal Infallibility, and the Offices of Ministry.

A. Justification by Faith

The doctrine of justification by faith taught and confessed in Article IV of the *Augsburg Confession* (1530) and the *Apology of the Augsburg Confession* (1531) became central in the Lutheran-Roman Catholic Dialogues after Vatican II. Dialogue VII took up the doctrine of justification by faith. The previous six dialogues dealt with the Nicene Creed, Baptism, Eucharist, Ministry, Papal Primacy, Teaching Authority and Infallibility, all of which achieved a remarkable degree of convergence of teaching, if not what one can call consensus. The seventh dialogue began in 1978 and did not conclude with a final statement until 1985, declaring "A fundamental consensus on the gospel is necessary to give credibility to our previous agreed statements on baptism, on the Eucharist, and on forms of church authority. We believe we have achieved such a consensus."[275] To explicate this statement further it is stated: "Our entire hope of justification and salvation rests on Christ Jesus and on the gospel whereby the goodness of God's merciful action in Christ is made known; we do not place our ultimate trust in anything other than God's promise and saving work of Christ."[276]

Gerhard Forde was one of the participants who did not agree that consensus had been reached. Lindbeck reflected on his experience in this dialogue saying, "On justification, it appears to be the Lutherans who are boxed in. On this question they often give the impression of being less open to diversity and less ecumenical than their Catholic partners."[277] The ecumenical problem is that some Lutherans require consensus on the doctrine of justification with Catholics and other denominations as a precondition of pulpit and altar fellowship, while they do not even enjoy consensus among themselves. This fact became glaringly obvious at the Helsinki convention of the Lutheran World Federation in 1963, when the leading Lutheran theologians representing their respective churches failed to agree on

---

275. H. George Anderson, T. Austin Murphy, and Joseph A. Burgess, editors, *Justification by Faith*, Lutherans and Catholics in Dialogue VII (Augsburg, 1985), 74.

276. *Justification by Faith*, Lutherans and Catholics in Dialogue VII, 16.

277. George Lindbeck, "Article IV and Lutheran/Roman Catholic Dialogue: The Limits of Diversity in the Understanding of Justification," *Lutheran Theological Seminary Bulletin* 61 (1981), 39.

justification, and adjourned the meeting without reaching a consensus. There were too many inner-Lutheran differences to be reconciled, from the forensic view of gnesio-Lutherans, to the modern existentialist view by which the kerygma brings about a new self-understanding, to the new Finnish interpretation that affirms the real presence of Christ in faith.[278]

The LWF Assembly in Helsinki proved that there is no consensus among Lutheran Churches worldwide on the doctrine of justification, so how can they require it when they meet Roman Catholics in dialogue? In fact, Lindbeck argued "that Lutherans cannot by their own principles insist on the Roman Catholic dogmatization of the *sola fide* as a condition for church fellowship. They ask only, in the historic phrase, for the 'freedom of the gospel.' ... To demand that the *sola fide* be accepted as a prior condition for church fellowship is to betray the Reformation by turning what professed to be a reform movement in the Church universal into self-enclosed sect."[279]

B. Papal Infallibility

The First Vatican Council in 1870 dogmatically declared that when the Bishop of Rome speaks officially *ex cathedra*, he possesses infallibility in defining doctrine on faith and morals, and such declarations are of themselves irreformable with no need for the Church to consent. After Vatican II Catholic theologians debated about the meaning of the doctrine of infallibility. Some began to argue that it was dispensable,[280] others that it was indispensable but not of central importance. Lindbeck realized that the exercise of infallibility by the magisterium had become dysfunctional. "Radical surgery appears to be necessary....

---

278. *Union With Christ. The New Finnish Interpretation of Luther*, eds. Carl E. Braaten and Robert W. Jenson (Eerdmans, 2008).

279. George Lindbeck, "Article IV and Lutheran/Roman Catholic Dialogue," 50.

280. Hans Küng, *Infallible? An Inquiry* (Doubleday, 1971).

As this theory has come to be understood that is practiced in Roman Catholicism, it is clearly at odds with present needs. It does not conform to what many contemporary Catholics, no less than non-Catholics, think of as the demands of the gospel; the monarchical papalism which is associated with it seems dangerously anachronistic, and it is clearly unecumenical. Pope Paul himself, as we know, has spoken more in sorrow than in anger of the irony that the office with supposedly infallible power which is supposed to be the prime servant of unity has in fact become the chief point of division between the churches."[281] As dark as this picture is of papal infallibility, at the same time Lindbeck acknowledged that it is so deeply ensconced in modern Catholicism that getting rid of it would spell complete disaster. "It would rupture the continuity and shatter the unity of the Roman communion. Certainly if this were done abruptly, schism would result, and the Catholic Church would become another Protestant denomination or congeries of denominations, all competing for the Roman name but without the substance."[282]

As one of the leaders in the official Lutheran-Roman Catholic dialogues, Lindbeck made a valiant effort to find a breakthrough so that both sides might reach an agreement that the doctrine of infallibility need not be church-dividing, despite their ongoing differences. He published a book and many articles to that end, listed in a footnote below.[283] Before Vatican II virtually all Lutheran and Catholic theologians would

---

281. George Lindbeck, "Infallibility," *The Church in a Postliberal Age*, 123.

282. George Lindbeck, "Infallibility," *The Church in a Postliberal Age*, 123.

283. George Lindbeck, *Infallibility* (Marquette University Press, 1972). Also, George Lindbeck, "The Infallibility Debate," *The Infallibility Debate* (Paulist Press, 1971); "Papacy and *ius divinum:* A Lutheran View." *Papal Primacy and the Universal Church*, Lutherans and Catholics in Dialogue 5, eds, Paul C. Empie and T. Austin Murphy (Augsburg, 1974). "Papal Infallibility: A Protestant Response," *Commonweal* 102 (1975). "Lutherans and the Papacy," *Journal of Ecumenical Studies* 13 (1976). "The Reformation and the Infallibility Debate," *Teaching Authority and Infallibility in the Church*. Lutherans and Catholics in Dialogue 6, 102-19.

agree with a statement Lindbeck made: "There appears to be no more possibility of reconciling Protestant and Catholic views on infallibility than squaring the circle."[284] In the aftermath of Vatican II, however, the prospects of reconciliation seemed to appear more hopeful. Hans Küng and Walter Kasper both argued against what they called 'a priori infallibility,' by which they meant a magisterial authority that is automatic, quite apart from whether the content of what is dogmatically affirmed is scriptural or consistent with church tradition. From the point of view of the Reformation there can be no objection to the concept of infallibility. Lutherans affirmed the infallibility of the Bible because of its gospel content, the message of salvation on account of the person and work of Christ. The New Testament confession that "Jesus is Lord" is absolutely essential to Christian identity so that to deny it would sound a death knell. That is a biblical sense of infallibility. So infallibility in itself is not the problem. Lindbeck writes, "From this point of view, the original Reformation tradition, like historic Christianity in general, is just as deeply committed to infallible dogmatic propositions as is the Catholic.... The problem of *a priori* infallibility, then, is the real sticking point. This is the view that, for example, 'When the Pope declares that he is speaking definitively on a *de fide* question or as the supreme teacher of the Church, then such a declaration, in the standard traditional theory, is *a priori* inerrant.... it requires no *a posteriori* verifying tests in scripture, tradition or the present faith of the Church.'"[285] That would in principle give the teaching office a "blank check." The Pope can decide whatever he wants going solo. But no one seriously believes this. The interpretation among the leading Catholic theologians, including Karl Rahner and Walter Kasper, is that magisterial pronouncements seek support and verification in the light of Scripture and church tradition.

---

284. George Lindbeck, "Infallibility," *The Church in a Postliberal Age*, 125.
285. George Lindbeck, "Infallibility," *The Church in a Postliberal Age*, 138.

Now to Lindbeck's conclusion, after his lengthy, subtle, sophisticated analysis. "We must now observe in conclusion, there is no contradiction between dogmatically possible Roman Catholic positions on infallibility and the hypothetical Reformation view.... If ecumenicity and reception by the Church were added to the conditions for the recognition of a teaching as infallible, then Protestants who stand with the Reformers would have to ask whether they are not simply permitted but required to agree with their Catholic brethren."[286] Lindbeck admits such a putative reconciliation is purely theoretical and abstract. It does not equate to the real ecclesial realities all the churches confront in the real world. Lindbeck's hypothetical reconciliation "amounts to no more than saying that one can conceive of a new hermeneutical setting, different from past and present ones, in which the doctrinal propositions on infallibility would no longer be incompatible.... It seems unlikely that these requirements will be met in the foreseeable future."[287]

We are back to square one. The dogma of papal infallibility as it is understood and practiced in the Roman Church is not acceptable to Eastern Orthodox Christianity or the ecclesial heirs of the Reformation. This is not a trivial matter, but does it need to constitute a barrier to full communion between the churches? Lindbeck says, "No." I agree. Most Lutheran churches around the world welcome Roman Catholics to join their celebrations of the Lord's Supper. The official position of Rome is not reciprocal. Geoffrey Wainwright, Anglican professor emeritus of theology at Duke Divinity School, humorously commented on papal infallibility after a lecture at Notre Dame University, "The Pope has spoken *ex cathedra* only twice, on his own infallibility and on the Assumption of Mary, and he was wrong both times."

---

286. George Lindbeck, "Infallibility," *The Church in a Postliberal Age*, 141.
287. George Lindbeck, "Infallibility," *The Church in a Postliberal Age*, 141.

C. The Church and the Offices of Ministry

Ecclesiology was understandably high on the agenda in the multilateral dialogues involving the Orthodox, Roman Catholic, and Anglican Churches. The Protestant Churches were outplayed and had a lot of catching up to do. Comparing and contrasting their different doctrines of the church based on their respective denominational confessional statements would not reconcile their glaring diversity. Lindbeck embarked on a different approach, starting with a biblical theology of the Church rather than with the history of its post-biblical traditions. At Vatican II there were several equally acceptable definitions of the Church, such as, sacrament of unity, institution of salvation, and people of God. The weight of biblical research leads Lindbeck to opt for the phrase, the "messianic pilgrim people of God," as the starting point for thinking about the church. The people of God image has been appropriated by both Catholic and Protestant theologians. For these reasons Lindbeck says, "This is the way of viewing the Church which currently has the greatest *prima facie* claim to ecumenical catholicity.[288]

A scholarly consensus exists on what the Bible means when it speaks of the Church as the people of God. Granted, there are other images of the Church that might be regarded as equally important, such as, body of Christ, worshiping assembly, or community of the Spirit. Lindbeck asserts that he will proceed in response to an "ecumenically mandated hypothesis that the Church was primarily the people of God in the biblical writings."[289] The use of this hypothesis yields some important insights. 1. The early Christians were a Jewish sect. They believed in a crucified and resurrected Messiah, and though these believing Jews welcomed uncircumcised Gentiles into their fellowship, they continued to think of themselves as Jews, legitimate people of Israel. 2. The story of Israel was their story.

---

288. George Lindbeck, "The Church," *The Church in a Postliberal Age*, 147.
289. George Lindbeck, "The Church," *The Church in a Postliberal Age*, 148-149.

The story was prior to whatever images, concepts, and doctrines of the Church developed as explanation. 3. The Hebrew Scriptures were the only inspired Bible of the first Christians. They did not have the New Testament to ground their identity. The history of Israel was their history, their only history. 4. The faith of the first Jewish Christians in Jesus as the promised Messiah made such a profound difference that they saw themselves in a new way as members of the body of Christ. The dawning of a new age was a continuation of the story of Israel. Lindbeck endorsed Krister Stendahl's phrase, "honorary Jews," to describe the Gentile Christians.[290]

This original biblical view of the relation between Israel and the Church did not survive for long. The opposition between synagogue and church led to mutual anathemas. By the second century the Church became exclusively Gentile; anti-Judaism evolved. The original one people of God became split in two, the old and the new. Israel could be seen as the type and the Church as the antitype, the fulfillment. Yet, the early church fathers set a limit to the rejection of Israel and the Hebrew Scriptures among the Gentile Christians in their struggle against Gnosticism and Marcionitism. The rest of church history records many horrific chapters of anti-Jewishness, starting with the conversion of the Roman Empire to Christianity, turning those who had been persecuted into persecutors, culminating in the Holocaust of the twentieth century.

Meanwhile, systematic ecclesiology, whether Catholic or Protestant, did not recover the biblical story of the people of God. Lindbeck suggests there are good reasons to start over again with the biblical theology of the Church as the people of God. He writes, "There are a number of familiar ways in which the present period is becoming more like the Christian beginnings than the intervening ages. Christendom is passing and Christians are becoming a diaspora. The antagonism of the Church to the

---

290. Krister Stendahl, *Paul Among Jews and Gentiles* (Fortress Press, 1976), 37.

Synagogue has been unmasked (we hope definitively) for the horror it always was. Ecclesial pretensions to fulfillment have become obnoxious to multitudes of Catholics and Protestants alike. Some of the reasons for distorting and then rejecting the scriptural people-of-God ecclesiology are disappearing, and perhaps its original version is again applicable."[291]

What would ecclesiology look like today if constructed in terms of the biblical concept of the people of God? Lindbeck offers a few descriptions. The Church would think of its identity and mission continuous with Israel's, not as a rupture in the biblical story. God elects a people to be a sign and a witness to who God is and what he has done. Election comes first and the story of his people follows. "The primary mission of the chosen people is to witness to the God who judges and who saves, not to save those who would otherwise be damned (for God has not confined his saving work exclusively to the Church's ministrations). It testifies to the God whether or not it wills to do so, whether it is faithful or unfaithful. The final consummation which has begun in Christ is proleptically present in this people and nowhere else, but so is also the eschatological judgment."[292] Lindbeck's concept of the church's mission will undoubtedly rankle the feelings of many Evangelical missiologists when he says the primary mission of the Church is not to save souls but to be a witness to the nations concerning the God who acts in history during this time between the times. Might this come dangerously close to selling short the missionary mandate of the risen Jesus who told his disciples "that repentance and forgiveness of sins should be preached in his name to all nations, beginning from Jerusalem?" (Luke 24:47). Lindbeck might be implicitly protesting the many ill-begotten evangelistic crusades in the name of Jesus motivated by the expansionist aims of Western colonial powers.

---

291. George Lindbeck, "The Church," *The Church in a Postliberal Age*, 155.
292. George Lindbeck, "The Church," *The Church in a Postliberal Age*, 157.

An ecclesiology renewed in line with Lindbeck's ecumenical proposal will need structures to carry out its mission. At this point Lindbeck for the most part sticks with the great tradition, maintaining that it is better to reform past structures than to replace them. The most essential, ecumenically beyond dispute, are the parochial ministries of word and sacrament. What has been and still is disputed are the church-wide structures of the historic episcopacy and papacy. Lindbeck disapproves of the widespread Protestant attitude that holds that structures are *adiaphora*, matters of theological indifference. According to this view the decision should be purely pragmatic, whatever works to get the job done. No, that won't work because in the life of communities tradition is the umbilical cord essential to continue their identity into the future. Thus for Lindbeck those Protestants who reject the historic three-fold ministry as recommended in the Lima Text, *Baptism, Eucharist and Ministry,* have the burden of proof. There are two factors to keep in mind; the three-fold ministry of bishop, priest/pastor, and deacon was the practice of the early church and this ministry is presently maintained by three-quarters of Christianity worldwide. Thus, Lindbeck concludes that it is incumbent on churches that do not have it to adopt it for the sake of church unity. Theologians from various ecclesial perspectives have debated the question whether the historic episcopate is of the *bene esse* (well being), the *plene esse* (full being), or the esse (essential) to the very nature of the church. Lindbeck does not take a position on this question one way or another. But this is his final statement on the matter: "It is to this episcopally unified church that all the major Christian traditions owe their creeds, their liturgies and, above all, their scriptural canon. If these latter are inexpugnable, why not also the episcopate? ... The historic episcopacy (with or without the papacy, for the latter is impossible without the former but not vice versa) is the only ministry that exists to promote the unity and mutual responsibility for the worldwide church. Those churches which lack it have no substitute. To the degree that they are concerned

185

about unity and mutual responsibility, it is to this ministerial ordering of the Church they need to turn."[293]

4. Postliberal Theology and Ecumenism

George Lindbeck was the leading American Lutheran ecumenical theologian before, during, and after the Second Vatican Council. He wrote two books on Roman Catholicism, *The Future of Roman Catholic Theology* (Fortress, 1970) and *Infallibility* (Marquette University Press, 1972). We have already dealt with his role as a delegated observer at Vatican II during all four sessions (1962-1965). For two decades he was a member of the Lutheran-Roman Catholic Dialogues both in the United States and Internationally, representing the Lutheran World Federation. It was out of his vast ecumenical experience that Lindbeck puzzled over the question, how is it possible for two parties in dialogue, say, Lutherans and Catholics, to reach basic agreement on a doctrine historically in dispute, despite the fact that both sides continue to affirm their traditional convictions, whether it be on Justification, Baptism, the Lord's Supper, the Offices of Ministry, or Papacy. When reports made headlines that Lutherans and Catholics had reached a consensus on justification by faith, for example, laity and clergy, including theologians, greeted the headlines with suspicion, consternation, or downright rejection. Gerhard Forde led the chorus of naysayers on the Lutheran side as did Avery Dulles, S.J., on the Catholic side. Lindbeck did not question the integrity or competence of the dialogue participants; they truly believed they had reached a consensus without having to surrender an iota of their long held positions on the doctrine in question.

Lindbeck was motivated to write his major theological book, *The Nature of Doctrine, Religion and Theology in a Postliberal Age,*

---

293. George Lindbeck, "The Church," *The Church in a Postliberal Age*, 163, 164.

to answer the question how it can be that a doctrine that once divided churches is now no longer church-dividing. How can two churches reach doctrinal reconciliation without either side having to make any doctrinal change? This slim book of 138 pages was intended "as prolegomena to a book I have been long trying to write on the current status of agreements and disagreements of the major Christian traditions."[294] Such a book never appeared; its content, however, is substantially available in the more than one hundred articles on ecumenical topics Lindbeck published in various journals.[295]

Lindbeck begins his discussion of the nature of doctrine by distinguishing three theories of doctrine currently practiced. The first is "cognitive propositionalism" characteristic of the pre-modern classical Christian tradition. This is the view that holds that a doctrinal proposition is true or false depending on its adequacy to the reality to which it refers. The classical epistemological maxim is *"adaequatio rei et intellectus."* According to Thomas Aquinas truth is the agreement of thing and intellect (*veritas set adaequatio rei et intellectus*). The truth or falsity of a proposition does not depend on who says it or the cultural context in which it is said. If it was once true, it is always true. Thus to assert that "God raised Jesus on the third day" is commonly held by biblical Christian orthodoxy as a true proposition, true in the first century among believing Jews and true in the twentieth century by believing Christians. Propostionalism "emphasizes the cognitive aspects of religion and stresses the ways in which church doctrines function as informative propositions or truth claims about objective realities.... For a propositionalist, if a doctrine is once true, it is always true, and if it is once false, it is always

---

294. George Lindbeck, *The Nature of Doctrine. Religion and Theology in a Postliberal Age* (Westminster Press, 1984), 8.

295. Bruce Marshall has produced a bibliography of Lindbeck's books, articles, and reviews in *Theology and Dialogue. Essays in Conversation with George Lindbeck*, ed. Bruce D. Marshall (University of Notre Dame Press, 1990), 283-298.

false."[296] Lindbeck thinks this theory of religion and doctrine became discredited by Immanuel Kant whose critical philosophy demolished "the metaphysical and epistemological foundations of the earlier regnant cognitive-propositionalist views."[297] Yet, he also admits, seemingly to contradict himself: "Classical propositionalism is by no means dead or wholly discredited. There are thinkers of great contemporary philosophical sophistication, such as Peter Geach, who emphasize the cognitive dimension of religion (or at least Christianity), and for whom church doctrines are first of all truth claims about objective realities."[298] Then he names G. K. Chesterton and C. S. Lewis in that camp. Even Hans Frei, Lindbeck's Yale colleague and best friend, opined in his review of *The Nature of Doctrine,* "half under my breath, I will confess to some *qualified* sympathy for the moderate propositionalists."[299]

A second theory of doctrine Lindbeck calls "experiential-expressivism." This view "interprets doctrines as noninformative and nondiscursive symbols of inner feelings, attitudes, or existential orientations ... particularly congenial to the liberal theologies influenced by the Continental developments that began with Schleiermacher."[300] This approach was expressed in different ways by such eminent theologians and phenomenologists of religion as Rudolf Otto, Mircea Eliade, Rudolf Bultmann, Paul Tillich, Karl Rahner, Bernard Lonergan, and David Tracy. Yet, these thinkers "all locate ultimately significant contact with whatever is finally important to religion in the prereflexive experiential depths of the self and regard the public or outer features of religion as expressive and evocative objectifications (i.e. nondiscursive symbols) of internal experience."[301] The reduction of theology

---

296. George Lindbeck, *The Nature of Doctrine*, 16.

297. George Lindbeck, *The Nature of Doctrine*, 20.

298. George Lindbeck, *The Nature of Doctrine*, 24.

299. Hans W. Frei, "Epilogue: George Lindbeck and *The Nature of Doctrine*," *Theology and Dialogue*, ed. Bruce D. Marshall, 279.

300. George Lindbeck, *The Nature of Doctrine*, 16.

301. George Lindbeck, *The Nature of Doctrine*, 21.

to experience is not new in the history of Christianity; it was the hallmark of ancient Christian Gnosticism. The essence of Gnosticism, old and new, is the notion of the self as one with the divine source, from whose abyss experiences are verbalized at the level of consciousness, providing inputs for theological reflection. Thus, Harold Bloom can say, "The God of American Religion is an experiential God, so radically within our own being as to become a virtual identity with what is most authentic (oldest and best) in the self."[302]

Paul Tillich is on Lindbeck's list of experiential-expressivists. It is true that Tillich does say that everything we say about God is expressed in religious symbols. The only non-symbolic statement which is possible is that God is being-itself.[303] However, this is what Tillich wrote about the role of experience: "Experience is the medium through which the sources 'speak' to us.... Experience is not the source from which the contents of systematic theology are taken but the medium through which they are existentially received.... Christian theology is based on the unique event Jesus the Christ, and in spite of the infinite meaning of this event it remains this event and, as such, the criterion of every religious experience. This event is given to experience and not derived from it. Therefore, experience receives and does not produce.... The systematic theologian is bound to the Christian message which he must derive from other sources than his experience under the criterion of the norm."[304] It would seem that Tillich does not altogether fit Lindbeck's description of experiential-expressivism.

Lindbeck proposes a third theory of doctrine, not to supplement cognitive propositionalism or experiential-expressiveness but to replace them with his own alternative cultural-linguistic

---

302. Harold Bloom, *The American Religion* (Simon and Schuster, 1999), 259.

303. Paul Tillich, *Systematic Theology*, Vol. I (The University of Chicago Press, 1951), 239.

304. Paul Tillich, *Systematic Theology*, 40, 42, 46.

scheme. But he does not construct this theory from scratch. For his understanding of the cultural side he draws from the works of Max Weber, a German sociologist, and Émile Durkheim, a French social scientist. On the linguistic side Lindbeck works with Ludwig Wittgenstein's philosophy of language, suggesting that doctrines are like the rules of a game. Lindbeck also draws on the anthropology of Clifford Geertz in his understanding of the nature of religion, one that he calls a "cultural-linguistic" approach. These non-theological disciplines provide the framework for Lindbeck's rule theory of church doctrine. Doctrines function as the authoritative rules of a religious community that govern its discourse, attitudes, and actions. Becoming a member of a church "is to interiorize a set of skills by practice and training. One learns how to feel, act, and think in conformity with a religious tradition."[305] If one wishes to learn Chinese, one needs to learn the rules of grammar. If one wishes to play soccer, one must learn the rules of the game. If one wishes to be a member of a Christian community, one must learn the rules (the doctrines) that govern its way of thinking, speaking, and conduct.

Lindbeck mixed quite a cocktail of non-theological disciplines to serve as prolegomena of Christian dogmatics proper. A bit of sociology, anthropology, and linguistic philosophy prepares the way for Christian theological reflection that serves the church, its ministry, and mission. Hans Frei raised a question exactly on this point. "Karl Barth is famous for telling us that prolegomena to dogmatic theology are part of dogmatic theology itself. Schleiermacher, by contrast, suggested that prolegomena are distinct from theology.... Am I right in thinking that in this respect, though certainly not in others, Professor Lindbeck's cultural-linguistic theory of religion functions in a way that is closer to Schleiermacher."[306]

---

305. George Lindbeck, *The Nature of Doctrine*, 35.
306. Hans Frei, "Epilogue: George Lindbeck and *The Nature of Doctrine*," *Theology and Dialogue*, ed. Bruce D. Marshall, 279-280.

Lindbeck applies his cultural-linguistic approach to deal with the relation between world religions. He believes it is impossible to construct a Christian theology of the world religions, because they do not share a common ground. The world religions are simply different; they "have incommensurable notions of truth and of experience.... This cultural-linguistic approach proposes no common framework ... within which to compare religions."[307] The truth of each religion must be understood within its own grammar of faith; there is no one universal grammar that fits all religions.

As the son of missionary parents Lindbeck had to have thought often about the salvation of people of other religions or of no religion at all. The biblical-Christian belief is that salvation is by Christ alone appropriated through faith alone (*fides ex auditu*). Rahner famously taught that non-Christians who have no conscious faith in Jesus Christ may have an implicit faith; he called them "anonymous Christians." Lindbeck does not accept such a maneuver. Instead, he proposes a "prospective" theory of salvation. "The proposal is that dying itself be pictured as the point at which every human being is ultimately and expressly confronted by the gospel, by the crucified and risen Lord. It is only then that the final decision is made for or against Christ; and this is true, not only of unbelievers, but also of believers.... We must trust and hope, although we cannot know, that in this dreadful yet wondrous climax of life no one will be lost."[308]

Ten years after the publication of *The Nature of Doctrine* there appeared a German translation for which Lindbeck wrote a very interesting and revealing Foreword. He reminds his readers that his book was supposed to be "preliminary to a larger work, a comparative dogmatics which would deal with the present status and future possibilities of overcoming the ecclesial divisiveness of historic doctrinal differences between the major Christian

307. George Lindbeck, *The Nature of Doctrine*, 49.
308. George Lindbeck, *The Nature of Doctrine*, 59.

traditions.... In the meanwhile, however, my intended audience had largely vanished."[309] What he meant is that ecumenism had entered a bleak winter. Konrad Raiser, the Executive Secretary of the World Council of Churches wrote a book that signaled the new situation, *Ecumenism in Transition: A Paradigm Shift in the Ecumenical Movement?* He expressed the widespread sense that church leaders and ecumenists had lost interest in removing the doctrinal roadblocks in the way of Christian unity. Now they were interested in their common struggles for "Justice, Peace, and the Integrity of Creation." *The Nature of Doctrine* had been written for doctrinally committed ecumenists, but now they were scarcely anywhere to be found. Mostly conservative theologians, Catholic and Evangelical, interested in pursuing a postliberal theology, were the ones engaged in discussing every chapter and verse of Lindbeck's book. However, postliberal theology did not supplant the liberal theology of the experiential-expressivist approach. Their tribe continued to be dominant in the American Academy of Religion, in University Departments of Religious Studies, as well as in the Denominational Theological Schools now aflood with feminist, liberationist, and religious pluralistic theologies.

Lindbeck concluded his "Foreword" by asking, "What are the prospects for the post liberal cultural-linguistic approach which this book recommends?"[310] His answer is that its future in theological circles does not seem bright, because religious people are very individualistic and experientially oriented and for the most part are not interested in being shaped by communal loyalties. Those few who got on board the postliberal cultural-linguistic approach of Lindbeck's book "are unlikely to have much influence on the general course of theology in the

---

309. George Lindbeck, "Foreword to the German Edition of *The Nature of Doctrine*," *The Nature of Doctrine*, 197.

310. George Lindbeck, "Foreword to the German Edition of *The Nature of Doctrine*," *The Nature of Doctrine*, 199.

churches for the foreseeable future.... Both conservative and liberal resistance to postliberal outlooks seems likely to prevail."[311]

Lindbeck was struck by a brain aneurism in 2009 which greatly slowed him down. He spent his final years in an assisted living center in Florida. His accomplishments were recognized far and wide. He was awarded five honorary doctorates, from the University of Notre Dame (1966), Augustana College (1966), University of Munich (1980), Upsala College (1984), and Gustavus Adolphus College (1988). George Lindbeck was a frequent contributor to the work of the Center for Catholic and Evangelical Center that the Jensons and Braatens founded in Northfield, Minnesota, in 1991, and he was a member of its first Board of Directors. His last thoughts were appropriately on ecclesiology, how to think of the church true to Scripture and relevant to the contemporary situation. Such an ecclesiology, he said, must start with what he called "Israel-ology." In a scriptural narrative approach Israel and the Church cannot be separated; they are one elect people. Lindbeck's legacy will continue to inspire and instruct those committed to thinking ecumenically for the sake of all the churches in this post-Christendom age.

---

311. George Lindbeck, "Foreword to the German Edition of *The Nature of Doctrine*," *The Nature of Doctrine*, 200.

Rev. Dr. Robert W. Jenson was born on August 2, 1930, in Eau Claire, Wisconsin, the son of a Lutheran pastor of the Norwegian Lutheran Church in America. He received a B.A. in 1951 from Luther College, Decorah, Iowa, and an M.Div. from Luther Seminary in 1955. After graduation Jenson taught for two years in the Department of Religion and Philosophy of his alma mater Luther College. In 1957 he enrolled as a student in the theological faculty of Heidelberg University and received a theological doctorate with honors in 1960. He also went to Basel, Switzerland, to study with Karl Barth, and eventually published a revision of his doctoral dissertation on his theology entitled *Alpha and Omega*. In 1960 Jenson returned to teach in the Religion Department of Luther College, where he taught until 1966. His next move was to Oxford University to serve as Dean and Tutor of Lutheran Studies at Mansfield College for a term of three years. Upon returning to the States he became professor of systematic theology at Lutheran Theological Seminary in Gettysburg, and taught there from 1968 to 1988. Jenson then accepted a position to teach in the religion department of St. Olaf College for a decade. In 1998 he went to Princeton, New Jersey, to serve as the director of the Center for Theological Inquiry at Princeton Theological Seminary and held the title as Senior Scholar for Research. Robert Jenson was co-founder (with Carl E. Braaten) of the Center for Catholic and Evangelical Theology in 1991 and was associate editor of *Pro Ecclesia: A Journal of Catholic and Evangelical Theology*. Jenson died in his home on September 5, 2017.

Nine

Robert W. Jenson

Lutheran Systematic Theology

obert Jenson (1930-2017) was born in Eau Claire, Wisconsin, where his father was a pastor of a congregation of the Norwegian Lutheran Church of America. He attended Luther College, majoring in philosophy and the classics. In 1951 he enrolled at Luther Seminary, St. Paul; that is where we first met. Neither of us at the time could have guessed that the Jensons and the Braatens would soon become not only best friends but life-long collaborators on many projects having to do with theology and the church. During the year of 1957 we were both graduate students of the faculty of theology of Heidelberg University. I was there to write my doctoral dissertation for Harvard University on the Christology of Martin Kähler and Jenson was beginning a three year program to earn a theological doctorate. The Heidelberg faculty of theology was without doubt the strongest in the world at that time. Of his experience Jenson recalled, "I went to Germany to study for the doctorate because that was still where the action was. Just imagine my *rigorosum* — the sudden-death oral exam — which was conducted by Gerhard von Rad, Günther Bornkamm, Hans von Campenhausen, Peter Brunner and Edmund Schlink."[312] On the recommendation of Peter Brunner, his "doctor-father," Jenson went to the University

---

312. "An Interview with Robert W. Jenson," (https://religion-online.org).

of Basel, Switzerland, to study with Karl Barth and to write a dissertation on his theology.[313] While at Heidelberg Jenson met Wolfhart Pannenberg, a beginning instructor of theology known as a Privatdozent, whose lectures on nineteenth century German theology made a tremendous impact on Jenson. Pannenberg's signature themes of revelation, history, resurrection, eschatology, and Trinity coalesced into a new departure in theology which Jenson creatively developed in constructing his own theology.

Robert Jenson accepted a teaching position at Luther College with his head full of new theology unfamiliar to his teaching colleagues. He introduced students to new hermeneutics of biblical interpretation, new dogmatics that incorporates pre-Reformation patristic and medieval resources, and new methods in constructive theology influenced by Immanuel Kant, Georg Hegel, and Friedrich Schleiermacher. Any mention of evolution or biblical criticism was equally taboo. That was too much to tolerate for his fellow members in the religion department. They accused him of heterodoxy, perhaps even heresy. So they brought their concerns to the College president, presenting him an ultimatum — either Jenson has got to go or they will all resign en masse. The president decided to keep Jenson and to let them have their choice. That gave Jenson the opportunity to build an entirely new department of religion of younger scholars with Ph.D.s, which happened to include Gerhard Forde.

Jenson's next move was to serve for three years (1966-1969) as the Dean and Tutor of Lutheran Studies at Mansfield College, Oxford University. In 1967 I was fortunate to receive a Guggenheim Fellowship for a sabbatical year of study at Oxford University. So we were together again, exchanging ideas from week to week on books we were writing. That was the year that Martin Luther King Jr. and Bobby Kennedy were assassinated

---

313. A revised edition of Jenson's dissertation was published with the title, *Alpha and Omega: A Study in the Theology of Karl Barth* (Thomas Nelson & Sons, 1963).

and the Vietnam War was escalating. We and our spouses were radicalized, motivating us to participate in anti-war protests.

1. Jenson's Early Writings

The first thing that comes to mind after trying to grasp the whole of Jenson's thought is that he was truly a complete theologian. The first book Jenson wrote after the publication of his work on Barth is *A Religion Against Itself*, a title obviously inspired by Barth's Commentary on Paul's *Epistle to the Romans*. As the title suggests this slim book was an attack on religion in the name of the gospel of God's Son, Jesus of Nazareth. Here Jenson laid down the tracks that would carry his ideas forward in his later writings. It was a foretaste of what was to follow, a resolute concentration on the gospel and all its corollaries. "The gospel is a narrative of what happened with Jesus, spoken with the claim that this story tells the final destiny of those who hear it told.... The gospel purports to be about the end of the human story."[314] So what is theology? Jenson is already clear that the task of theology is to accomplish one thing, to teach what can be known of God by the explication of what happened with Jesus. "Thereby all our talk of what happened with Jesus will become talk about God — so that Christian theology will become what its name has always suggested, one great statement about God.... A truly Christian doctrine of God is a description of Jesus Christ.... God is what Jesus of Nazareth accomplished in life, what got done in the course of his history. God is the future, the hopes and possibilities, opened by the events of this man's life."[315] To thicken the plot Jenson boldly affirms what many modern theologians discount or deny, that God is the one who raised Jesus from the dead. "'The one who raised Jesus from the dead' is the believer's identification of God, the answer

---

314. Robert W. Jenson, *A Religion Against Itself* (John Knox Press, 1966), 15, 16.
315. Robert W. Jenson, *A Religion Against Itself*, 29, 30, 33.

197

to the question of who it is that is worshiped instead of the God of religion.... 'Whoever raised Jesus, he is God.'"[316]

In this book Jenson also adumbrates the specific theological theme that brought him well-deserved fame, identifying the Triune God of the Bible by his proper name, Father, Son, and Holy Spirit. "Asked, 'Which God do you worship?' The church has replied, 'We worship the triune one,' The first point to get across is that to the question, 'Who is God?' 'The Triune God' and 'The one who raised Jesus' are the same answer. If God raised Jesus, then God is separate from Jesus. Yet apart from what happens with Jesus, there is no God; God's reality *is* the history of Jesus."[317] With his writings on the Triune God Jenson joined an ecumenical group of theologians who made major contributions to the renewal of trinitarian theology in the twentieth century — Karl Barth and Jürgen Moltmann (Reformed), Karl Rahner, Walter Kasper, and Catherine LaCugna (Roman Catholic), Wohlhart Pannenberg and Eberhard Jüngel (Lutheran), and John Zizioulas (Orthodox).

The three years of teaching at Mansfield College, Oxford University, turned out to be productive of two seminal works on eschatology, the spinal column of Jenson's gospel-centered revisionary metaphysics.[318] The eschatological theology of hope had become the topic *de jour*, with the best-selling books of Wolfhart Pannenberg and Jürgen Moltmann taking center stage. Jenson wrote a book that analyzes the logic of the language of hope, entitled *The Knowledge of Things Hoped For. The Sense of Theological Discourse.* This work provides the epistemology for an eschatological view of the meaning of world history and personal existence, creating at the same time a synthesis of the Continental futurist theology of hope and the Anglo-Saxon tools

---

316. Robert W. Jenson, *A Religion Against Itself,* 35.

317. Robert W. Jenson, *A Religion Against Itself,* 35.

318. Robert W. Jenson, *Theology as Revisionary Metaphysics. Essays on God and Creation* (Cascade Books, 2014).

of linguistic analysis. Jenson also reaches back to two giants of classical theology, comparing Origen's account of the language of images and Thomas Aquinas' notion of analogy to the contemporary language of hope for Christian faith and discourse. Jenson's years at Oxford brought forth a second work on the theology of Karl Barth, entitled *God after God. The God of the Past and the God of the Future, Seen in the Work of Karl Barth.* This book focuses on Barth's trinitarian theology in relation to what Jenson perceives as our contemporary post-religious situation. He ends his book with a *critical* appropriation of the futurist theology of hope of Wolfhart Pannenberg.

Non-specialists in Barth's theology will find much in Jenson's composition highly abstract and complicated. Decode this locution, for example: "If God's temporality is the temporality of *death* and *resurrection*, then he does indeed project himself toward a future — and just so overcomes our dream of timelessness. It will not do merely to say in the abstract that God's omnipotence is the openness of history to man; we must say very concretely that God is omnipotent as the self-abandonment of the Cross, that is because he so perfectly accepts all our action upon him that his presence is ineradicable."[319] Out of our experience together in Oxford we co-authored a book which introduced our take on the regnant theology of hope, entitled *The Futurist Option.*

2. The Gettysburg Years

During Jenson's third and final year at Oxford University he was given the opportunity to choose whether to return to teach religion at Luther College, or to accept an invitation to teach systematic theology at the Lutheran Theological Seminary in Gettysburg, Pennsylvania. He wrote to me for my advice. He felt a strong loyalty to his alma mater where he had been in-

---

319. Robert W. Jenson, *God after God. The God of the Past and the God of the Future, Seen in the Work of Karl Barth* (Bobbs-Merrill Company, 1969), 144.

strumental in building its religion and philosophy department and where he and his wife Blanche had many good friends. Luther College or Gettysburg Seminary? My answer was that a seminary would provide a more stimulating context for teaching churchly theology at the highest level and besides, Gettysburg would open doors to other forms of service to the church that a college in a small mid-western town never could. That seemed to me to be the case then; now I am not so sure that is equally true today. Jenson chose to go to Gettysburg Seminary where he taught theology for twenty productive years.

During Jenson's years at Gettysburg Seminary he laid the foundations for the systematic theology he would write after he left to teach at St. Olaf College. His first attempt to write a mini-system of theology bore the title, *Story and Promise. A Brief Theology of the Gospel About Jesus,* which became a classic, equally appreciated by beginning students, lay persons, and pastors. "Story" and "promise" are the two focal points of Jenson's understanding of what Christianity is all about, not only in this book but in all his later writings. "Let me try a premature summary formulation of the story and its promise. 'There has lived a man wholly for others, all the way to death; and he has risen, so that his self-giving will finally triumph.' Christianity is the lived-out fact of the telling ... of the narrative of what is supposed to have happened and to be yet going to happen with Jesus-in-Israel, and of the promise made by that narrative. All Christianity's special realities have to do with this tale."[320] It is wise to start with these easy to grasp twin concepts before wading into the deeper waters of Jenson's more complex iterations of the same in his two volumes of *Systematic Theology.*

What is the gospel? It is a story about the people of Israel and an Israelite named Jesus that spells good news for everyone willing to listen. And what is the church? It is a gathering

---

320. Robert W. Jenson, *Story and Promise. A Brief Theology of the Gospel about Jesus* (Fortress Press, 1973), 1.

where such gospel-communication takes place. What then does the church's gospel have to do with "God," the most notoriously ambiguous word ever spoken? Martin Luther said that "whatever your heart clings to and confides in, that is really your God."[321] If that is true, then gods are a dime a dozen; religion breeds idolatry of all sorts. In this connection Jenson writes, "The gospel is entirely uninterested in claiming that there is some God or other — that 'God exists.' It is interested only in claiming that a specific putative God is indeed God: the God identified by what happened in Israel with Jesus. By 'God' the gospel means 'whoever and whatever it was that raised Jesus from the dead.' ... We identify which God we take to be the real one by narrative statements about Israel and Jesus."[322] These are samples of the way Jenson starts with clear and distinct statements that ordinary believers might have learned in Sunday School. That would please Jenson, because he always intended to create a theology that explicates the story and promise of the biblical God of the gospel that is the substance of what Christians believe.

What is most remarkable about *Story and Promise* is that as a mini-systematic theology it already contains the nucleus of every doctrine Jenson would subsequently develop at great length and in great detail in his two volumes of *Systematic Theology*. Thus, the reader already learns how Jenson constructs the doctrine of the triune God in a unique way. The longest chapter introduces the doctrine of the Trinity, entitled, "The God of the Promise." "The doctrine of the Trinity is only a particular expansion of the identification of God as the one who raised Jesus.... We identify God by narration about Jesus-in-Israel.... The whole business about the 'Trinity' begins by believers saying flat out: Jesus *is* God.... Jesus is the possibility of picking out

---

321. *Large Catechism*, "Explanation of the First Commandment."

322. Robert W. Jenson, *Story and Promise. A Brief Theology of the Gospel about Jesus* (Fortress Press, 1973), 5-6.

God, of indicating God.... We have to say that apart from what happened and will happen with Jesus, the God of the gospel would not occur. It is in this sense that Christian theology has said that God *is* Jesus."[323] So how does the triplicity of God come about for Jenson? So far we have God and Jesus, God as the one who raised Jesus. Here is Jenson's way of thinking of the oneness and threeness of God at once. "Thus we arrive at a triple identification of God. It is triple — rather than, say, double or quadruple — because time is past, present and future; and what we are trying to analyze is the way in which the gospel identifies an event in time as itself the embrace around time. First, God is identified as Jesus; when we try to pick God out, to point at him, we have nothing whatever to point to but the man Jesus. Second, God is identified as one to whom Jesus is related as to the authority and origin of his destiny: God is the one Jesus called 'Father.' Third, God is identified as the futurity of this relation, as what comes of Jesus' self-giving to 'the Father.'"[324]

While at Gettysburg Jenson co-authored with Eric Gritsch a textbook entitled *Lutheranism. The Theological Movement and Its Confessional Writings*. A church historian and a systematic theologian collaborate in producing an apologia for a Lutheran understanding of the gospel. The basic theme throughout is that Lutheranism is a confessional movement within the broad stream of the catholic tradition. The authors explicate the article of justification by faith apart from the works of the law as a proposal of dogma to the church catholic. Yet, the authors are keenly aware that contemporary Lutheranism needs to be reformed by this article as much as the Roman Church of the sixteenth century to which this article was addressed as the norm of orthodoxy. "The church is now in at least as desperate need of reformation as it was in the sixteenth century, and by the very

---

323. Robert W. Jenson, *Story and Promise*, 113, 114.
324. Robert W. Jenson, *Story and Promise*, 115.

same criterion as then."[325] The authors elaborate justification by faith and all its essential corollaries — Christology, church, ministry, sacraments, and the Christian life. In a final section they discuss some of the fuzzy issues in Lutheranism — church unity, the two kingdoms doctrine, authority in the church, and *adiaphora* in the Christian tradition. From this classic a generation of seminarians, teachers, and pastors learned the essentials of Lutheranism to face the intramural challenges of ecumenism and the extramural challenges of secularism.

In the 1970s I was invited to join the Workgroup on Constructive Theology convened by the Department of Theology of Vanderbilt University. Its purpose was twofold: to promote collaborative work among systematic theologians and to identify the issues on which they might profitably work together. After meeting for three years, members of the Workgroup succeeded in collaborating on a textbook for use in college and university schools of religion, entitled *Christian Theology: An Introduction to Its Traditions and Tasks*, edited by Peter C. Hodgson and Robert King. Although I found the book deeply flawed in that it privileged the post-Enlightenment theology of modern Protestantism at the expense of the classical Christian tradition that produced the creeds of the Church confessing the Trinitarian and Christological dogmas. Yet, the concept of doing theology in a collaborative way seemed to me an excellent one. I brought the idea to Robert Jenson, my chief collaborator; let us select a group of Lutheran theologians to write a textbook of Christian dogmatics for use in our seminaries. And so in 1984 we co-edited a two volume work of *Christian Dogmatics*, each of us writing two chapters. In addition the group was composed of Gerhard Forde, Philip Hefner, Paul Sponheim, and Hans Schwarz, each of whom also contributed two chapters. We have discussed this work before in our chapters devoted to the thought

---

325. Eric W. Gritsch and Robert W. Jenson, *Lutheranism. The Theological Movement and Its Confessional Writings* (Fortress Press, 1976), 134.

of Forde, Hefner, and Sponheim. Since Schwarz was born and educated in Germany, though teaching at Southern Lutheran Seminary, we did not portray his theology in this book.

It was fitting for Robert Jenson to write the Second Locus on "The Triune God" and the Eighth on "The Holy Spirit." Since Jenson had already written a splendid book on the Sacraments, taking into account new thinking that had emerged in the bi-lateral ecumenical dialogues, it fell to him to do the same for this textbook.[326] Jenson had also written his first major work on the Trinity, *The Triune Identity. God According to the Gospel*, following up on the germinal insights he espoused in *Story and Promise*. He analyzed the formula, "Father, Son, and Holy Spirit," as the appropriate name for the God identified in the Bible in two ways, first, as the "God who liberated his chosen people Israel from Egypt" and second, as the "God who raised Jesus of Nazareth from the dead." This approach is diametrically opposed to the classical idea of the timelessness of God, a theme that Jenson will drive home with relentless conviction and passion in his *Systematic Theology*, Volumes I & II. Jenson's two works on the Trinity were written only two years apart, so understandably both have the same content, often the very same words. This posed no problem because Fortress Press was the publisher of both treatises.

The only other major work that Jenson wrote during his Gettysburg years was on Jonathan Edwards entitled *America's Theologian. A Recommendation of Jonathan Edwards*. This took me by surprise when it came out, because Edwards was a Calvinist pure and simple, and Jenson was not given to using especially laudatory words on John Calvin and theologians of the Reformed branch of Protestantism. The two exceptions are Karl Barth and Jonathan Edwards. In a footnote Jenson offers this comment: "Little attempt has been made to paper over the

---

326. Robert W. Jenson, *Visible Words. The Interpretation and Practice of Christian Sacraments* (Fortress Press, 1978).

many holes in my knowledge of my predecessors. Thus, e.g., although two notable Calvinists, Jonathan Edwards and Karl Barth, will repeatedly appear in the following, Calvin himself appears rarely; it is simply a fact that I have never been able to muster either sympathy or antipathy for this admittedly great thinker."[327]

What then did Jenson find so interesting and compatible in Edward's theology? The Edwards I learned about in American church history was the Puritan preaching about "Sinners in the Hands of an Angry God," hell fire and damnation. Jenson, to the contrary, found much to his liking in Edward's theology. He entitled his book, *America's Theologian. A Recommendation of Jonathan Edwards* (Oxford University Press, 1988). Jenson treats Edwards with great respect and admiration, accentuating Edwards' conception of beauty and harmony as well as his critical appreciation of the Enlightenment, especially the works of Isaac Newton and John Locke. Edwards became president of Princeton University in 1758 and sadly died a month later from a smallpox inoculation. He played an important role in the First Great Awakening, and is remembered for his fiery sermons. Jenson's way of according Jonathan Edwards the highest honor is to call him "America's theologian," although some of Jenson's admirers would now wish to transfer such an accolade to Jenson himself. Richard J. Neuhaus writes: "So, is Robert Jenson America's theologian? Not in any exclusive sense, to be sure, but I think the answer is Yes. In the preface to the book on Edwards, Jenson writes, 'I have exercised my reflection on him for many years now and have found that America has indeed an American theologian and that I am, for better or worse an American Christian.' It follows that Jenson is an American Christian theologian. There is no doubt that he is God's theologian, which is to say the church's theologian, first.... Just so

---

327. Robert W. Jenson, *Systematic Theology*, Volume 1: *The Triune God* (Oxford University Press, 1997), 38, n41.

(if I may borrow Jenson's signature phrase) is Robert Jenson America's theologian."[328]

3. The Systematic Theology of Robert Jenson

Robert Jenson was a systematic theologian par excellence. When he published the two volumes of *Systematic Theology*, George Lindbeck commented that the work is not really a systematic theology. One wondered what he could have meant, if he had read the books. Lindbeck had been so steeped in reading the great medieval scholastic systems of philosophical theology *à la* Thomas Aquinas or Duns Scotus, that he might have thought that theology needed to be founded on a philosophical prolegomena, whether based on Plato, Aristotle, or Plotinus. Or, in modern times systematic theologians, like Schleiermacher, Ritschl, or Tillich, constructed their systems on the philosophical thought of Kant, Hegel, or Schelling. So perhaps Lindbeck thought that Jenson was really writing dogmatics as his mentor Karl Barth unapologetically did. Lindbeck was not the only one to miss the key to Jenson's theological method. Jenson declared war against the classical way of doing theology, whether it be that of Origen in the East or Augustine in the West, that started with a general foundational doctrine of God, also called natural theology, which presupposed the timeless God of the Greeks. He called the God of the classical tradition "the unbaptized God." Jenson started and ended his systematic theology with the "baptized God" of the Bible, who is available to human beings in the gospel narrative — and only there — of the crucified and resurrected Jesus of Nazareth, who is the Son/Logos of God the Father.

---

328. Richard J. Neuhaus, "Jenson in the Public Square," *Trinity, Time, and Church. A Response to the Theology of Robert W. Jenson*, ed. Colin Gunton (Eerdmans, 2000), 250-251.

A. The Task of Theology

The word "theology" is often used as reflection on anything that has something to do with a particular religion or religious experience in general. Jenson uses the word "theology" in a very specific sense. Theology is the thinking of the Christian church that serves the communication of the gospel. He puts it even more simply: "Theology is the thinking internal to the task of speaking the gospel.... The church's specific enterprise of thought is devoted to the question, 'How shall we get it across, in language, with signs other than linguistic.... or by other behavior of our community, that Jesus is risen and what that means?'"[329] Of course, one has to ask, what is that gospel the church is called to speak? Jenson offers a succinct answer: "'He is risen' was — and is — the gospel."[330] The task of Christian theology is to reflect critically on the practices the church deems essential to perform if this proposition is believed to be true. "The church has a mission to see to the speaking of the gospel, whether to the world as message of salvation or to God as appeal and praise."[331] The question is often posed, is theology a "speculative" or "practical" discipline? Jenson's answer is that of the Reformation (e.g. Philip Melanchthon and Johann Gerhard); theology is a practical discipline, a *habitus practicus,* in distinction from the medieval scholastic idea of theology as a speculative discipline. The work of the theologian must examine the practices of the church asking the question, "Does this teaching or other practice further or hinder the saying of the gospel?"[332] This is more difficult as well as more important than doing theology as "experiential expressionism," to use Lindbeck's term for the most popular way in liberal Protestantism. The nineteenth century German theologian, J. C. K. von Hofmann, expressed the

---

329. Robert W. Jenson, *Systematic Theology*, Vol. I, 5.

330. Robert W. Jenson, *God After God*, 157.

331. Robert W. Jenson, *Systematic Theology*, Vol. I, 11.

332. Robert W. Jenson, *Systematic Theology*, Vol. I, 11.

idea this way, "I, the Christian, am the object of knowledge for me, the theologian."[333] Karl Barth attributed this approach to Friedrich Schleiermacher, who made religious feelings the data for theological reflection. Jenson accepted Barth's criticism because it turns theology into anthropology, away from God and the works of God to human beings and their subjective states of mind and spiritual experiences.

The gospel is not the sum total of religious experiences or moral values, although these may be relevant effects of the receptive hearing of the gospel. The gospel is a witness to an event that happened in space and time — the resurrection of Jesus — on the third day after his crucifixion. Jenson asks a question long debated in the history of theology, must a theologian be a believer? The mainstream of the theological tradition maintained that theology is composed of "mixed articles." Some of them are considered to be true whether one is a believer or not, such as, there is a God, and God is omnipotent, omniscient, omnipresent, and so forth. This was called a *theologia irregenitorum* — a theology of the unregenerate — which religious thinkers have held quite apart from Christianity. Mixed articles are truths that can be known by the light of reason according to philosophical principles. This teaching was held by the seventeenth century Lutheran dogmaticians, David Hollaz, Abraham Calov, Johann Quenstedt, and others, and in this respect they were in line with the medieval scholastic theologians. Jenson thinks that this is a mistaken way that led to a lot of theological confusion with deleterious effects on Christian preaching and witness. Jenson's criticism is that the unbaptized elements, the truths that pagans and Christians supposedly share alike, provided the foundations on which the whole edifice of Christian theology was built. Since they were supposedly 'natural' and 'rational,' the mixed articles of natural theology became the judge of the special articles of divine revelation. They formed the prolegomena of both Protestant

---

333. Robert W. Jenson, *Systematic Theology*, Vol. I, 12.

and Catholic dogmatics. Jenson refers to them as "systematically pompous prolegomena"[334] There are no such mixed articles in Jenson's prolegomena. Jenson intends that everything in his systematic theology owes its inclusion to how it derives from its relation to the gospel, the good news that Jesus lives and reigns beyond the tomb. "Theology is reflection internal to the act of tradition, to the turn from hearing something to speaking it. Theology is an act of interpretation: it begins with a received word and issues in a new word essentially related to the old word. Theology's questions is always: In that we have heard and seen such-and-such discourse as gospel, what shall we now say and do that gospel may again be spoken?"[335]

B. Theology According to the Biblical Narrative

When we briefly discussed Jenson's book, *Story and Promise*, we identified the seeds that blossomed to the full in his *Systematic Theology*. The structure of this theology is based on the biblical narrative or drama of the ways God is revealed by his actions of creating, redeeming, and consummating the world, in other words, by the works of the one God in three personal identities, Father, Son, and Holy Spirit. There is no other God than the one identified by the temporal events in the biblical narrative. At this point Jenson was joining a parade displaying the dramatic narrative character of biblical revelation. The original revelation does not consist of a body of true propositions mined out of the 66 books of the Bible. Hans Frei led the charge with the publication of *The Eclipse of Biblical Narrative*. About the same time Hans Urs von Balthasar published the first of four volumes of *Theodrama*. That was followed by *Why Narrative? Readings in Narrative Theology*, eds. Stanley Hauerwas and L. Gregory Jones. "If we say the Christian God is the God identified by the biblical narrative, we must also say there is 'the' biblical narrative only as

---

334. Robert W. Jenson, *Systematic Theology*, Vol. I, 11.
335. Robert W. Jenson, *Systematic Theology*, Vol. I, 14.

we read the temporally, culturally, and religiously various documents of Scripture as witness to the continuing action of one and the same agent.... We will follow the one biblical narrative, to identify the one biblical God, only as we read the Bible by the purpose for which the church assembled this book in the first place, to be in its entirety and all its parts witness to Jesus' Resurrection and so to a particular God."[336]

No theologian has written a systematic theology without recourse to a metaphysics of one kind or other. Even the ancient Creeds of the Church made use of metaphysical concepts to explain the Trinitarian and Christological dogmas — *ousia, physis, homoousian, hypostases, idiomata, persona,* etc. The Greeks developed metaphysical systems without any knowledge of the Bible or the gospel. Very early in the history of the church theologians appropriated the available metaphysical categories to expound their beliefs derived from the gospel. Jenson follows his mentor, Karl Barth, in making metaphysics the handmaid of the gospel drama, rather than being the Procrustean bed into which the evangelical truths must be made to fit. Jenson wrote this of Barth's theology: "The *Kirchliche Dogmatik* is an enormous attempt to interpret all reality by the fact of Christ; indeed, it can be read as the first truly major system of Western metaphysics since the collapse of Hegelianism."[337]

C. The Incarnation of the Logos

Jenson mounts a severe criticism of the traditional Christological idea of the *logos asarkos*. The idea of the *logos asarkos* is that the Word of God, the Second Person of the Trinity, pre-exists his incarnate state in the human being Jesus. That is, once he existed within the eternal Trinity without the flesh (*asarkos*); since the incarnation he exists as well in the flesh (*ensarkos*.). The fathers of the ancient church expended a lot of time, energy, and even

---

336. Robert W. Jenson, *Systematic Theology*, Vol. I, 58.
337. Robert W. Jenson, *Systematic Theology*, Vol. I, 21.

blood trying to solve the Christological paradox, how Jesus Christ can be one person with two natures fully divine and fully human. How can he be fully human without being a human person (*prosopon*). Jenson locks horns with this ancient beast of a problem and flat out denies the idea of a *logos asarkos*. There never was a Logos without the flesh (*ensarkos*). Jenson writes, "What in eternity precedes the Son's birth to Mary is not an unincarnate state of the Son, but a pattern of movement within the event of the incarnation, the movement to incarnation, as itself a pattern of God's triune life."[338] Jenson has taken a lot of flak for this departure from the *cantus firmus* of traditional ecclesiastical Christology, in refusing to accept a distinction between the eternal Son and the Logos in the flesh.

It is interesting that most of Jenson's critics represent the Reformed tradition which tended to stress the difference between the divine and the human states of bring, whereas Jenson's Lutheran instinct is to stress the unity of the divine and the human. It is noteworthy that Jenson increasingly gravitated to the Byzantine theology of Eastern Orthodoxy. Maximus the Confessor and John Damascene were special favorites. It is also the case that his doctrine of the Trinity owes a great deal to the Eastern theology of the three great Cappadocians, Gregory of Nazianzus, Gregory of Nyssa, and Basil of Caesarea. Jenson called for correction of Augustine's way of constructing the doctrine of the Trinity and was critical of his dominating influence on virtually all subsequent Western Trinitarian theologies.[339] Classical Lutheran Christology leaned more toward the Alexandrian monophysite interpretation of Chalcedon whereas the Reformed Christology was the opposite, leaning more toward a dualistic separation of the divine and human natures characteristic of the Antiochene tradition. Jenson did not want to attribute some of the acts of Jesus to his divine nature and others to his human nature. "Given

---

338. Robert W. Jenson, *Systematic Theology*, Vol. I, 141.
339. Robert W. Jenson, *Systematic Theology*, Vol. I, 113.

the incarnation, what we call the humanity of Christ and the deity of Christ are only actual as one sole person, so that where the deity of the Son is, there must be Jesus' humanity, unabridged as soul and body."[340] The difference between the Reformed and the Lutherans on Christology, the former emphasizing the duality of the natures and the latter their unity, became pronounced in the Marburg Colloquy (1529) between Martin Luther and Huldreich Zwingli. Zwingli argued that Christ could not be in the bread because he was sitting at the right hand of God, so the words, "This is my body," must be taken figuratively. Luther countered that Christ was not restricted to one place. The words were meant to be taken literally.

4. A Decade at St. Olaf College (1988-1998)

In 1988 Robert Jenson left Gettysburg Seminary to join the religion department of St. Olaf College in Northfield, Minnesota. Three years later I decided to retire early from the Lutheran School of Theology at Chicago in order to link up with Jenson in Northfield to found a Lutheran center for theological research and renewal. In 1991 we co-founded the Center for Catholic and Evangelical Theology. We were often asked to explain why we chose such an ambiguous title. After all, it was commonly thought that Catholic meant Roman and Evangelical meant conservative Protestant. Both of us agreed that catholic and evangelical properly understood define what it means to be Lutheran. So there is no good reason to surrender these good words to popular misunderstanding. Luther's own words kept ringing in our ears: "I ask that people make no reference to my name; let them call themselves Christians, not Lutherans. What is Luther? After all, the teaching is not mine. Neither was I crucified for anyone. St. Paul, in I Corinthians 3:22, would not allow the Christians to call themselves Pauline or Petrine, but

---

340. Robert W. Jenson, *Systematic Theology*, Vol. I, 203.

Christian. How then could I — poor stinking maggot-fodder that I am — come to have people call the children of Christ by my wretched name? Not so, my dear friends; let us abolish all party names and call ourselves Christians, after him whose teaching we hold."[341]

At the same time we launched a new theological journal to be named *Pro Ecclesia. A Journal of Catholic and Evangelical Theology*, now in its thirtieth year and recognized worldwide as a leading ecumenical publication. Being together in Northfield gave us the opportunity to collaborate on many additional projects, which I will enumerate with some elaboration. 1. We co-edited *A Map of Twentieth Century Theology: Readings from Karl Barth to Radical Pluralism*. 2. We hosted two "Call to Faithfulness Conferences," to deal with the neuralgic issues facing Lutheranism in America, especially those that surfaced within the Evangelical Lutheran Church in America. The Conferences were sponsored by the editors of three independent Lutheran journals: *dialog, Lutheran Forum*, and *Lutheran Quarterly*. Around a thousand pastors and lay persons attended each of the conferences, making church officials at Higgins Road in Chicago nervous. They had reason to worry because most of the speakers were well known for calling attention to the ways the new church was drifting from its confessional standards. 3. In order to pass the baton of writing dogmatics on to a younger generation of scholars Jenson and I invited around twenty younger theologians representing ecumenically engaged churches to form what we called "The Dogmatics Colloquium." The group met regularly twice a year from 1992-1995 in Northfield, writings papers for critical discussion that eventually resulted in the publication of a book, *Knowing the Triune God*, edited by James Buckley and David Yeago. The editors dedicated the book "To the Braatens and Jensons for their generosity, hospitality, and patience." This experiment proved that doing

---

341. *Luther's Works*, Vol. 45, 70-71.

theology in a collegially ecumenical way can be fun, especially with all the coffee breaks, happy hours, and gourmet cuisine our spouses, Blanche and LaVonne, provided. The experience also resulted in forming close bonds of friendship and enduring collaborative relationships. 4. On behalf of the Center for Catholic and Evangelical Theology we sponsored a seminar on the new Finnish interpretation of Luther. We invited Tuomo Mannermaa and three of his closest associates — Simo Peuro, Antti Raunio, and Sammeli Juntunen — from the Institute for Systematic Theology of the University of Helsinki to lead the seminar. The new Finnish paradigm focussed on Luther's doctrine of justification, moving away from a purely forensic juridical idea to a more mystical and ontological interpretation, using the formula of "the real presence of Christ in faith." I am not a Luther scholar so I listened and had much to learn. I had written a book on *Justification, The Article by Which the Church Stands or Falls* (Fortress Press, 1990) at a time when I knew nothing about the Helsinki Finns. My book was not on Luther's doctrine but on the Lutheran doctrine of justification, based mostly on German and Swedish sources. The outcome of the seminar was the publication of a book we co-edited, *Union With Christ. The New Finnish Interpretation of Luther.* 5. As Lutheran theologians we were heirs of a tradition that privileged the patristic theological consensus of the first five centuries (*consensus quinquesaecularis*) over what is pejoratively called the theology of the Dark Ages, a time period between the fall of the Roman Empire and the Renaissance (500-1400 A.D.). So we got the challenging idea of organizing a study tour of Rome, Greece, and Turkey. The theme was "Christianity and Culture: East and West." We were twenty in the group. Jenson provided the background lectures as we traveled from site to site. The purpose of the tour was to learn about the encounter of Christianity with the culture of the Graeco-Roman world of antiquity. To prepare for the trip we suggested that everyone read the great book by Charles Norris Cochrane, *Christianity and Classical Culture. A Study of Thought and Action from Augustus to Augustine.* The tour also gave us the opportunity to inquire into the reasons for the division between the Eastern and Western branches of Christendom that occurred in 1054 A.D., and what is being done in the modern ecumenical movement to heal the breach. 6. The Center sponsored a consultation on the future of ecumenism that was composed of a select group of ranking ecumenical theologians. We were proposing that the Center undertake a major study on ecclesiology and ecumenism, and we were seeking expert counsel. The group consisted of Roman Catholic, Orthodox, Anglican, Reformed, Methodist, Pentecostal, and Lutheran theologians. By the time the group was ready to convene its first session, Jenson had left St. Olaf College to become the Senior Scholar for Research at the Center of Theological Inquiry in Princeton, New Jersey. We decided that Princeton would be a convenient place to meet, as we did twice a year, three days at a time, for three and half years. The study group produced two publications: one was *The Princeton Proposal for Christian Unity*, which we entitled *In One Body Through The Cross* and the other was the Background Papers for the Princeton Proposal entitled, *The Ecumenical Future.* The reception of this ecumenical overture was mixed. Ecumenism had moved on to consider matters of peace and justice. Churches were putting ecumenical dialogues on the back burner, worrying more about inclusivity, diversity, identity, declining membership and stewardship. In our judgment the ecumenical work for Christian unity is a perennial responsibility of the separated churches, even when the weather is not so congenial outside.

The Center for Catholic and Evangelical Theology is now thirty years old, during which time it has planned and organized scores of theological conferences, mostly in the Midwest and in the East, and most of these conferences have seen the light of day in print form. To access all of this information and more one may Google "Center for Catholic and Evangelical Theology."

5. Jenson Goes To Princeton (1998-2017)

In 1998 Jenson started a new chapter in his long and and prolific career as a church theologian at the Center of Theological Inquiry of Princeton Seminary. The second volume of his *Systematic Theology* was published the year after he arrived. Were there any surprises? Most of what appeared in this book had been prefigured in his previous writings, for example, in his chapters on the Trinity, the Holy Spirit, and the Sacraments in the two volumes of *Christian Dogmatics* that we co-edited — with one interesting exception. In the book on *Lutheranism*, co-authored with Eric Gritsch, Jenson presented a strong defense of the traditional Lutheran understanding of the doctrine of justification through faith alone apart from the works of the law. As we already noted, he wrote, "The Lutheran proposal of dogma has one great theme: justification by faith alone, apart from works of law." Without rejecting what he wrote in *Lutheranism,* Jenson presents a modified version of justification in his *Systematic Theology*, because in the meantime he had encountered the new Finnish School of Luther Interpretation. In agreement with Mannermaa and the Finns, now Jenson writes: "Justification is 'a mode of deification,'"[342] and in support he quotes no less than Martin Luther: "By faith the human person becomes God."[343] Jenson heaps lavish praise on Mannermaa and his disciples. "The following may not much resemble what readers expect from Luther. His texts in fact contain what will here be cited from them, but standard Luther exegesis, conducted mostly by liberal Protestants or philosophical existentialists, has tried to explain these systematics as too metaphysical and therefore tending to Catholicism. Luther is praised, indeed, as theology's great deliverer from ontological thinking. The contrary has now been demonstrated in detail from the texts, by a sustained cooperative research project at the University of Helsinki, sometimes

---

342. Robert W. Jenson, *Systematic Theology*, Vol. II, 296.
343. Robert W. Jenson, *Systematic Theology*, Vol. II, 296-297.

referred to as the 'Mannermaa school' of Luther research.... The received scholarly understanding of Luther must now be taken as in large part discredited."[344] One wonders whether this is not at the same time an implicit self-criticism.

Mannermaa was delighted to discover this turn in Jenson's thinking. Mannermaa's ground-breaking work is entitled, *Der Im Glauben gegenwärtige Christus,* a formula almost identical with Luther's in his *Commentary on Galatians, In ipse fide Christus adest.* Both say that Christ is present in faith. Mannermaa wrote: "There is no doubt that Jenson follows Luther in his interpretation of Christ as gift (*donum*) received through faith. Faith is understood here as a real participation in God, and such participation occurs equally in the Holy Spirit as well as both in and with Christ. Justification from the perspective of *donum* is clearly a triune event, but this characterization does not yet capture the complex meaning of justification. Justification from the perspective of *favor Christi,* that is, from the perspective of forgiveness and of the abolition of the wrath of God, also has its foundation wholly in the triune life."[345] To simplify what seems overly complicated, the Christ who is present in faith is ontologically present as very God himself, as the Creed of Nicaea confesses. There is a real exchange between Christ and the believer, so that the one who is really present in faith is God himself. Thus, according to the Finnish view which Jenson shares, a bridge is thereby built between Luther and the Orthodox idea of salvation as deification or *theosis.* Also in this respect the idea of deification connects Jenson to his favorite church fathers, the Cappadocians. He quotes Basil as saying that the final result of the Spirit's work in us is "endless joy in the presence of God, becoming like God, and ... becoming God."[346]

---

344. Robert W. Jenson, *Systematic Theology*, Vol. II, 293-294.

345. Tuomo Mannermaa, "Doctrine of Justification and Trinitarian Ontology," *Trinity, Time, and Church,* ed. Colin Gunton, 142.

346. Robert W. Jenson, *Systematic Theology*, Vol. II, 311.

The idea of salvation as deification brings us to the closing section of nearly every dogmatic treatise ever written by a Christian theologian, ancient or modern — eschatology. Christian eschatology is the answer to the question, What does the gospel promise? The answer is, "The gospel promises inclusion in the triune community by virtue of union with Christ and just so in a perfected human community."[347] This straightforward Christocentric statement spares us from letting our imaginations run riot in the field of biblical apocalyptic symbolism in the futile attempt to create an account of the last things. The notion of a chronological sequence of events piling up at the end of world history is ruled out because it diverts attention from Christ as the sole foundation of Christian hope. The entire hope for the future is directed to Christ. He is the one and only way of entry into the life of the triune God. "Thus the Eschaton is the inexhaustible event of the triune God's interpretation of created history by the life of the one creature Jesus. The Eschaton is infinite created life, made infinite in that it is the life of creatures seen by the Father as one story with the story of the Son and enlivened by the Spirit who is the Telos of that story."[348]

Will everyone finally participate in the everlasting future promised in the gospel of Christ? We have seen how the theologians we have covered in this book have struggled to answer the question, "Will all be saved in the end?" Does God really desire all to be saved and come to the knowledge of truth? (I Timothy 2:4). What about people of other religions who know not Christ? Jenson answers, "If followers of other religions enter the Kingdom proposed by the gospel, this is not because they have arrived at the salvations proposed by their religions. Quite apparently, all religions are not different ways to the same place."[349] Though there is no salvation except through the gospel,

347. Robert W. Jenson, *Systematic Theology*, Vol. II, 311.
348. Robert W. Jenson, *Systematic Theology*, Vol. II, 319.
349. Robert W. Jenson, *Systematic Theology*, Vol. II, 310.

this does not rule out the possibility that people outside the church, people who have not heard the gospel, may be saved. Jesus said, "It is easier for a camel to go through the eye of a needle than for a rich man to enter the kingdom of God." When the disciples heard this, they were greatly astonished, saying, "Who then can be saved?" But Jesus looked at them and said to them, "With men this is impossible, but with God all things are possible" (Matthew 19:24-26). Jenson uses his own words to address the same issue: "If a partial or complete *apokatastasis* of those outside the people of God is to take place, it can only be by an eschatological address of the gospel, about the circumstances of which it would be entirely useless to make guesses."[350]

So much more could be written to describe and explain the inexhaustible riches of Jenson's thought,[351] but I will bring this chapter to a close with some of Jenson's own final and finest words that conclude his two volumes of *Systematic Theology*. The section is simply entitled, "Telos," only half a page in length. Jenson ended his first volume, reflecting on the beauty of God, with the statement: "God is a great fugue."[352] He ends his second volume on the same note: "The last word to be said about God's triune being is that he is 'a great fugue'.... The end is music."[353] That will keep the heavenly choirs of angels and archangels eternally busy glorifying God. *Soli deo gloria*!

---

350. Robert W. Jenson, *Systematic Theology*, Vol. II, 364.

351. Jenson continued to write many articles and essays while at Princeton, including two exegetical commentaries on Ezekiel and the Song of Songs. This confirms what we wrote in our introduction that Jenson was a complete theologian, deeply anchored in the Bible, Church History, the History of Doctrine, Medieval Theology, Reformation and post-Reformation Theology, Modern Theology from the Enlightenment to Contemporary Theological Thought.

352. Robert W. Jenson, *Systematic Theology*, Vol. I, 236.

353. Robert W. Jenson, *Systematic Theology*, Vol. II, 369.

 **Rev. Dr. Paul R. Hinlicky** is Professor of Luther Studies at Roanoke College, Salem, Virginia. Before coming to Roanoke College in 1999 he was professor of systematic theology at the Evangelical Theological School of Jan Comenius University in Bratislava, Slovakia, from 1993-1999. In 2010 Hinlicky began teaching part time for the Institute of Lutheran Theology. He received a B.A. in 1974 from Concordia Senior College in Fort Wayne, Indiana, an M. Div. in 1978 from Christ Seminary-Seminex in St.Louis, and a Ph.D. in 1983 from Union Theological Seminary in New York. He was ordained a Lutheran minister in 1978 in the Lutheran Church of America, a predecessor body of the Evangelical Lutheran Church in America. While still a graduate student at Union Theological Seminary Hinlicky served as a pastor of several New York parishes. For four years Hinlicky held the position as Research Associate for the Department for Church in Society of the Lutheran Church in America. Then Hinlicky became the pastor of Immanuel Lutheran Church in Delhi, New York from 1985 to 1993. Hinlicky served as editor of *Lutheran Forum* from 1988 to 1993. Hinlicky has also been a member of the editorial councils of *dialog*, *Lutheran Quarterly*, and *Pro Ecclesia*. Paul Hinlicky and his wife Ellen are amateur farmers; they own and manage a family farm of 83 acres, raising fruits and vegetables, as well as chickens, pigs, and bees.

Ten

Paul R. Hinlicky

Lutheran Critical Dogmatics

Paul R. Hinlicky is currently the Tise Professor of Lutheran Studies at Roanoke College in Salem, Virginia, where he has taught for more than twenty years. Before coming to Roanoke College he was Visiting Professor of Systematic Theology at the Protestant Theological Faculty of Jan Comenius University in Bratislava, Slovakia, from 1993-1999. He also teaches part-time for the web-based seminary, the Institute of Lutheran Theology, Brookings, South Dakota. Hinlicky received a B.A. from Concordia Senior College, Fort Wayne, Indiana, an M.Div. from Christ Seminary-Seminex, St. Louis, Missouri, and a Ph.D. from Union Theological Seminary, New York. In 1978 he was ordained into the Lutheran ministry of the Lutheran Church in America, a predecessor body of the Evangelical Lutheran Church in America. From 1985-1993 Hinlicky served as the pastor of Immanuel Lutheran Church in Delhi, New York.

Paul Hinlicky has been a prolific writer of articles, book reviews, editorials, and monographs on a wide variety of subjects. He was the editor of *Lutheran Forum* from 1988-1993. His academic articles have been published in *Pro Ecclesia, Lutheran Quarterly, dialog – A Journal of Theology, Currents in Theology and Mission, Word and World, Journal of Ecumenical Studies, The Cresset, Journal of Lutheran Ethics,* and others. In addition Hinlicky has contributed to various books, such as Conference

Proceedings, *Festschrifts*, and the like. All of these occasional writings are based on wide-ranging research that prepared the author for an outpouring of books written between 2009 and the present. A great number of Hinlicky's published materials have been saved for posterity by inclusion in his *magnum opus*, *Beloved Community: Critical Dogmatics after Christendom,* a huge volume of nearly a thousand pages in rather small print.

Paul Hinlicky has never hesitated to tell his readers exactly what he thinks, and what he thinks has often rubbed people the wrong way. In this respect it can be said with no exaggeration that he joins the company of Lutheran dogmaticians and ethicists we have chosen to portray in this volume. Once when he was irked being disparaged as just another "white voice," he offered a self-revealing comment: "The color of my skin tells you next to nothing about me.... Though this is not the forum, I would be happy to supply further details of my ancestral story, being the grandchild of despised Slavic immigrants in WASP America, growing up poor on the wrong side of the tracks, being orphaned by a church schism in my youth and in adulthood being black-listed in my own declining denomination."[354] This is a sample of Hinlicky's keen awareness that a person's social location and cultural particularity contribute to his or her theological subjectivity with hermeneutical significance.

1. Paul Hinlicky's Luther Interpretation

Paul Hinlicky wrote two major works that preceded and prepared the way for the publication of his systematic theology, *Beloved Community. Critical Dogmatics after Christendom.* One was *Paths Not Taken: Fates of Theology from Luther Through Leibniz.* The second was *Luther and the Beloved Community. A Path for Christian Theology after Christendom.* Both of them

---

354. Paul Hinlicky, "Response to Contributors," *Pro Ecclesia*, Vol. XXVI, No. 2, 181-185.

secured his reputation as a *bona fide* Luther-Scholar, but not of the garden-variety. In his Leibniz-book Hinlicky laments that the history of Lutheranism did not follow a path that Luther would have envisaged, zigzagging from the period of Lutheran Scholastic Orthodoxy, to its diametrical opposite in Halle's Lutheran Pietism, followed by Enlightenment Rationalism, failing to reform Christianity by the gospel and to develop a public theology for ordering society. Hinlicky works through the philosophical influences of Baruch Spinoza and Immanuel Kant, overcoming Cartesian dualism, and then charts a new path forward for Christian theology inaugurated by Karl Barth and subsequently developed in the systematic theologies of three great Lutheran theologians deeply influenced by Barth — Wolfhart Pannenberg, Eberhard Jüngel, and Robert W. Jenson. Hinlicky's theology is best understood in this post-Barthian lineage, with this caveat. All four of these Lutheran theologians are committed to overcome a lack of attention to the Third Article of the Creed — the Holy Spirit. Jenson wrote an illuminating article entitled, "You Wonder Where the Spirit Went,"[355] in which he attributed Barth's low sacramentology to lack of attention to Pneumatology. Hinlicky pointed to the exact same deficit in modern Lutheranism, when he writes about how the Holy Spirit disappeared in Lutheranism and, agreeing with Jenson, claims that it never reappeared in Barth.

In *Luther and the Beloved Community. A Path for Christian Theology after Christendom,* what immediately meets the eye is two of the terms that reappear in the title of his systematic theology, *Beloved Community. Critical Dogmatics after Christendom.* The term, "after Christendom," is clear enough; Hinlicky believes that the era of the amalgamation of Christianity and society is passé. The church can no longer count on being propped up and in sync with the secularized society that now prevails in

---

355. Robert W. Jenson, "You Wonder Where the Spirit Went," *Pro Ecclesia*, 2 (1993), 296-304.

Europe and America. On this point Hinlicky is in agreement with Stanley Hauerwas' thesis in *After Christendom*. But what is the meaning of "Beloved Community?" What is its origin? Hinlicky gives credit to Josiah Royce and Martin Luther King Jr. for whom "Beloved Community" was an important concept; both of these Christian thinkers, one a philosopher and the other a preacher, were also influential on Hinlicky's thought in many ways. For Josiah Royce the "beloved community" was conceived of as an eternal place of rest and infinitely blessed, hence eschatological. For Martin Luther King Jr. the beloved community was thought of more as a society characterized by justice, equal opportunity for everyone, and love for one's fellow human beings, hence sociological. Hinlicky appropriated the concept of "Beloved Community" for his own constructive theology of the Holy Trinity, which functions as the framework of all its parts.

As a Lutheran theologian building a system of dogmatics for the twenty-first century Hinlicky retrieves aspects of Luther's theology that he deems suitable for the well-being of the church and its mission today. "Permit me to acknowledge from the outset that the Luther who appears in the pages to follow will be 'my' Luther, Luther as I appropriate him, for which I, not Luther, am responsible."[356] He does not repeat, he does not re-pristinate "*was Doctor Luther sagt.*" Instead, what Hinlicky offers his readers is a creative appropriation of the doctrinal theology of the mature Luther, especially on the Trinity and Christology. Hinlicky explained his intention this way: "In *The Substance of Faith: Luther's Doctrinal Theology*, with Mickey Mattox and Dennis Bielfeldt, we demonstrated the salience of the older Luther's return to academic method and canonical hermeneutic to clarify logically classical Christian dogmatic assertions as something needful in the life of the churches reformed by the Word of God. We accordingly lifted up the evident seriousness with

---

356. Paul Hinlicky, *Luther and the Beloved Community* (Eerdmans, 2010), xviii.

which the elder Luther applied himself to dogmatic questions in Trinitarian theology."[357]

Luther and the Beloved Community consists of three main parts, with a total of ten chapters. The first part deals with the doctrine of the Trinitarian God. Its first chapter indicates that for Luther doctrine based on the Word of God is "the bread of life." The second chapter takes up Christology, going against the stream of modern biblical historical criticism that attempts to reconstruct the Jesus of history as he actually was. Luther's Christology starts at the other end, with the incarnation of the Son of God, such that the divine attributes are communicated to humanity (*communicatio idiomatum*). Who is Jesus? He is the Son of God, one of the Trinity, who truly suffered under Pontius Pilate and died bearing the sins of the world. In chapter three Hinlicky shows that Luther's doctrine of the atonement combines aspects of all three of the main theories, victory (Aulén), substitution (Anselm), and moral example (Abelard). Chapter four provides a Trinitarian interpretation of the law-gospel dialectic, saying "yes" and "no" to Barth's famous criticism of Luther's view.

Part Two deals with theological anthropology, in two chapters. Chapter five undertakes a novel interpretation of Luther's most controversial writing, *De servo arbitrio*. *The Bondage of the Will* is the usual translation, but Hinlicky prefers "*On Bound Choice*." Luther said, "You can burn all my books except for two, *The Bondage of the Will* and the *Small Catechism*." Hinlicky does well to rescue this controversial book for theology today, despite the fact it has been an embarrassment to most of later Lutheranism, especially the Pietists and the Liberals. Hinlicky sees the work as an example of apocalyptic theology rather than as a philosophical treatise, as it was understood not only by Erasmus but also by Luther's ally, Melanchthon. "What Luther says about human nature and the human plight is said strictly

---

357. Paul Hinlicky, *Luther and the Beloved Community*, xv.

in light of the revelation — concretely, the resurrection of the Crucified — not then as spontaneous self-understanding or even as a labored, rational account of experience. This apocalyptic reading yields a rich and suggestive idea of the new agency of Christ by the Holy Spirit active in the redemption of the body of the Beloved Community."[358]

Chapter six deals with the theology of the body, Luther's theology of marriage, controversial issues of sexual ethics, and suggests that the Church today could restrict its public marital blessing for heterosexual couples and at the same time openly recognize the value of same-sex unions. Here Hinlicky is walking a tight rope, careful not to fall too much to one side of the other. "This possibility of recognition, argued by using Luther as resource, admittedly falls painfully short for those seeking the public blessing of same-sex union.... Why is it necessary theologically to maintain that homophile desire is disordered, that is to say, not the will of God articulated in the Genesis passage, as Christologically interpreted? As it is necessary theologically to maintain that even marital love is afflicted by concupiscent desire for an infinity of objects, it is by analogy necessary also to maintain that polymorphous sexual desire is disordered; attraction to the same sex intrinsically refuses the procreative purpose of God, from which the blessing of Genesis 1:26-28 obviously cannot be separated. Nor is there any other 'blessing' from the Word of God for the church to pronounce over a marriage."[359]

Part Three consists of chapters seven through ten. Readers have had to wait to nearly the end of the book to find out what the author thinks about "the article by which the church stands or falls," the act of God by which sinners are justified (made right before God) by grace alone, through faith alone, on account of Christ alone. This chapter will not enchant conservative Lutheran theologians whose approach is to repristinate the traditional

---

358. Paul Hinlicky, *Luther and the Beloved Community*, xxi.
359. Paul Hinlicky, *Luther and the Beloved Community*, 215.

jargon in defense of the doctrine, which historically has been used as a club against other denominations as well as against other Lutherans who do not fit the mould. Hinlicky warns, "Even those who self-identify as 'radically' Lutheran,[360] for all their alienation from conservative confessionalism or ecclesiastical Lutheranism, still want to appropriate Luther under the mantle of *the* Reformation, *the* Protestant principle, *the* Scripture principle, *the* doctrine of justification. It never occurs to them that this is more of the same self-privileging, which ineluctably contains within it the original demonization of the opponent. This is why repristination, whether conservative or radical, is not only hermeneutically impossible but morally suspect. It never occurs in such thinking, for example, that the sixteenth-century 'Reformation' might with equal justice be labeled the schism of Western Christianity."[361]

Hinlicky's discussion of the doctrine of justification turns to the recent hot debate on Luther's alleged misinterpretation of Paul. The New Testament theologian, James D. G. Dunn, framed the debate as "The New Perspective on Paul." The debate was initiated by two biblical scholars, E. P. Sanders[362] and Krister Stendahl.[363] The new perspective on Paul, critical of Luther, was championed further by N. T. Wright.[364] The debate has reached a stalemate; leading New Testament scholars have mounted

---

360. Our chapter on Gerhard Forde used the term"radical Lutheranism" to characterize his thought, because it was the term he chose himself.

361. Paul Hinlicky, *Luther and the Beloved Community*, 224.

362. E. P. Sanders, *Paul and Palestinian Judaism. A Comparison of Patterns of Religions* (SCM Press, 1977).

363. Krister Stendahl, a Swedish Lutheran New Testament theologian, was perhaps the first to challenge Luther's interpretation of the law and justification in his famous essay about the "introspective conscience of the West," in *Paul Among Jews and Gentiles* (Fortress Press, 1976).

364. N. T. Wright, *The Climax of the Covenant: Christ and the Law in Pauline Theology* (Fortress Press, 1991). And, *Paul in Fresh Perspective* (Fortress Press, 2005).

strong counter-criticisms, such as, Peter Stuhlmacher,[365] J. Louis Martyn,[366] and Stephen Westerholm.[367] Hinlicky tackles this disputed subject by going beyond the old and new perspectives on Paul in sections entitled, "Sanders' Misidentified Insight," "Stendahl's Misplaced Conscience," "Käsemann's Critique of Salvation History," and "Beyond the Old and New Perspectives." Hinlicky's conclusion is that Luther can still help as a resource for a renewed understanding of the law and justification without necessarily defending all of his exegetical assertions. He asks, "Can Luther help? It depends of course on what kind of help he might offer. Certainly exegesis from the sixteenth century cannot settle critical-historical disputes of the twenty-first. Nor is it a matter of superimposing a 'Lutheran' dogmatic formulation about the righteousness that prevails before God."[368]

Chapter eight reconstructs Luther's catholic ecclesiology which has been largely neglected in various patterns of Protestant deformation. Luther's vision of the church can be seen in substantial agreement with the *communio* ecclesiology highlighted at Vatican II. The ninth chapter takes up an assortment of issues bearing on the church's encounter with the world in modern times — political theology, the challenge of Marxism, the struggle for peace and justice, the ministry of Martin Luther King Jr., and the doctrine of the two kingdoms. The tenth chapter offers an interpretation of Luther's *theologia crucis*, a theme popularized by books on the subject by Walter von Loewenich[369] and Jürgen Moltmann,[370] and also in need of clarification in light of feminist

---

365. Peter Stuhlmacher, *Revisiting Paul's Doctrine of Justification: A Challenge to the New Perspective* ((InterVarsity Press, 2001).

366. Louis J. Martyn, *Galatians. The Anchor Bible* (Doubleday, 1997).

367. Stephen Westerholm, "Did Luther Get Paul Right on Justification?" *Preaching and Teaching the Law and the Gospel of God*, ed. Carl E. Braaten (ALPB Books, 2013).

368. Paul Hinlicky, *Luther and the Beloved Community*, 248-249.

369. Walter von Loewenich, *Luther's Theology of the Cross* (Augsburg, 1976).

370. Jürgen Moltmann, *The Crucified God* (HarperCollins, 1974).

concerns. Hinlicky's book on Luther ends with an appendix on Luther's demonization of his opponents, an indefensible trait that he claims stems from his apocalyptic theology.

This brief survey of Hinlicky's Luther interpretation omits many insights readers interested in the future of our Lutheran heritage would welcome. His interpretation of justification involves a social dimension, inclusion of the excluded in the beloved community, beyond, that is, the kind of individualist introspection that Krister Stendahl targeted. Not introspection, says Hinlicky, which tends to fit a purely forensic view of justification, but extra-spection, which entails seeing oneself in a new community with God and one's fellow believers. Readers would also benefit from Hinlicky's rich dialogues with the greatest theologians in Western Christianity, Augustine and Anselm, as well as his interactions with modern greats like Karl Barth, Dietrich Bonhoeffer, Robert Jenson, and Oswald Bayer. But in the end, the epitaph of this book would read — Hinlicky discovers in Luther what the doctor ordered to treat what ails so much of contemporary Christian theology. On to his *magnum opus!*

2. The Critical Dogmatics of Paul Hinlicky

Paul Hinlicky's book on Luther's theology was a perfect springboard for him to undertake his next big project, a voluminous system of theology, *Beloved Community. Critical Dogmatics after Christendom.* It was published in 2015. In the Preface Hinlicky writes: "What I now lay before the reader is a life's work of reflection on the troubled state and future prospects in Euro-America of the message that improbably emerged out of ancient Palestine two millennia ago and is still on its journey through the nations on the way to the coming of the Beloved Community of God. Along the way, the message found a remarkable spokesperson in a talented and troubled being, Martin Luther. While I have found many other teachers of the faith, as will be amply evident

229

in what follows, this work manifestly stands in the tradition of theological reflection within the Western Catholic Church that arose from Luther's witness to Jesus Christ."[371] Hinlicky's dogmatics is critical, even at times of his main interlocutor, Martin Luther. It is critical of the kind of Christian theology aligned with either of two trends, on the one hand, the Scylla of progressive social fads and political correctness rampant in mainline Protestant denominations, including the one to which he uncomfortably belongs as an ordained minister and, on the other hand, the Charybdis of the obscurations of conservative evangelical fundamentalisms, including some that bear Luther's name. Hinlicky's dogmatics is critical also in the sense that he eschews the kind of method that repristinates the theology of a particular period held to be sacrosanct, authentic, orthodox, inerrant, infallible, or whatever. There are no sacred cows in Hinlicky's system, as we shall see.

Hinlicky's *Critical Dogmatics* consists of four parts, each with two chapters, and it ends with a concluding doxology. Part One is the Prolegomena with two chapters. Chapter One deals with the knowledge of God and the discipline of theology which presupposes that such knowledge has been revealed to the pilgrim people of God and inscribed in the biblical narrative concerning Israel in its prophetic writings (Old Testament) and concerning the Israelite, Jesus of Nazareth, in the writings of his apostles (New Testament). Hinlicky believes that doing theology in a situation deemed post-Christendom and post-modern providentially provides theologians an opportunity to retrieve their knowledge from scriptural, patristic, and Reformation sources, largely ignored and even repudiated by theologians of Liberal Protestantism who regarded the Enlightenment as the critical watershed demanding a paradigm shift of theological method and reflection in light of the impact of biblical criti-

---

371. Paul Hinlicky, *Beloved Community. Critical Dogmatics after Christendom* (Eerdmans, 2015), xi.

230

cism, new scholarly disciplines, religious pluralism, and global secularization.[372]

Already in the first chapter Hinlicky makes the case for the resurrection of Jesus as the originating event of the gospel. Apart from the resurrection history would not have remembered Jesus, since he was hanged on the cross like scores of other criminals. "Historically speaking, it is the case that ... the history of Jesus of Nazareth does not as such account for the beginning of the gospel, since Jesus' end in ignominious disgrace and abandonment would have left Him forgotten like countless other victims of legalized injustice among the crucified of the world. Rather, the history of Jesus is remembered as the 'beginning of the gospel' from the perspective of an event that early Christianity named 'the resurrection.'"[373] But, many critical historians ask, did the resurrection of Jesus really happen as a real historical event in space and time? Robert Funk tells about how once he formulated the proposition, "The resurrection was an event in the life of Jesus," and presented it to members of the "Jesus Seminar." Then Funk writes, "My proposition was received with hilarity by several Fellows. One suggested that it was an oxymoron. Others alleged that the formulation was meaningless, since we all assume, they said, that Jesus' life ended with his crucifixion and death.... John Dominic Crossan confessed, 'I do not think that anyone, anywhere, at any time brings dead people back to life.'"[374] Hinlicky is a theologian and does not claim to be a critical historian, but this is what he says, "Theologians are entitled to their personal taste, and it is surely the case that one does not tastefully speak of 'resurrection' in polite circles today — anymore than first-century Athens

---

372. An example of such an approach can be seen in a text book entitled *Christian Theology. An Introduction to Its Traditions and Tasks*, eds. Peter Hodgson and Robert King (Fortress Press, 1982),

373. Paul Hinlicky, *Beloved Community, Critical Dogmatics after Christendom*, 20.

374. Robert Funk, *Honest to Jesus* (HarperCollins, 1996), 258.

(Acts 17:32). N. T. Wright, in his massive study, hit the nail on the head in this connection, however, when he wrote with emphasis: '*The fact that dead people do not ordinarily rise is itself part of early Christian belief*, not an objection to it. The early Christians insisted that what happened to Jesus was precisely something new; was, indeed, the start of a whole new mode of existence, a new creation. The fact that Jesus' resurrection was, and remains, without analogy is not an objection to the early Christian claim. It is part of the claim itself."[375] Treatment of the resurrection of Jesus belongs in the Prolegomena simply because it is now and always has been the *sine qua non* of the possibility of doing Christian theology for the communion of saints who believe in him as Savior and Lord.

Chapter two looks to the theologies of Augustine and Luther as well as to some contemporary scholars such as Jean Bethke Elshtain, Philip Cary, and Jean-Luc Marion to offer material criticism of the Enlightenment idea of the sovereign self. Then Hinlicky poses and answers at length four questions to bring the Prolegomena to a close. 1. Is God possible? His answer recounts how he overcame a love affair with Paul Tillich when he discovered the relevance of the Trinity in reading Barth and Jenson, which Hinlicky would go on to develop in a unique way in constructing his dogmatics. Hinlicky acknowledges what he learned from them: "Jenson has rigorously carried through on the insight of Luther and Barth that neither existence nor essence can be privileged in the question of God; that it is rather the Bible's personal and social, historical and narrative identification of God in our world that tells — as of first importance — *who* God is for us. At the same time, the understanding of the *who* brings a new understanding of the *what* and the *that* of God, as Jenson puts it: '...the gospel's God can be an object for us if and

---

375. Paul Hinlicky, Beloved Community. Critical Dogmatics after Christendom, 21-22. The quotation is from N. T. Wright, The Resurrection of the Son of God, vol. 3 of Christian Origins and the Question of God (Fortress Press, 2003), 712.

only if God is so identified by the risen Jesus and his community as to be identified *with* them."[376]

The second question: "Is Christ Necessary?" Luther and the Lutheran Confessions answer this question in spades, no need to look elsewhere. Christ is not necessary if we can merit the forgiveness of sins by acts we perform. Christ is not necessary if we can be justified before God by our reason and morality. Paul said in Galatians, "If justification were through works of the law, then Christ died to no purpose" (Gal. 2:21). Hinlicky sums up the discussion of the necessity of Christ with this thesis: "Christ the Crucified is made necessary when the prophetic critique of this world in the name of God is so penetrating — striking with the Baptist's ax to the root (Luke 3:9!) — that nothing less than the Messiah's cross can accomplish genuine reconciliation with Luther's 'real, not fictitious sinners.'"[377] Other scholars are cited to reinforce the idea of the necessity of Christ —Dietrich Bonhoeffer, Robert Bertram, and Daniel Bell.

The third question is: "Does Faith Justify?" The answer begins, "It all depends." If faith is understood as a good work that we humans are able to choose to do by our own free will, then the answer is no. Faith does not justify as an act that we are able to perform. Hinlicky warns against the distortion of some brands of Lutheranism that explain faith psychologically or existentially. He gives high marks to Regin Prenter and the Mannermaa Finnish School of Luther Research, who bring into play the role of Christology and Pneumatology in Justification. Hinlicky concludes this discussion on faith with an historically informative excursus on three types of Lutheranism that fiercely quarreled over the very doctrine that supposedly was at the heart of Luther's reformation, justification by faith alone — Orthodoxy, Pietism, and Liberalism.

---

376. Paul Hinlicky, *Beloved Community. Critical Dogmatics after Christendom*, 123.

377. Paul Hinlicky, *Beloved Community. Critical Dogmatics after Christendom*, 139.

The fourth question is: "Are the Scriptures Holy?" Hinlicky hits some inadequate answers on the head. One is the proof-texting method of Protestant Orthodoxy that could not withstand the rise of historical criticism. But the historical critical method tends to be equally arbitrary because critics are not as scientifically neutral as they often pretend. "Historical criticism is, or too often operates as, biblicism of a higher order."[378] Hinlicky's own answer aligns with Luther's understanding of the Bible as the Word of God. "A theology is 'biblical' if, and when, it thinks with the Bible taken as a canonical narrative that tells of the eternal Father who is determined by the costly missions of his Son and Spirit to redeem the creation and bring it to fulfillment. Theology is then thinking after God's thinking ... counting the cost that is the Christ crucified that makes grace free to sinners and their faith alone to justify."[379]

Hinlicky's prolegomena privileges four doctrines which he claims are normative for any Christian theology that aims to be orthodox and ecumenical. The first is the canon of Scripture from Genesis to Revelation that tells the story of the creation to consummation. The second is the Trinity, identified as such in the canonical story of the Father with his Son and Spirit as the one God. The third is second person of the Trinity who became a servant to liberate those enslaved. The fourth is the power of the Spirit who proceeds from the Father and the Son at work in preserving, redeeming, and fulfilling creation in the coming of the Beloved Community. These four doctrines are essential for ecumenical Christian theology and are normed in the shared forms of canon, creed, and confession. Admittedly, the last of these three remains in dispute, even though significant progress has been made in the many transactions of the modern ecumenical movement.

---

378. Paul Hinlicky, *Beloved Community. Critical Dogmatics after Christendom*, 173.

379. Paul Hinlicky, *Beloved Community. Critical Dogmatics after Christendom*, 172.

Within this cluster of canon, creed, and confession Hinlicky's dogmatics elevates two doctrines to a special place of normativeness, the Trinity and Justification by Faith. "In systematic theology, these two meta-doctrines of the Trinity and Justification by Faith, aside from any explicit treatment accorded to them, permeate the whole of this presentation so that they continually do the work of sorting and integrating the topics of traditional Christian belief."[380]

3. Innovative Treatment of the Trinity

The most innovative aspect of Hinlicky's dogmatics is the way he unfolds the traditional Christian doctrine of the Trinity. If the Christian doctrine of God is to be normed by the gospel, then it would seem to make good sense to start with the experience of receiving the gift of the gospel. That reception is the work of the Holy Spirit. The Apostles' Creed and the Nicene Creed each have three parts, the first with God the Father and creation, the second with God the Son and redemption, and the third with God the Holy Spirit, the church, and all the rest. That is following the order of being (*ordo essendi*). Hinlicky starts at the other end, following the order of knowledge (*ordo cognoscendi*) gained through experience. I know of no other systematic theology, Catholic or Protestant, that starts with Pneumatology, then Christology, and last Patrology. It remains to be seen whether any junior dogmaticians will follow Hinlicky's lead. In any case, in my mind, it is a worthy experiment that deserves careful attention and critical examination to discern if this approach has pragmatic teachable significance.

Hinlicky starts his doctrine of God with the three persons and not with the one. The leading medieval scholastic theologians, Thomas Aquinas and Duns Scotus, started with a chapter on the

---

380. Paul Hinlicky, *Beloved Community. Critical Dogmatics after Christendom*, 37.

oneness of God (*de deo uno*), setting forth what metaphysical reason can know. Hinlicky wrote a book entitled, *Divine Simplicity: Christ the Crisis of Metaphysics*, vigorously arguing that the traditional doctrine of God starting with what can be known of God by philosophy apart from the biblical revelation has caused great confusion. The church fathers constructed a synthetic doctrine of God, combining what Plato, Aristotle, and Plotinus taught about God via reason with what the Bible reveals concerning the acts of God in the history of salvation, culminating in the incarnation, death, and resurrection of Jesus Christ. Hinlicky follows the Trinitarian personalism of Karl Barth and Robert Jenson who deny that the true God can be known apart from what the Bible reveals. They rejected the view that Christian theology can properly superimpose a trinitarianism upon a prior monotheism. This approach has led to a colossal muddle, giving the doctrine of the Trinity an unstable place in the tradition of Christian theology. Karl Barth places the Trinity at the front of his *Church Dogmatics*, with the very first things to be said in the Prolegomena. He wrote, "The doctrine of the Trinity is what basically distinguishes the Christian doctrine of God as Christian."[381]

There was another Karl writing about the Trinity about the same time as Barth, Karl Rahner, who said some sobering things about the doctrine. "Christians are, in their practical life, almost mere 'monotheists.' We must be willing to admit that, should the doctrine of the Trinity have to be dropped as false, the major part of religious literature could well remain virtually unchanged.... The treatise on the Trinity looks itself in even more splendid isolation, with the ensuing danger that the religious mind finds it devoid of interest. It looks as if everything which matters for us in God has already been said in the treatise *On the One God*."[382]

---

381. Karl Barth, *Church Dogmatics*, ed. and trans. G. W. Bromiley (T.&T Clark, 1956), 1/1, 301.

382. Karl Rahner, *The Trinity*, trans. Joseph Donceel (Herder and Herder, 1970), 17.

Since Hinlicky starts his treatment of the Trinity with Pneumatology, in chapter three he takes up the doctrine of baptism, the initial point of contact between the Spirit and the human on the way to becoming Christian, a member of the body of Christ. Baptism is the Spirit's work of regeneration, bringing about union with the crucified and risen Christ. Hinlicky discusses the early Christian practices of baptism, the baptismal theologies of Martin Luther ("*Baptizatus sum!*"), Menno Simons, and Karl Barth. That leads him into the debate over the validity of infant baptism, which is theologically justifiable but becomes questionable when it is administered to all infants with no regard as to whether they will be brought up in the Christian faith. Karl Barth surprised many of his followers when in his ripe old age he rejected the practice of infant baptism. In defense of Barth one can point to the scandal he observed of a Christianity under Hitler in which millions of nominal Christians supported the evil regime and its genocidal policies of mass murder.

Chapter four continues to consider issues under Pneumatology, naturally the doctrine of sanctification, the ministry and mission of the church, with an excursus on the ordination of women. Hinlicky boldly speculates on the distinctive role of the Spirit within the immanent Trinity as the unifier of the Father and the Son. "Just as the origin of the persons is the Father who begets the Son and breathes the Spirit, the personal indivisibility of these Three distinct by way of origin is the eternal act of the Spirit, showering the Father's love on the Son and returning the Beloved Son to the Father in love, as active anticipation of God's ever-new future. In this respect the Father is Alpha and the Spirit is Omega in God."[383]

Part Three deals with Christology, also in two chapters. Chapter five focusses on Mary as *Theotokos,* a term used in the Eastern Orthodox Church for the one who gave birth to God

---

383. Paul Hinlicky, *Beloved Community. Critical Dogmatics after Christendom*, 322.

the Son, otherwise often translated as "Mother of God." This chapter deals principally with the truth of the Incarnation and its essential connection with eucharistic theology, rife with many controversies. In discussing the Lutheran emphasis on the "real presence" of Christ in his body and blood, Hinlicky regards the terms as redundant. "What other kind of presence could there be than 'real'?"[384] To say "real presence" is what Hinlicky calls "emphatic polemical rhetoric," used in controversy over the Lord's Supper. On the other hand, he regards the idea of a "symbolic presence" as an oxymoron. The bread and the wine are symbols of the body and blood of Christ, who is then considered not present but absent. "In this ceremony, with this bread and wine, the *man* Christ is present, i.e., as His *body-and-blood human reality born of Mary and suffered under Pontius Pilate* — or, He is not there as such at all."[385]

Chapter six begins with an attempt to show that the post-Vatican II dialogues between Lutherans and Catholics have reached a convergence on the doctrine of the Eucharist. "Both traditions acknowledge a 'manifold presence of Christ,' but specifically 'that in the Sacrament of the Lord's Supper, Jesus Christ, true God and true man, is present wholly and entirely, in his body and blood, under the signs of bread and wine."[386] In this chapter Hinlicky also discloses a core concept of his dogmatics, in that he goes to the East to retrieve the neo-Chalcedonian Christology of Cyril of Alexandria and couples it with the Western theological anthropology of Augustine. A Cyrilian Christ is the Savior of an Augustinian sinner. "Our claim

384. Paul Hinlicky, *Beloved Community. Critical Dogmatics after Christendom*, 479.

385. Paul Hinlicky, *Beloved Community. Critical Dogmatics after Christendom*, 480.

386. Paul Hinlicky, *Beloved Community. Critical Dogmatics after Christendom*, 499. Hinlicky is quoting from *Lutherans and Catholics in Dialogue*, eds. Paul C. Empire and T. Austin Murphy (Augsburg Publishing House), III: 189.

has been that nothing less than a Cyrillian Christ is soteriologically adequate to facing, engaging, and in the end overcoming the predicament of Augustinian humanity that is sinfulness."[387] The chapter ends with a discussion of the threefold office of Christ — priest, prophet, and king.

Part four complete's Hinlicky's treatment of the Trinity with his discussion of Patrology, the doctrine of God the Father. In Chapter seven he offers extended commentary on Matthew's version of the Lord's Prayer. In addressing God as Heavenly Father, Hinlicky contends, Jesus is acknowledging that God is the audience of theology. If that is so, then theology has more than one audience, because theology is written for the church to hear, to equip it to proclaim the gospel, to teach the articles of the faith, and to plan its mission to the nations. Chapter eight deals with the primary agency of the Father, the Creator of everything that is not God. This chapter also takes up the problem of evil and explains Hinlicky's concept of the theodicy of faith, drawing upon his book on Leibniz. It also deals with the concept of the existence of God, against the backdrop of Tillich's famous assertion that "God does not exist." When Paul Holmer of Yale Divinity School heard that Tillich made such an assertion, he said it shows that Tillich was an atheist. It might have been better for Holmer first to read what Tillich meant by what he said.[388]

Hinlicky's volume of dogmatics fittingly concludes with a "Doxology." Readers who have come this far will rejoice to praise

---

387. Paul Hinlicky, *Beloved Community. Critical Dogmatics after Christendom*, 567-568.

388. See Paul Tillich, *Systematic Theology* (University of Chicago Press, 1951), Vol. I, 204-208. Tillich wrote, "It would be a great victory for Christian apologetics if the words 'God' and 'existence' were very definitely separated except in the paradox of God becoming manifest under the conditions of existence, that is, in the christological paradox. God does not exist. He is being-itself beyond essence and existence." He says, God is the creative ground of essence and existence. As such God is real, beyond essence and existence applicable to created things.

God from whom all blessings flow. It has been a heavy read. Only those who have more than a sophomore's knowledge of the history of philosophy and theology will be able to delight in the to and fro of Hinlicky's dense argumentation and subtile nuances. The "Doxology" takes up the relevant themes of eschatology, including the hotly debated one of universal salvation, engaging the thought of David Hart.[389] I will end this review with the last words that Hinlicky wrote to end his book: "The Father remembers us better than we can remember ourselves, so that, purified by final conformation to Christ, in the resurrection the Spirit makes us all together new forever in His love. So it is that already now the church sings in anticipation, 'Glory to the Father and to the Son and to the Holy Spirit, as it was, is now and will be forever. Alleluia. Amen.'"[390]

4. Recent Monographs

After twenty some years of teaching at Roanoke College Paul Hinlicky looks forward to retirement. After the publication of his tome of dogmatics, Hinlicky continued to publish shorter books related to Luther and Lutheranism. I will close this review of Hinlicky's prolific work as a Lutheran dogmatician with brief notes on a few of his most recent writings. With his wife Ellen and son Will, Paul Hinlicky has a small farm in Virginia where the family is busy raising naturally grass-fed beef, chickens and honeybees. That's what I read online, which made me wonder when does he find time to write so much.

One of the most interesting of Hinlicky's books was written before the publication of his dogmatics. Its title is, *Before Auschwitz: What Christian Theology Must Learn from the Rise of Nazism* (Cascade Books, 2013). I wrote a blurb for the book I

---

389. David Bentley Hart, *The Beauty of the Infinite: The Aesthetics of Christian Truth* (Eerdmans, 2003).
390. Paul Hinlicky, *Beloved Community*, 893.

will repeat here: "Paul Hinlicky's interest is not merely to shed light on how it could happen that highly cultured and sophisticated German Christians could support the evil actions of Nazi anti-Semitism, but to suggest that we have no guarantee that something similar could not happen within American Christianity." That is a comment that seems even more apropos in America 2021. I know of no more informative book on the extent to which Christians were complicit in the rise of Nazism, some of them well known Lutheran theologians, Paul Althaus and Werner Elert. Before Auschwitz German church leaders believed that Hitler would be a great leader of the German people and help to build a *Volkskirche*. Instead, what came about was a deadly version of fascism. Hinlicky has a chapter on "The Not So Strange Theology of Adolf Hitler." This book is a gem and a must read for American Christian church leaders and theologians in our time.

In 2017 Hinlicky published a book rehearsing the events of the sixteenth century Reformation that led to Luther's excommunication by Pope Leo. The book's title is enough to whet one's appetite to take up and read — *Luther vs. Pope Leo: A Conversation in Purgatory*. In the Preface Hinlicky opines: "There must be a place in contemporary theology for thought experiments, such as the author now lays before the reader.... Let me confess right up front: I am no stylist. Genre-wise, I have birthed some kind of a monster in what follows: neither history nor theology but some fanciful, or, if you will, creative hybrid of the two that I am tempted to call 'ecumenical fantasy' ... as fanciful as putting Luther and Leo X together in an interminable purgatory may seem."[391] Even though Hinlicky may be right to call what he has written a work of fantasy, the author clearly has a sure grasp of both the history and theology of what was going on between Luther and Rome. Since the author's intent is to move the ec-

---

391. Paul Hinlicky, *Luther vs. Pope Leo: A Conversation in Purgatory* (Abingdon Press, 2017), IX.

umenical ball down the field, Hinlicky is aware that there will be conservative Lutherans as well as conservative Catholics of the Pre-Vatican II variety who will be unhappy with the words he has coming out of the mouth of both Luther and Leo.

Luther and Pope Leo have lengthy conversations in purgatory, where they have to share the same room, discussing the key issues that divided Lutherans and Catholics in the sixteenth century. The outcome is that they achieve the kind of reconciliation in the afterlife that mirrors the convergence that Lutherans and Catholics have reached on earth in their mutual signing of the "Joint Declaration on the Doctrine of Justification."

Hinlicky rejoices in the ecumenical progress that has been made between Lutherans and Catholics, and so quotes what Pope Francis said in authorizing the liturgy for the Week of Prayer for Christian Unity in 2017: "Separating that which is polemical from the theological insights of the Reformation, Catholics are now able to hear Luther's challenge for the church today, recognizing him as a 'witness to the gospel.' And so after centuries of mutual condemnations and vilification, in 2017 Lutheran and Catholic Christians will for the first time commemorate together the beginning of the Reformation."[392] This book is eloquent testimony to the ecumenical commitment of Paul Hinlicky, and reinforces his understanding of Luther's theology as fundamentally "Catholic."

In 2018 Hinlicky wrote another book on Luther's theology, this one entitled, *Luther for Evangelicals: A Reintroduction.* In teaching courses on religion and theology at Roanoke College, Hinlicky no doubt had many students who were "Evangelicals," not of the Lutheran kind but conservative Protestant. Undoubtedly also he became aware that Evangelicals know practically nothing about Luther, except that he started the Protestant Reformation by posting the 95 Theses on the door of the Castle

---

392. Paul Hinlicky, *Luther vs. Pope Leo*, XII.

Church. One could learn about that dramatic event from seeing one of the popular films on Luther. Hinlicky graciously welcomes Evangelical readers, presenting his book as "a scholarly project of liberating Luther from Lutheranism to make him available as a resource for the rest of the Christian world."[393] He chose to write on four Christian doctrines that would surely be of special interest to Evangelicals — the new birth, the Bible, evangelization, and atonement. Hinlicky sees the traffic of communication going in both directions: Luther's theology has much in common with the concerns of Evangelicalism; at the same time Evangelicals would benefit from Luther's teaching on these four topics. Hinlicky expounds Luther's key idea of the "joyous exchange" (*fröhliche Wechsel*) in explaining the atonement. On the cross Jesus does not only suffer the punishment sinners deserve, but out of unfathomable love he takes upon himself the sin itself. Thus atonement is a once-for-all act of divine liberation, which is good news for sinners always and everywhere.

In the second part of the book Hinlicky produces a masterful explanation of Luther's Catechisms, the Ten Commandments, the Apostles' Creed, the Lord's Prayer, and the Sacraments. In my knowledge of standard Evangelical theology, Luther's explanations of what is meant by each of the ten Commandments, the three articles of the Creed and the seven petitions of the Lord's Prayer would be readily digestible, but I would expect many would choke on the red meat that Luther serves up in explaining the three Sacraments, Baptism, Confession and Absolution, and the Lord's Supper. In his *Critical Dogmatics* Hinlicky offers strong evangelical catholic and orthodox teaching on each of the Sacraments, but here he tends to pull his punches a bit when addressing Evangelicals directly. Most usefully, this book would be an excellent choice for an ecumenical book club to read and discuss.

---

393. Paul Hinlicky, *Luther for Evangelicals: A Reintroduction* (Baker Academic, 2018), ix.

Hinlicky's most recent book is entitled, guess what, *Lutheran Theology. A Critical Introduction* (Wipf and Stock, 2020). I have to confess that I have not purchased or read this latest book released in May of 2020, but what I can do is transmit the publisher's blurb for the book.

In this book Lutheran theologian Paul Hinlicky makes the deeply conflicted origins of Lutheran theology fruitful for the future. Exploring this intellectual and spiritual tradition of thought through its major historical chapters, Hinlicky rejects essentialist projects, exposing the debilitating binaries such programs engender and perpetuate, to establish an authentic Luther-theology or Lutheran theology. Hinlicky excavates the ways that throughout a five-hundred-year tradition the legacy of Luther texts has been appropriated, retooled, subverted, or developed. Readers of this introduction will thus be critically equipped to make intellectually honest appropriations of the Luther legacy in the plurality of contemporary context in which the iteration of Christian theology will continue.

Rev. Dr. Carl E. Braaten was born in 1929 in St. Paul, Minnesota. He grew up in Madagascar where his parents were missionaries of the Norwegian Lutheran Church in America. There he attended a school for missionary children until his senior year of high school. He finished high school in 1947 at Augustana Academy in Canton, South Dakota. Braaten received a B.A. from St. Olaf College in 1951. He was a Fulbright Scholar at the Sorbonne University of Paris in 1952. From 1955 to 1957 he attended Harvard Divinity School, then he went to Heidelberg University to write his doctoral dissertation. He received a Th.D. from Harvard Divinity School in 1960. He received a Guggenheim Fellowship in 1967 to attend the University of Oxford. In 1958 he was ordained and served for three years as pastor of Lutheran Church of the Messiah in Minneapolis. At the same time he was also Instructor in theology at Luther Seminary. His next move was to teach systematic theology at the Lutheran Theological Seminary in Maywood, Illinois, which merged with other seminaries to become the Lutheran School of Theology at Chicago, where he served from 1961-1991. After retiring from seminary teaching he co-founded with Robert W. Jenson the Center for Catholic and Evangelical Theology, and served as its executive director from 1991 to 2001. Braaten was the founding editor of two journals, *dialog – A Journal of Theology* (1962) and *Pro Ecclesia: A Journal of Catholic and Evangelical Theology* (1992).

Eleven

Carl E. Braaten

Lutheran Ecumenical Dogmatics

I was born on January 3, 1929, in St. Paul, Minnesota. My two older sisters, Agnes and Arlene, and my older brother, F. Martin, were born in Fort Dauphin, Madagascar, where my parents were serving as missionaries of the Norwegian Lutheran Church in America. The family joke was that I was the only one in the family qualified by law to become president of the United States. My father was born in Telemark, Norway, and came to America for the same reason hundreds of thousands of other immigrants did — and still do! He attended Concordia College in Moorhead, Minnesota, then Luther Seminary in St. Paul, after which he and my mother went to the island of Madagascar to preach the gospel and plant the church of Jesus Christ.

So I grew up on the southern tip of the island, a teenager during the years of World War II, then returned to the United States for my senior year of High School. When I was writing my memoirs entitled, *Because of Christ,* I reflected on the significance of those first sixteen years of my life, living in a boarding school for missionary children, attending school in a white only colony, and with lots of teenage energy frustrated by the strict rules at the Missionary Children's Home that were meant to keep us safe. How did this experience influence my decision to become an academic theologian of the church? Our teachers led the whole school in Bible reading, prayers and hymn singing every day, we said prayers before and after every meal, we attended Sunday School, learned every word of Luther's *Small Catechism* by heart, got gold stars for memorizing many of the Psalms and red lettered passages of the Gospels, and attended lengthy church services every Sunday in the Malagasy language. We did all of this in a perfunctory way without questioning whether any of it was true or salutary. But I do remember questioning some of the things our teachers taught about the Bible. They had attended the Lutheran Bible Institute in Minneapolis, so supposedly they were qualified to teach the Bible. But that meant also that they were taught to believe everything in the Bible was literally true because God wrote it, and God does not contradict himself. Was Jonah really swallowed by a whale? Did Adam and Eve start the human race about six thousand years ago? Did Methuselah really live to the ripe old age of 969? Is John 3:16 literally true, that "God so loved the world that he gave his only Son, that whoever believes in him should not perish but have eternal life?" I left Madagascar believing that for sure, but cured of the kind of literalism based on the fundamentalist theory of biblical inerrancy. I left knowing I was a Christian and proud of my parents who forsook the fleshpots of American abundance for a sacrificial life of service for what seemed to be a godforsaken wilderness. Along with scores of other Lutheran missionaries they watered and the Spirit provided the growth so that the Malagasy Lutheran Church is now one of the largest in the world. I have never doubted they did the right thing, which I have implicitly acknowledged by making missiology a major focus of my teaching and writing.

In 1947 I graduated from Augustana Academy, a Lutheran high school (now defunct) in Canton, South Dakota. I received a B.A. from St. Olaf College in 1951, then went to Paris on a Fulbright Scholarship to study at the Sorbonne University. My project was to study the French atheistic existentialism of Jean-Paul Sartre and to compare it to the Christian existentialism of Sören Kierkegaard. Sartre was all the rage in Paris at that time. His plays were showing in the theaters. His first novel was entitled *Nausea,* which he considered his best. The main character is Antoine Roquentin, who is disgusted with his own existence. Sartre takes us into the depths of angst and despair, the twin effects of nihilism. Sartre's philosophical thought is spelled out in detail in a massive work, *Being and Nothingness.* Sartre was a master of turning everything into nothing. Reading *Nausea* made me nauseated. I quit working on my research project and turned to the writings of two major Neo-Thomists, Jacques Maritain and Étienne Gilson. This was the right cure for the nihilistic despair that Kierkegaard called the "sickness unto death."

From Paris I went to Luther Seminary and received an M.Div. in 1955. I did not do an internship as most of the students did because I planned to go on to study for a doctorate in theology which I knew would at best take three years. I was accepted at Harvard, Yale, and Chicago and chose Harvard for two reasons, Paul Tillich was leaving Union Theological Seminary in New York for Harvard Divinity School and, being virtually penniless, Harvard offered me a free ride. My second year at Harvard I became Tillich's student assistant, read and graded all of his students' papers, with some pushback from students who did not appreciate getting poor grades. The dean of the faculty, Douglas Horton, called me into his office and after a brief discussion gave me his blessing, and that was the end of that. Tillich was an enormously important person for me. With his letter of recommendation I was awarded the Sinclair Kennedy Traveling Fellowship which supported me and my family for a year of graduate study at the University of Heidelberg. That was the year I began a life-long friendship with Wolfhart Pannenberg (1928-2014) and Robert W. Jenson (1930-2017) who also, along with Paul Tillich, became my most important teachers — geniuses all three of them. At Heidelberg I wrote my doctoral dissertation on the historical Jesus, focussing on Martin Kähler's book, *Der sogennante historische Jesus und der geschichtliche biblische Christus.* I did it because Tillich told me to. I wondered why. Kähler happened to have been Tillich's professor of dogmatics at Halle University, whose criticism of the nineteenth century critical historical inquiry into the life of Jesus was key to Tillich's own Christology. Kähler was writing on the historical Jesus at the same time Albert Schweitzer published his famous *The Quest of the Historical Jesus;* both of them reached virtually the same negative conclusions without knowing anything about each other's work. About a decade later Tillich wrote another letter of recommendation, this one in support of my application for a Guggenheim Fellowship at Oxford University. This was another year when Jenson and I could exchange ideas about current trends in theology and plan to corroborate on future projects.

After a year in Heidelberg I returned to Minnesota and in 1958 I was ordained into the ministry of the Evangelical Lutheran Church (ELC) and served for three years as the pastor of the Lutheran Church of the Messiah on the north side of Minneapolis. The ELC had a rule that a person had to be ordained for five years before becoming a seminary professor. Alvin Rogness, president of Luther Seminary, intended for me to join the faculty as a professor of theology, but I had served as a pastor for only three years when I received a call to teach at the Lutheran Theological Seminary in Maywood, to succeed George Forell who had before that succeeded Joseph Sittler. I could not refuse. I taught at the Lutheran School of Theology at Chicago for thirty years (1961-1991), took an early retirement to join Robert Jenson in Northfield, Minnesota, to found the Center for Catholic and Evangelical Theology in 1992, with the invaluable assistance of our wives, Blanche and LaVonne. I served as its executive director and also as the editor-in-chief of *Pro Ecclesia: A Journal of Catholic and Evangelical Theology* for fifteen years. I retired a second time to live in beautiful sunny Sun City West, Arizona, which has weather similar to what I grew up with in Madagascar. There are very few days when the weather is too wet for tennis.

1. The Priority of Eschatology

When I made the transition from being a student of theology to becoming a teacher of seminary students, the decision I had to make to get a platform on which to stand theologically seemed to be made for me when I bonded with Wolfhart Pannenberg in Heidelberg. He was charting a path forward beyond the greatest theologians of the post-War era, Karl Barth, Rudolf Bultmann, and Paul Tillich. I knew that no matter how much I learned from each of them, I could not follow in their footsteps. Barth was too much in the Reformed tradition and to some extent hostile to Luther and Lutheranism, especially on law and gospel, the two kingdoms of God, and Zwinglian on the sacraments. Bultmann was too much a demythologizing reductionist in the modernist tradition of German Protestantism; his kerygma floated in the air not grounded in real historical events; Paul Tillich was too much in the speculative tradition of German Idealism, somehow wrongly branded as a Heideggerian existentialist by the religious press in America. I was looking for a different way and Pannenberg was out in front pointing to a new direction in theology. When I wrote my first book, *History and Hermeneutics*, I was under the spell of Pannenberg's influence. I identified eight problem areas on which theologians from different schools of thought were working: the theological use of the historical-critical method; our knowledge of the Jesus of history; the resurrection of Jesus, fact or fantasy; the role of the Old Testament in the history of salvation; scriptural hermeneutics; and the meaning of eschatology. I summarized the state of each problem, compared various types of solution, then concluded each chapter showing how Pannenberg's theology was offering solutions which I attempted to set forth and defend. Pannenberg welcomed the book and thanked me for introducing his thought to the English-speaking public.

On my first sabbatical I was privileged to go to Oxford University on a Guggenheim Fellowship with the intention to write a "little dogmatic" in my own voice, yet acknowledging that I was riding a wave set in motion by the new theology of hope advocated by Wolfhart Pannenberg and Jürgen Moltmann, and buttressed by Ernst Bloch's *Das Prinzip Hoffnung* (Frankfurt: Suhrkamp Verlag, 1959) and Fred L. Polak's *Image of the Future* (Dobb's Ferry, NY: Oceana Publications, 1961). In the Preface of my book, *The Future of God. The Revolutionary Dynamics of Hope*, I wrote: "Whether one cut his theological eyeteeth more on Barth, Bultmann, or Tillich, the feeling is quite general that we can hardly go on the way we have been going. But how do we begin again? Where do we go from here? ... This book on the concept of the future works in alliance with a new movement in modern theology that grasps the gravity of the issues which confront the church and its theology today. The new place to start in theology is at the end — eschatology. The rediscovery of the role of eschatology in the preaching of Jesus and of early Christianity has been one of the most important events of recent theological history.... Hope is a word whose correlate is the future. As a questioning being, man is oriented in hope toward the future. The concepts of 'hope' and 'future' are crucial in the new theology that begins with eschatology."[394]

Chapter one of *The Future of God* deals with anthropology in light of a phenomenology of hope. The gospel of the crucified and risen Christ is the answer to the question of hope for the human condition. The story of Jesus is told within the horizon of the eschatological hope of Israel. After the crucifixion of Jesus one of his disciples said, "We had *hoped* that he was the one to redeem Israel" (Luke 24:21). On trial before King Agrippa, Paul testified, "I stand here on trial for *hope* in the promise made by God to our fathers, to which our twelves tribes *hope* to attain, as they earnestly worship day and night. And for this *hope* I am accused by Jews, O king! Why is it thought incredible by any of you that God raises the dead?" (Acts 26:6-8).

---

394. Carl E. Braaten, *The Future of God. The Revolutionary Dynamics of Hope* (Harper & Row), 1969), 9, 10.

Chapter two deals with God as the power of the future. It answers the question of who and what and where God is by his self-revelation in Jesus Christ. Theologians of the ancient church adopted the neo-Platonic idea of the "*Logos spermatikos*" to express their belief that something of God was previously revealed in general everywhere through the Logos in the world and in human experience. In Jesus of Nazareth God is revealed in particular and definitively as the Logos in the flesh. This means that some aspects of divinity could be known apart from Jesus, apart from the history of Israel, by the channels of natural theology. Theologians we have written about in this book are critical of the traditional kind of natural theology according to which God can be known in advance of his self-definition in the history of the Messiah Jesus. I make an argument in this book for a new kind of natural theology focussed on serious inquiry into the conditions of human experience that give rise to the question of God. This is what I claim: "Natural theology today is a doctrine not of God, of his being and nature, but of the human being in quest of personal identity and meaning. Man cannot cease asking the question of God. It is not natural for man to be an atheist.... In asking the question of God, man will continually project images of reality, dream dreams, or make myths which purport to give an ultimate answer. Not these answers, but the conditions that give rise to the question are of interest to a Christian natural theology."[395]

Chapter three deals with the cross of Jesus, one of the great themes in Luther's theology. Luther's Latin dictum was: "*Crux sola est nostra theologia.*" Luther was echoing Paul who said he wanted to know nothing "except Jesus Christ and him crucified" (I Cor. 2:2). Some theologians boost a theology of the cross at the expense of the resurrection. In a secular age it is easier to believe that a man died than that he rose from the dead. The theology of the cross presupposes the resurrection of Jesus. If

---

395. Carl E. Braaten, *The Future of God*, 63.

Jesus had not been raised from the dead, his death on a cross would not have been remembered by anyone. The apostles — the first theologians — were faced with the question: If Jesus has been raised, why was he crucified? What is the meaning of the cross? They searched their Hebrew Scriptures for clues to understand the meaning of Jesus' death on the cross. They recorded their beliefs and interpretations in the New Testament. Luther inherited a theological tradition that provided various speculative theories that try to explain the meaning of the cross. There are four main ones: 1) The Ransom Theory of the Atonement (Origen of Alexandra); 2) The Satisfaction Theory (Anselm of Canterbury); 3) The Moral Exemplary Theory (Peter Abelard); 4). The *Christus Victor* Theory (Martin Luther's view, according to Gustaf Aulén). I have dealt with these theories in previous chapters. In none of my writings have I latched on to any single one of these theories, although I have tried to understand and have certainly preached the Scriptural motifs which have given rise to the traditional full-blown theoretical explanations. My view is, first, that the theories indulge in speculations, pretending to know more than has been revealed in Scripture, and second, that they raise too many questions to which there are no good answers.

Rather than adopt one of the traditional theories I have tried to go behind them into the actual story of Jesus' life and death as presented in the New Testament. Reinhold Niebuhr once said that the most simple confession of Christian faith, one that underlies all the very complicated theories of the atonement is that "Christ died for our sins." Christ did something *for us* that we could not do for ourselves; in other words, Christ is our elected representative. Wolfhart Pannenberg developed the concept of "representative" in a section of his Christology, entitled "Jesus as Representative of Men before God."[396] Dorothee Soelle also explained the concept of "representation" in her book, *Christ*

---

396. Wolfhart Pannenberg, *Jesus—God and Man*, trans. Lewis L Wilkins and Duane A. Priebe (Westminster, 1968), 195-207.

the Representative.[397] The death of Jesus was not an isolated act of representation. Jesus entire life represented the kingdom of God in his parables and miracles, bringing its healing power to the sick and the dying, its forgiveness to sinners and outcasts, and hope to the poor and powerless. The cross is not a single instrument of salvation apart from the whole self-surrendering service of Jesus as God's anointed delegate in a world of anti-divine powers — sin, death, and the works of Satan. The cross was the destiny of a life that dared to represent God's love by granting unconditional forgiveness and freedom for life already in the present. The cross of Jesus represents the depths of God's love to us. Jesus is the representative in whom God and human beings exchange hope for each other. Because of Jesus' cross God has a reason to hope for us; on account of Jesus' resurrection we have been given a reason to place our hope in God. We can adopt Luther's phrase and call it "the happy exchange." An exchange occurs in the cross — from God to us and from us to God. God has delegated Jesus to be both his representative and ours, by raising him from the dead, by identifying himself with Christ's suffering, and his pain with ours. Faith is the act by which we let Jesus be our representative, of letting Jesus' death be for us, so that we may hope to share in his victory, find reconciliation with God through him, and live even now the life of freedom that the power of love can bring.

As our representative Jesus does not replace us. On his cross he died for us, but not instead of us. We still have to suffer; we still have to die. His suffering and his death are not a substitute for ours. But now we know that we no longer have to die alone on a Godforsaken hill "outside the gate" (Heb. 13:12). We will die in a communion of his love, in the assurance of the forgiveness of sins, and with the hope born of Easter for a life with God forever. Because Jesus died the death of a sinner as one without

---

397. Dorothee Soelle, *Christ the Representative: An Essay in Theology after the "Death of God,"* trans. David Lewis (Fortress, 1967).

sin, he can be our representative. Because he died the death of the guilty as the guileless man, he can be our representative. He can be our representative because in his resurrection God accredited him as the One who has what we lack and who lacks what we have. He has the right credentials to be the ambassador of the human race before God. He goes before us into death and new life, pleading our case and to make room for us in the future of God. Looking at the cross of Jesus from the side of God, we can view it as God's participation in human suffering. Jesus is God's representative, the One in whom God shares most deeply in the suffering of all humankind. This means that we do actually believe in a God who suffers. As the Japanese theologian Kazoh Kitamori writes, "Only a suffering God can help."[398] In view of Jesus' suffering, the person we confess to be "true God," it is hard to believe in a God who would keep his distance from the suffering of "his only beloved Son." The ancient church condemned Patripassionism in its condemnation of Sabellius's modalist interpretation of the Trinity. The issue of the pain and suffering of God is being rethought by the twentieth century theologians engaged in the renewal of the doctrine of the Trinity, as we have discussed in previous chapters of this book.

Christian hope is based on faith in Jesus of Nazareth as the resurrected Son of God; through the event of the resurrection God proved to be the power of the future beyond the finality of death. By raising Jesus from the dead, God confirmed Jesus' claim to authority. Jesus spoke and acted as though he were on the inside of God's will for the world. The resurrection of Jesus was God endorsing the cause of Jesus, vindicating his claim to represent the future of God's coming kingdom in his earthly ministry. Two things are of utmost importance in the Christian confession that on "the third day he rose from the dead" — that it happened and what it means. To locate its meaning elsewhere than in the event itself, as Bultmann's demythologizing program

---

398. Kazoh Kitamori, *Theology of the Pain of God* (John Knox Press, 1965).

does, is more unbelievable than the event itself. A slew of modern Protestant theologians teach that the resurrection of Jesus never happened, but believing it should still remain an option for gullible and weak-minded Christians. Schubert Ogden once said in my hearing that Wolfhart Pannenberg cannot be very smart, as some in the room (including me) seemed to think he is, because he believes that Jesus really did rise from the dead. My view is that to be a Christian is to confess that God is the power who "raised Christ Jesus from the dead" (Rom. 8:11) and "who gives life to the dead and calls into existence the things that do not exist" (Rom. 4:17). If God is stripped of this means of his self-identification, we will have to count ourselves among those "who have no hope" (I Thess. 4:13). To be without hope is to be future-less, to live without trust in the power of God to meet us on the other side of our death. Without faith in the God who creates new life from death, we will be at the mercy of the God of wrath (I Thess. 1:10). This is our confession: In Jesus we meet the living God of love who proves to be God by raising up new life from death. God did this first with Jesus, igniting our hope that the One who is the eschatological power of the future will in the end do the same for us.

We turn now to reconceptualizing the doctrine of the Trinity in light of eschatology. We have dealt with the creative contributions to the doctrine of the Trinity by Ted Peters, Robert Jenson, and Paul Hinlicky. I will add my two cents worth very briefly. The presence of God in Jesus of Nazareth and through his Spirit in the church lead to an eschatological concept of the tri-unity of God. The root of the doctrine of the Trinity is God's self-definition in the person of Jesus and the sending of his Spirit. Paul Tillich called for a "reopening of the trinitarian problem," which Karl Barth accomplished to the great benefit of a whole generation of dogmatic theologians. This can be done in different ways. Pannenberg, Peters, Jenson, and Hinlicky follow Barth, but not down to every detail, to be sure. The doctrine of the Trinity, I suggest, should be constructed within the horizon of an eschatological concept of the power and presence of God's future in relation to the world. The First Article of the Creed confesses God the Creator of all that is. A new eschatological orientation views the doctrine of creation from the perspective of its goal in the kingdom of God whose universality and futurity Jesus announced and anticipated in his own ministry and love for the world. "The God who created 'in the beginning' is not antecedent to the world, progressively being left behind in the primordial past as the world goes forward. God is precedent to the world as its original future, so that the beginning of the world occurs from the power of its end. What is needed ... is an eschatology of creation that starts with Jesus' proclamation of the coming kingdom of God and its initial arrival (the firstfruits) in the new creation of his resurrection life.... The *archē* has no privilege of dominion over the creative rights of the *eschaton*. The power of the future is free to create new things, which have not been scheduled from the beginning in the primeval origins.... The *eschata* of the future are not an echo of the *prōta*.... The starting point for a Christin doctrine of the world as creation is not the account of its genesis in *Genesis*; rather it is the account of its neogenesis in the arrival of God's creative future in the resurrection of Jesus — the prolepsis of the new creation."[399] This revised version of the doctrine of creation frees it from the pagan protological myth of origin so that the dominion of the past is ruled out.

A comment is in order on the word "prolepsis." Prolepsis is a figure of speech in which something future is represented as though it already exists, as though the "not yet" is "already now." The New Testament tells the story of Jesus of Nazareth as the one in whom the future of God's kingdom is already present in his words and deeds. How does the Holy Spirit fit into this picture of the proleptic presence of the Infinite in the finite reality of human experience (*finitum capax Infiniti*)? The Holy Spirit was experienced in the early church as the presence of the power of

---

399. Carl E. Braaten, *The Future of God*, 103, 104.

the future (God) which had proleptically appeared in Jesus of Nazareth. The Apostle Paul viewed the Spirit as the power of God raising Jesus from the dead. Whenever Jesus is confessed as Lord, there the Spirit is active. The Spirit calls and keeps believers in the community of Christ. Because Christ is one with God (*vere deus*), the Spirit he sends as his indwelling presence in believers is also "*homoousios*" with God the Father. "The doctrine of the Trinity is, thus, the most adequate interpretation of the eschatological structure of God's self-revelation in Jesus of Nazareth and in the Spirit who creates a community of believers who already participate in the future of God, and thus exist toward the future as the proleptic sign and sacrament of a new world."[400] Because the kingdom of God was proleptically present and active in the life, death, and resurrection of Jesus, the community that the Spirit created in his name is a new creation, the prolepsis of a new world. Thus, the starting point for a definition of the church must begin with the kingdom of God in the message and ministry of Jesus. Eschatology precedes ecclesiology.

Not only was eschatology taking center stage in theological discussion in the 1960s, the idea of revolution was equally becoming a hot topic. Christian theology could simply ignore it or do what it had often done before, join the counter-revolutionaries. Oscar Cullmann, Swiss New Testament theologian, published a book on Jesus and the revolutionaries in the aftermath of the Paris revolution of students in 1968, stating, "In all the current discussion regarding the relationship of Jesus of Nazareth to the phenomenon of revolution, the key factor is Jesus' attitude to the situation and movements of *his time*."[401] I believed that the Christian response to any social or political movement must be determined by applying a Christological criterion. Here I follow Friedrich Schleiermacher's statement

---

400. Carl E. Braaten, *The Future of God*, 107.

401. Oscar Cullmann, *Jesus and the Revolutionaries*, trans. Gareth Putnam (Harper & Row, 1970), viii.

that only that is essentially Christian that can be "related to the redemption accomplished by Jesus of Nazareth."[402] I knew that flirting with revolution is like playing with fire, so I thought it wise to apply what I had learned about the historical Jesus to answer the question, was Jesus a revolutionary or not? Still under the spell of the rediscovery of apocalyptic eschatology in the New Testament and early Christianity, I wanted to develop a Christian understanding of revolution shaped by the ministry and message of Jesus. Ernst Käsemann famously wrote, "Apocalyptic was the mother of all Christian theology."[403] I published a book that bore the title, *Christ and Counter-Christ. Apocalyptic Themes in Theology and Culture.* One of the chapters deals with the "The Revolutionary Jesus." I will limit what I wrote in this book to my portrayal of Jesus of Nazareth, his way of being, speaking, and acting. Even though this was written more than fifty years ago, I have not learned anything in the meantime to change my mind. Jesus was a unique kind of revolutionary.[404] He was not one of the Zealots who wanted to bring in the reign of God by force, aiming to drive the Romans out. But why did Jesus die by crucifixion, the Roman method of executing political agitators? He called Herod a "fox," he spoke against kings who oppress the people. At the same time he called upon his followers not to resist evil and not to draw the sword. Instead, they are to love their enemies and to be peacemakers. He did not endorse the existing order but neither did he endorse its overthrow by violent means. Somehow Jesus got an unsavory reputation, charged for being "a glutton and a drunkard, a friend of tax collectors and sinners" (Matt. 11:19).

---

402. Friedrich Schleiermacher, *The Christian Faith*, eds. H. R. Mackintosh and J. S. Stewart (T. & T. Clark, 1928), 52.

403. Ernst Käsemann, "The Beginnings of Christian Theology," *Journal for Theology and the Church*, ed. Robert Funk (Herder and Herder, 1969), Vol. 6, 17.

404. Carl E. Braaten, "Apocalyptic Theology of Revolution," *Christ and Counter-Christ. Apocalyptic Themes in Theology and Culture* (Fortress Press, 1972), 101-118.

It is difficult to get a complete grasp of Jesus' revolutionary life-style. The Marxists dis it as "opium for the masses," as being non-political, soft and irrelevant. It is true that Jesus did not offer a blueprint for a perfect society; he did not call for specific institutional reforms. There is no evidence that he was a social reformer or political revolutionary, yet he was caught in the web of political involvement. The temptation story does picture Jesus in the grip of a political temptation. Satan offered to make a deal so that he could possess the kingdoms of this world. The masses wanted to hail Jesus as a political Messiah. It was Jesus' apocalyptic eschatology that empowered him to resist the political temptation as of the devil. Jesus said, "My kingdom is not of this world" (John 18:36). The twentieth century had three great religious leaders with enormous political influence, Mahatma Ghandi, Martin Luther King Jr., and Nelson Mandela, who owed their practice of non-violence to the influence of Jesus. They would perhaps be the first to acknowledge that their imitation of Jesus' way in the world was at best only partial. They had no messianic pretensions.

Jesus' unique kind of revolution can be summarized briefly by eight points. 1. Jesus called for change, not radical change but *total change*, a complete break with the present orders of existence. A revolutionary reversal of cosmic proportions will be preluded by chaos and catastrophe. 2. Jesus was engaged in a struggle to exorcize *demonic powers* of evil, of which political parties and programs are only representative. I once preached a sermon in chapel claiming that "Demons are strong, but Jesus is stronger." One of my colleagues of Bultmannian persuasion asked me, "Do you really believe in demons?" Demons are "isms" that possess people's minds and command their absolute loyalty. Today we know such demons by other names, Nazism, Communism, Fascism, Racism, Xenophobia, Anti-Semitism, and the like. Are these isms demonic? Figure it out! 3. Jesus was a prophet; he could read the *signs of the times*, by which present realities can be seen to point beyond themselves. 4. The Kingdom of God is near at hand, Jesus said; its imminence calls for radical conversion. "You must therefore be perfect, as your heavenly Father is perfect" (Matt. 5:48). 5. Jesus said his followers are to love their enemies; that calls for a complete surrender to unconditional love — love to God and to fellow human beings. History shows that it is all too easy and natural to curse, hate, and kill those on the opposite side, but Jesus' revolutionaries are told to pray for those who persecute them. 6. The tables must be turned, so that up is down and down is up. "Blessed are the poor." "Woe to you that are rich." One of the better slogans of liberation theology was "God's preferential option for the poor." The conspicuous inequality between the rich and the poor is completely unacceptable, in full contradiction of the will of God. 7. Jesus' vision of the way things should be calls for a reversal of roles, so that "The last shall be first, and the first shall be last" (Mark 10:30). "For what is exalted among men is an abomination in the sight of God" (Luke 16:15). Jesus' followers do not aim to be "number one." Their aim is to excel in service to their fellow human beings, not to seek to lord it over others. 8. When things seem hopeless, they may be *birth pangs* of a better future. The darkest hour may give way to the glimmerings of light. Salvation may come through suffering; the misery of the moment may not last for long. Black Friday was soon followed by the light of Easter. A hope-filled sermon could be preached on each one of these eight signs.

In 1974 I published a book entitled *Eschatology and Ethics* in which I claimed that eschatology is "the key to Christian ethics."[405] I observed that the most prominent contemporary ethicists completely ignore eschatology. Reinhold Niebuhr was allergic to the theme of the kingdom of God in ethics as he was in reaction to the role it played in Walter Rauschenbusch's theology of the Social Gospel. When he was informed that the idea of the kingdom of God was making a come-back in the theology of Wolfhart

---

405. Carl E. Braaten, *Eschatology and Ethics. Essays on the Theology and Ethics of the Kingdom of God* (Augsburg Publishing House, 1974).

Pannenberg, Niebuhr said, "We've been through this business of the Kingdom before."[406] Eschatology played no role in the ethics of Paul Ramsey[407] and James Gustafson.[408] It is irresponsible for Christian ethicists to ignore eschatology if what T. W. Manson says is true: "We must recall the fact that the ethic of the Bible, from beginning to end, is the ethic of the kingdom of God."[409] Amos N. Wilder backed up this finding in his book, *Eschatology and Ethics in the Teaching of Jesus*. Pannenberg's was not the sole voice crying in the wilderness of contemporary Christian ethics. Richard Hiers, an American New Testament theologian, also linked ethics radically to eschatology. Like Pannenberg he revived the futurist view of the kingdom in the teachings of Jesus held by Albert Schweitzer and Johannes Weiss. For Hiers the future eschatological kingdom in the message of Jesus is the moving agent of his ethical teachings.[410] I applied the idea of a futurist eschatology to the issues of politics, social welfare, and ecology.[411]

2. The Centrality of Christ

My major focus in writing theology has been on the Second Article of the Creed, "I believe in Jesus Christ!" When Jenson and I decided to co-edit a textbook of *Christian Dogmatics*, I was assigned the Locus on "The Person of Jesus Christ." It continues to be a textbook, mostly in Lutheran seminaries, almost four

---

406. Quoted in Richard Neuhaus' Introduction to Wolfhart Pannenberg's *Theology and the Kingdom of God* (Westminster Press, 1969), 32.

407. Paul Ramsey, *Basic Christian Ethics* (Charles Scribner's Sons, 1951).

408. James M. Gustafson, *Christian Ethics and the Community* (United Church Press, 1971).

409. T. W. Manson, *Ethics and the Gospel* (Charles Scribner's Sons, 1960), 65.

410. Richard Hiers, *Jesus and Ethics* (Westminster Press, 1968) and *The Kingdom of God in the Synoptic Tradition* (The University of Florida Press, 1970).

411. I wrote two chapters on ecology. "Toward an Ecological Theology," in *Christ and Counter-Christ*, 119-134. And, "Caring for the Future: Where Ethics and Ecology Meet," in *Eschatology and Ethics*, 175-187.

decades later. Its strength is that it is multi-authored. There is not one Lutheran theologian trusted with the truth, the whole truth, and nothing but the truth. The Christology I wrote for the textbook aimed to present what has been commonly accepted, transmitted, and taught within the mainstream of the classical Christian tradition. After dealing with "The Nature and Method of Christology" I tackled the question of the right starting point in constructing a Christology for the church today. Traditionally Christology started "from above." The Christological dogma of the ancient church started with the incarnation as recounted in the first chapter of John's Gospel. It was the revealed doctrine of the church and the norm by which every heresy was anathematized. Modern theologians asked by what authority is it decided that the church today needs to be bound by the conciliar decisions of the first five centuries, of Nicaea and Chalcedon. I accepted the virtual consensus among theologians today that the ancient Christological dogma must be shown to be a legitimate interpretation of the New Testament narratives of Jesus of Nazareth as the Christ (Messiah) of God. That is doing Christology (from below). But the danger is that starting Christology "from below" will lead to a "low Christoology," all too common among modern liberal Protestant theologians. A "low Chrstology" is an interpretation of Jesus as "merely human," which was the Ebionitic or Adoptionist heresy in ancient Christianity. I settled for a mediating position: "Despite the current preference for doing Christology from below, starting with what can be known about the historical Jesus, Christological reflection is a hermeneutical process in which the movements 'from above' and 'from below' are not so much mutually exclusive as dialectically related in a comprehensive understanding of the identity and meaning of the person of Jesus the Christ. The process of interpretation extends from the contemporary act of faith within the believing community to the past-historical fact of Jesus interpreted by the apostolic kerygma as the Christ."[412]

---

412. Carl E. Braaten, "The Person of Jesus Christ," *Christian Dogmatics*, eds. Carl E. Braaten and Robert W. Jenson (Fortress Press, 1984), Vol. I, 479.

Chapter 2 starts with the historical Jesus and his message of the kingdom of God. The explicit Christology of the early church is founded on the transition from Jesus' proclamation of the kingdom of God to the early church's Easter gospel announcement of the resurrection of Jesus. Chapter 3 retraces the ground covered by the ancient church fathers, steering a middle course between extremes to the right (Docetism) and to the left (Adoptianism), that is, between the denial of the union of God and humanity in the person of Jesus and the denial of the duality of their respective natures. The formula "one person in two natures" preserved the apostolic message of the gospel that salvation is procured by meeting the true God in the true man Jesus. Chapters four and five go into greater detail explicating traditional issues bearing on the true humanity and the true divinity of Jesus Christ. Chapter six discusses the two states of being in the experience of Christ, the state of humiliation (*status exinanitionis*) and the state of exaltation (*status exaltationis*) of Jesus Christ. The essence of the Gospel story is the participation of God in the human condition for the salvation of humankind and the fulfillment of the world. Chapter seven concludes the Christology with a presentation of the uniqueness and universality of Jesus Christ. The claim of the gospel is that the uniqueness of Jesus Christ lies in his universal meaning, that this concrete historical individual is the key to the universal fulfillment that God intends for all his creation.

Christology continued to be the main focus of my theological work. This came to expression in the title I chose for my theological memoirs, *Because of Christ*. I sent the manuscript to Eerdmann's Publishing Company with the title, *Propter Christum*, a familiar phrase to Lutheran students of theology. The editor would not accept it; Americans don't know Latin. I had also thought of using another Latin phrase, familiar to Lutherans, *Was Christum treibt*. Everything we do in the church is on account of Christ — our preaching, teaching, evangelizing, stewardship, and yes, even good works. Christ is the center of my existence as a Christian; he is the reason I became a theologian. *Propter Christum* is elaborated *in extenso* by the three Lutheran slogans — *solus Christus, sola gratia,* and *sola fide,* which became the core principles in my Lutheran book, *Justification, The Article by Which the Church Stands or Falls.* One year after publishing my memoirs, I returned to write another book on my favorite theme, *Who Is Jesus? Disputed Questions and Answers.*[413] That was half a century after the publication of my dissertation on Martin Kähler.[414] I continued to search for the best answers to the disputed questions in Christology, among them being: What can we know about Jesus of Nazareth, given the modern methods of historical science? How do Christians come to believe in Jesus as their personal Lord and Savior? How do we know whether or not Jesus really did rise from the dead? Why do Christians believe that Jesus of Nazareth, a human being like the rest of us, is really, truly, and fully God? Is Jesus unique in the sense that he is the one and only way of salvation? Was it for our sake or for God's sake that Jesus had to die on the cross? What Jesus of Nazareth the founder of the Christian Church or was it rather his apostles? What does believing in Jesus have to do with politics and things like that?

Searching for answers to questions like these began in earnest when I studied under Paul Tillich at Harvard Divinity School, 1955-1957. This search deepened and became intensely critical the year I was at the University of Heidelberg, when Rudolf Bultmann was at the peak of his influence. That year I met Roy A. Harrisville, a New Testament theologian and also on a Lutheran World Federation Fellowship. We were both rather stunned by Bultmann's existentialist interpretation of the kerygma, his program of demythologizing, and his view of the

---

413. Carl E. Braaten, *Who Is Jesus? Disputed Questions and Answers* (Eerdmans, 2011).

414. *The So-Called Historical Jesus and the Historic Biblical Christ,* by Martin Kähler, translated, edited, with an Introduction by Carl E. Braaten (Fortress Press, 1964).

historical Jesus, and much more. When we returned to America we collaborated in editing two volumes on Bultmann's theology. The first was entitled *Kerygma and History. A Symposium on the Theology of Rudolf Bultmann*, translated and edited by Carl E. Braaten and Roy A. Harrisville (Abingdon Presss, 1962). The second one to follow was *The Historical Jesus and the Kerygmatic Christ. Essays on the New Quest of the Historical Jesus*, translated and edited by Carl E. Braaten and Roy A. Harrisville (Abingdon Press, 1964). While we were not card-carrying disciples of Rudolf Bultmann, we found his correlation of existentialist analysis with a biblical theology of revelation very interesting and challenging. We thought his approach might be the source of a new tradition that radicalizes the Reformation understanding of justification by faith alone. Bultmann's proposals forced the best scholars in Germany and America to answer the question, how did it happen and what does it mean for faith today that Jesus of Nazareth became proclaimed as Christ in the kerygma of the first Christians? Jesus the proclaimer became the Christ proclaimed in a matter of a few years. I came away from all these efforts to understand Bultmann's theology and that of his critics grateful that the questions were sharpened but convinced that the answers were insufficient, chiefly for the reason that these scholars, biblical and philosophical, were treating Christology exclusively as a modern critical-historical enterprise in discontinuity from the Christological creeds and canons of the ancient church. My indebtedness to Martin Kähler proved to be an invaluable resource to deal with the new quest of the historical Jesus inspired by Bultmann and his pupils.

3. Mission: The Mother of Christian Theology

I was scheduled for a second sabbatical for 1974-1975. As a family we had taken three study trips to Europe, to Paris on a Fulbright in 1951, to Heidelberg on a LWF Fellowship in 1957, and to Oxford on a Guggenheim in 1967. What should we plan to do next? The answer came by a letter from the Lutheran

Church in America with the good news that I had been awarded a Franklin Clark Fry Fellowship worth $10,000 for sabbatical use. My imagination soared. As a child of missionaries I never lost interest in the worldwide mission of Christianity. The Braaten family was deeply invested in the global mission of the church. My parents retired from the mission field in Madagascar after thirty years of service. My brother Martin became a missionary to the French Cameroons. My sister Agnes returned to Madagascar as the wife of a medical missionary. I had once been recruited to be a missionary to Africa, but I felt called by God to be a theologian of the church. But here was an unexpected opportunity to play a positive role to advance the cause of world evangelization. I planned a lecture tour around the world, to visit and teach at the seminaries of the churches founded by missionaries in Asia, Africa, and South America. Would I have anything worthwhile to say? Theologically I was prepared to combine two wide-ranging convictions: first, the eschatological beliefs of the apostles launched the earliest gospel mission to the nations and, second, the apostolic imperative to tell the story of Jesus was the "mother of all Christian theology." My plan was to start my journey in Japan to teach for a quarter at the Lutheran Seminary in Tokyo. I gave the lectures in English and had a skillful Japanese theologian to translate. These lectures became the contents of my first book on missiology, *The Flaming Center. A Theology of the Christian Mission.*

The more I studied early Christian origins I became aware of the alliance between eschatology and mission in the Bible and the history of Christianity. Mission is the function of the kingdom of God in world history. The church's role in this scheme is to serve as God's agent for mission. The church inherited from Israel the idea of being the chosen people of God for mission. The Hebrew prophets got the idea that their God is the Lord of all the nations. They believed in the universality of their God, but they did not make it their mission to preach to the nations. Paul was the first Jew to take the gospel to people other than Jews, believing that he was commissioned by the risen Christ on

268

the road to Damascus to bring the message of salvation to the uttermost parts of the earth. When Jewish Christians met Greek pagans, Christianity became a universal amalgamated religion. By the fourth century Christianity had become the established religion of the Roman Empire. The church gained significant political influence. Thus, its Christian mission expanded its horizon beyond purely religious matters to the wider world of philosophy and culture. The modern period confronted the church with a new challenge, the discoveries of modern science. At first Christian theologians tried to debunk the science, then baptized it, realizing that the scientific enterprise presupposes a Christian view of the world as creation.

In working on a Christian theology of world mission in today's world one inevitably encounters the pluralistic theology of world religions, promoted by a number of Anglo-American philosophers of religion who base their hypothesis on a neo-Kantian religious epistemology. In 1930 William E. Hocking headed up a commission to examine the missionary enterprise of American Protestantism. The commission's report, entitled *Re-Thinking Missions,* concluded that the Christian mission has come to a fork in the road. The traditional idea that God promised salvation for the world through "no other name" than that of Jesus Christ can no longer be sustained. The results of the Christian encounter with other religions indicate that all religions are equally ways of salvation. Sone of the more popular champions of the pluralistic theory of religion are Wilfred Cantrell Smith, John Hick, and Paul Knitter, and the number of those who follow them in today's departments of religion in colleges, universities, and seminaries is legion. I have written four books in which I have tangled with the devotees of the pluralistic hypothesis: 1. *The Flaming Center. A Theology of the Christian Mission* (1977); 2. *The Apostolic Imperative. Nature and Aim of the Church's Mission and Ministry* (1985); 3. *No Other Gospel! Christianity among the World Religions* (1992); 4. *That All May Believe. A Theology of the Gospel and the Mission of the Church* (2008).

I am fully aware that it has been a battle lost not only among the teachers of religion and theology but also in the Divisions of Global Mission of the Mainline Protestant Denominations. The belief is widespread that Christianity is one religion among many and that it is in no position to assert either the finality or the normativity of Jesus Christ and the gospel of salvation in his name. The Gnostics of old shared the same relativistic belief. Are there not many revealers of the mysteries of God? Are there not many savior figures, at least one or more for every religion? Is not the apostolic claim a myth that Jesus is unique with universal meaning that we moderns have outgrown? In this brief account of my work as a Lutheran theologian with an ecumenical commitment to visible church unity expressed in common structures of governance, sacramental fellowship, community service, and world mission, I approached the question of God's revelation and its significance for salvation with the following convictions. "We are evangelical catholics standing in the Lutheran confessional tradition, and we hold certain truths to be solidly based on divine revelation attested by Holy Scripture. We propose four dogmatic propositions to which all Christians ought to subscribe if they are faithful to God's revelation in Jesus Christ. First, Jesus Christ is the personal event in whom God's final revelation has already occurred, so that we do not 'wait for another' (Matt. 11:3). Second, faith in Jesus as the Christ means real personal participation in God's eschatological salvation. Third, the church is the community of believers who must proclaim Jesus of Nazareth as the sole Savior of humankind until God's kingdom arrives in its final glory. Fourth, God's will is that all shall be saved and that the whole creation, now in a struggle for life, will at least reach its fulfilling future in the reign of God through Jesus Christ our Lord."[415]

---

415. Carl E. Braaten, *No Other Gospel. Christianity among the World's Religions* (Augsburg Fortress, 1992), 2-3.

The systematic theological problem is how to conceive the attainment of the universal goal of salvation by means of the particular once-for-all revelation in Jesus of Nazareth. My response to this problem has preoccupied my thinking throughout my life, way before I became a theologian. One of my chapters is entitled, "Christ is God's Final Revelation, Not the Only Revelation." I am not a Barthian. I believe the Bible is clear, as Paul is quoted as saying in Acts 14:17 that "God has not left himself without a witness." In Romans 1:18-20 he elaborated this claim that supports the traditional idea of a twofold revelation of God, first, through the creation, as Paul says, "Ever since the creation of the world, his invisible nature, namely, his eternal power and deity, has been clearly perceived in the things that have been made." And second, standing in the middle of the Areopagus, Paul witnessed to the Athenians, saying,"Now God commands all men everywhere to repent, because he has fixed a day on which he will judge the world in righteousness by a man whom he has appointed, and of this he has given assurance to all men by raising him from the dead" (Rom. 17:30-31). Luther certainly affirmed two things, a general revelation of God apart from the Bible and the history of salvation culminating in Christ. Contemporary Lutheran theologians for the most part affirm a broad understanding of God's revelation at work in the religions without any necessary connection with the Bible and the Christian tradition. I have in mind such dissimilar theologians as Nathan Söderblom, Paul Tillich, Paul Althaus, Carl Heinz Ratschow, Gustaf Wingren, Edmund Schlink, and Wolfhart Pannenberg. There are different ways to conceptualize the relation of what God has revealed though the media of nature, history, and religion to what God has revealed in the specific biblical history of salvation in Israel and in Christ. I am sure I have not written the last word, but thinking on this theme has been one of the major passions of my life as a theologian. Above I have written about a new kind of natural theology that involves a "question and answer" dialectic.

4. Ecclesiology and Ecumenism

My ecumenical awakening occurred coincidentally with the convocation of the Second Vatican Council by Pope John XXIII (1962-1965). In 1966 I was asked by the Rev. Dr. Robert Marshall, Bishop of the Northern Illinois Synod of the Lutheran Church in America, to give an ecumenical address on a Lutheran assessment of Vatican II. I did that and it made quite a stir. The title of my address was, "The Tragedy of the Reformation and the Return to Catholicity." It was printed in *The Record* of the Lutheran School of Theology in 1965. The editor of *Una Sancta*, a Lutheran ecumenical journal, edited by the Rev. Richard John Neuhaus, printed an abbreviated version of my address under a different title, "Rome, Reformation, and Reunion." The "Religious News Service" reported that I was calling for Lutherans to "return to Rome," that the reforms called for by the Reformation had been achieved. The New York Times ran the news story with the title, "Lutheran Favors Unity with Rome; Braaten says Reformation Has Accomplished Aims." The *Christian Century* ran an editorial rejecting my alleged proposal entitled, "Protestant Hara-Kiri." To make a long story short, the editor of *Una Sancta* excised some of my actual words: "If evangelical catholics harbor hope of reunion with Roman Catholics, they certainly do not and cannot mean return to the Roman Catholic Church as Roman. The concept of 'return' is inadequate simply because it suggests that the Protestant party is the prodigal wanderer who comes home, while the Roman Church is the waiting Father. There has been prodigality on both sides, and the Roman side has not been standing still. Furthermore, the concept of 'return' which grates upon Protestant nerves does not reflect Pope John's admission that responsibility is divided, and there is equal blame on both sides. The idea of a mutual advance converging upon the future fulfillment of what is valid on both sides is a better working hypothesis. It does not require either side to deny its own history, but through further historical development, it

272

allows for future reconciliation."[416] There would have been no story making headlines in seemingly every village newspaper if that paragraph had been included. In my recent book, *My Ecumenical Journey*, I did my best to set the record straight. "The editor of *Una Sancta*, Richard John Neuhaus, chose to delete the paragraph that made clear that I did not propose that Protestants 'return to Rome' as though they could accept it as their new home. But the cat was out of the bag, and once something appears in the news, many people are gullible enough to believe it must be true. This experience taught me never to believe the headlines or news reports until they are carefully fact checked."[417] A few years later Richard John Neuhaus "returned to Rome."

In the chapter on Robert W. Jenson I already told about the founding of the Center for Catholic and Evangelical Theology and its journal, *Pro Ecclesia: A Journal of Catholic and Evangelical Theology.* Precisely at the same time I was voicing criticism of the Evangelical Lutheran Church in America, lamenting its drift towards becoming just another liberal Protestant denomination. In June, 1990, Robert Jenson and I took the lead in organizing the two "Call to Faithfulness Conferences" held at St. Olaf College in 1990 and 1992. Jenson asked, "To whom or to what are we to be faithful?" His answer was: "To the particularity of the God of the Bible, the God of the Exodus, narrated in the Old Testament, and the God who raised Jesus from the dead, proclaimed by the apostles. The root of the doctrine of the Trinity is grounded in the biblical story of the God who saves and whose proper name is Father, Son, and Holy Spirit. The attempt to exchange the Triune name of God for some other triadic metaphors is a tell tale sign that gnosticism had reared

---

416. Carl E. Braaten, "The Tragedy of the Reformation and the Return to Catholicity, *The Record*, Lutheran School of Theology at Chicago (August, 1965), Vol. 70, No. 3, 13-14.

417. Carl E. Braaten, *My Ecumenical Journey. Ecumenical Experiences and Perspectives of an Evangelical Catholic Theologian* (ALPB Books, 2018), 32.

418. Robert W. Jenson, "A Call to Faithfulness, *dialog – A Journal of Theology* 30.2 (Spring, 1991), 90-97.

its head."[418] One of Jenson's memorable phrases is often quoted, "A church ashamed of God's name is ashamed of her God." Our concern was not solely for the soul of Lutheranism, but that our church would be a worthy ecumenical partner in the ongoing quest for church unity. We were convinced that there is no ecumenical future for churches captive to the cultural trends of a bankrupt secularized Christianity. I called attention to the church's unfaithfulness to the apostolic imperative to bring the gospel to the nations, as though the evangelistic mission had become obsolete. There are still many corners of the world that have never seen a missionary and never heard the gospel. What has changed? We have changed. The Call to Faithfulness conferences did not prevent the downhill trend in the ELCA. In 2009 a schism had become unpreventable, and the North American Lutheran Church was born in protest. Lord have mercy!

Serious ecumenical commitment requires a lot of healing in all the churches engaged in the quest for Christian unity. Jesus prayed that "They they may all be one ... that the world may believe" (John 17:21). Ecclesiology, missioiogy, and ecumenism move forward in lock step. In 2011 I was surprised and honored by a Festschrift,[419] edited by two friends sharing a common vision, one a former doctoral student, Alberto L. Garcia, a Missouri Synod professor of theology, and the other a Catholic sister, Susan K. Wood, a professor of theology at Marquette University. The contributors were fellow travelers on the ecumenical trail, participants in the conferences and publications of the Center for Catholic and Evangelical Theology as well as editors or authors of its ecumenical journal, *Pro Ecclesia:* Robert W. Jenson, Gabriel Fackre, Frank C. Senn, Timothy George, Joseph L. Mangina, Michael Root, Susan K. Wood, Alberto L. Garcia, Cheryl Peterson, and James M. Childs. May their tribe increase!

---

419. *Critical Issues in Ecclesiology. Essays in Honor of Carl E. Braaten*, eds. Alberto L. Garcia and Susan K. Wood (Eerdmans, 2011).

During this period of time I made a modest contribution to ecumenical ecclesiology in my book, *Mother Church.* The search for an ecumenical ecclesiology is one of the most creative achievements of the twentieth century. Lutheran Bishop Otto Dibelius signaled its emerging significance in a book entitled, *Das Jahrhundert der Kirche* (*The Century of the Church*). Catholic theologian, Romano Guardini, wrote after World War I: "An event of incalculable importance has begun: the church is awakening in people's souls."[420] Several decades ago David Yeago wrote an article entitled "Why Ecclesiology Is So Hard for Lutherans." Compared to Orthodox and Roman Catholic theologians what Lutherans have written *de ecclesia* is pretty thin stuff. I wrote my book in the conviction that Lutherans need to rediscover the idea and experience of the church as mother, a concept shared by many fathers of the ancient church. Martin Luther wrote, "I embrace the church, the communion of saints, as my holy mother, and in a conscious act of faith I make my own all the spiritual blessings that the church represents." In his *Large Catechism* Luther wrote that the Holy Spirit "has a unique community in the world. It is the mother that begets and bears every Christian through the Word of God."[421] No doubt he had read the church fathers of the ancient church who said, "You cannot have God for your Father unless you have the church for your Mother."[422] "Mother church" is more than a lovely metaphor; it underscores our identity as offspring of the bride of Christ; it signifies nourishment as we receive from her hands the very body and blood of our Lord Jesus Christ.

The last book I have written is a one volume dogmatics entitled, *The Christian Faith. Ecumenical Dogmatics* (Cascade

---

420. Quoted by Joseph Ratzinger, "The Ecclesiology of the Second Vatican Council," *Communio* II (Fall, 1986), 239.

421. Martin Luther, "Large Catechism," *The Book of Concord*, ed. and trans. Theodore Tappert (Fortress Press, 1959), 416.

422. Numerous citations are provided by Henri de Lubac in *The Motherhood of the Church* (Ignatius Press, 1975), 47ff.

Books, 2020). With this subtitle I was walking in the footsteps of my professor of dogmatics at Heidelberg University, Edmund Schlink, who entitled his great one volume work, *Ecumenical Dogmatics*. Mine were baby steps compared to his giant steps. Edmund Schlink was an official Lutheran observer at Vatican II and wrote an informative report on its proceedings entitled "After the Council."[423] Before this I had written two specifically Lutheran books that I did not claim to be ecumenical in orientation. The first one is entitled, *Principles of Lutheran Theology* (Fortress Press, 1983). A revised edition of this book was published in 2007, and continues to be used as a textbook. The other Lutheran book is entitled, *Essential Lutheranism. Theological Perspectives on Christian Faith and Doctrine* (ALPB Books, 2012). The book now in your hands is definitely a Lutheran book, no doubt my last. Though the twelve theologians treated in this book are all self-avowed Lutherans, at the same time they all undoubtedly had the intention of writing theology for the whole Christian *oecumene,* and perhaps half of them would define their Lutheranism more closely as meaning evangelical catholic.

Conclusion

Readers of this book will encounter a load of dogmatics, perhaps an overload. We have written it for the sake of the next generation of dogmaticians. Every generation needs to build on what has gone before, and then pass on the doctrines of the faith to the best of their ability to the next generation. It works like a bucket brigade. If amnesia sets in and one generation neglects to pass on the heritage of dogmatics, the future of faith will suffer the consequences. Dogmatics is a churchly discipline that formulates the doctrines of the Christian faith for the present

---

423. Edmund Schlink, "After the Council," *Ecumenical and Confessional Writings*, Vol. I, ed. and trans. by Matthew Becker (Vandenhoek & Ruprecht, 2017), 239-536.

situation. The Lutheran dogmaticians featured in this book practiced the discipline of dogmatics for the sake of the whole Christian Church they were committed to serve. In that sense they were aware of their ecumenical responsibility, addressing not merely the needs of the denomination to which they belong.

Christian dogmatics is like a comprehensive circle of understanding and experience that has a center. Those of us writing Christian theology and ethics for the church today share a common confession of faith: Jesus Christ is the center of the faith we seek to understand. We could surely agree to the Christological norm formulated by Paul Tillich: "the new Being in Jesus as the Christ is our ultimate concern." This prevents the theology we are writing from being primarily an expression of our personal religious experiences, though those experiences shine through everything we believe, teach, and confess. Theology is not autobiography, yet one's personal experience of faith is quintessential in doing theology. Thus, I have tried to highlight something of the personal story of each the authors.

These Christian theologians, dogmaticians and ethicists, are committed to the proposition that the substance of the faith they aim to express is grounded in a particular history, the history of God — the triune God — narrated in the sacred writings of Israel and the Church, the Hebrew and Christian Scriptures, the Holy Bible. Their denomination bears the name of its founder, Martin Luther, who was a great biblical scholar and expositor. The Reformation tradition that followed Luther was faced with the question of authority — by what authority do they dare to oppose the authority of the Pope, the Vicar of Christ, and Bishop of Rome? What was the authority to which Luther appealed against the highest authorities of church and empire? It wasn't reason, experience, dogma, or magisterium. Was it Scripture? That sounds right, but that set in motion a history of conflict over the meaning of *sola scriptura*. Lutherans became divided and the division continues to this day between two kinds of confessionalism — fundamentalism, with its doctrine of biblical inerrancy, and revisionism, with its Christocentric hermeneutics. The *Formula of Concord* does not settle the dispute; it simply says: "Holy Scripture remains the only judge, rule, and norm according to which as the only touchstone all doctrines should and must be understood and judged as good or evil, right or wrong." The authors in this book do not espouse the fundamentalist option, according to which the Holy Spirit dictated every word of the Bible, proving its inspiration and inerrancy. The biblical writers were merely amanuenses, secretaries taking dictation. The upshot is that there is no distinction between the Word of God and the words of the Bible. As modern Lutheran theologians we follow Luther's Chrstological canon of biblical interpretation: the gospel of the free grace of God and justification through faith alone. What counted for Luther was the material contents of each book of the Bible and not merely its formal place as one of the books included between its covers. Thus Luther said, "And this is the true test by which to judge all books, when we see whether or not they inculcate Christ.... Whatever does not teach Christ is not yet apostolic, even though St. Peter or St. Paul does the teaching. Again, whatever preaches Christ would be apostolic, even if Judas, Annas, Pilate or Herod were doing it.[424] The catchphrase often repeated by Lutherans is "*was Christum treibt.*" Many denominations and theologians who affirm the fundamentalist version of *sola scriptura* contradict each other, and even have gone to war and shed each other's blood over it. For us the hermeneutical question is how to interpret the Scriptures, and we believe Luther got it right.

The theologians in his book do not agree on method in dogmatic construction. Traditional systematic theology would use philosophy in its prolegomena, either that of Plato, Aristotle, or Plotinus. In modern theology a vast away of philosophical options has been available for theologians to use, from Kant and

---

424. Martin Luther, "Prefaces to the Books of the Bible," *Luther's Works*, Vol. 35, 225-411.

Hegel to Whitehead and Heidegger. No thanks, some of the theologians in this volume have said, following the prohibitive dicta of Karl Barth in this respect. Christian theology does not need to ride on someone else's elephant. That does not mean that philosophical concepts are to be jettisoned. Even Karl Barth said something to the effect that one could find philosophical noodles in his theological soup. That is true for every theologian, willy nilly; the question is whether the prolegomena of a system of theology is duty bound by a prior decision in favor of a particular philosophical system, its epistemology and ontology.

It is pretty clear that the theologians in this volume may well agree on what counts as formal authority in theology, but that does not guarantee consensus on matters of doctrinal substance. The evidence is clear that doctrinal pluralism abounds in contemporary Lutheranism. This goes beyond the minor matter of diversity into more serious matters bearing on orthodoxy and heresy. But who is to judge? I have been reticent to act like an umpire, calling balls and strikes, although some of my observations may have crossed the line. There are two most sensitive areas of concern, one has to do with the doctrine of the Trinity, i.e., the proper name of God as Father, Son, and Holy Spirit and on the relations between the three persons (identities) and their respective works in creating, redeeming, and sanctifying the world and humankind. The other has to do with Christology, the one person of Jesus Christ as both fully God and fully man, and the associated doctrines of the Son of God incarnate, his life, death, and resurrection. Without going into explicit comparative descriptions, I could not observe anything approaching consensus on these two central doctrines that define Christian orthodoxy. With regard to the doctrine of the Trinity, the spectrum runs from the modalist interpretation of the Trinity on the left to the personalist interpretation on the right. With regard to the doctrine of the Person of Jesus Christ, the distinction is between those who function with a low Christology on the left and those who affirm a high Christology on the right. I will let readers discern the distinctive differences among the twelve theologians featured in this book. When they all get to heaven, they will have time to engage in a celestial symposium to discuss who was right and who was wrong, and let Christ be the judge.

In their co-authored book, *Lutheranism. The Theological Movement and Its Confessional Writings*, Robert W. Jenson and Eric Gritsch suggested that the doctrine of justification by faith alone apart from works of law is a Lutheran proposal of dogma. If this is the case, as I believe it is, one would think that the doctrine would unite Lutherans ever since and around the world. What we have written about this doctrine in this book indicates that nothing could be farther from the truth. From the very beginning the doctrine of justification by faith was used by Lutherans as a norm to identify errors on the side of their opponents. Instead, Lutherans have wrangled about exactly how to explicate it from the beginning until now. That became glaringly embarrassing at the Lutheran World Federation meeting in Helsinki in 1963 which failed to draft an uptodate consensus statement on the doctrine of justification by faith. Lutheran dissensus on the doctrine is also highlighted by the Mannermaa School of Luther Research that provides an alternative interpretation of justification to a radically forensic view of the doctrine. In addition when Catholics and Lutherans at the highest official levels signed a "Joint Declaration on the Doctrine of Justification," many Lutherans greeted it with incredulity. Such is the unhappy fate of the doctrine which is supposed to be "the article by which the church stands or falls." The group of theologians in this volume replicates the same fate.

Lutheran theologians have not agreed on the doctrine of the law, namely, its function in relation to the gospel. The first confessing Lutherans disagreed on the place of good works in the order of salvation, one party (Georg Major) saying "good works are necessary for salvation" and the other (Johann Agricola) saying that "good works are injurious to salvation." Antinomianism was a threat to the Lutheran understanding of the gospel of salvation in the first generation of Lutheranism. And it still rears its head in present-day Lutheranism. After 500 years Lutheran theologians have reached no consensus on the so-called "uses of the law." Our report indicates that the question regarding the third use of the law, that is, whether it is the proper function of the law to guide the behavior of Christians, still remains in dispute. So it remains so among theologians we have discussed. The truth is that doctrinal confusion is a liability affecting every church, including the Roman Church which claims to have the advantage of an infallible arbiter.

On matters of ecclesiology and ecumenism the differences among these twelve theologians are quite noticeable and significant. One of the twelve claimed to be proud of owning a pin that says in red letters, "Beware! This man has no ecclesiology." Another one will endorse the patristic slogan, "If you don't have the church for your mother, you won't have God for your Father." A few of the twelve were hard at work on the ecumenical agenda pursing church unity; others were satisfied with the notion that Christian unity is a matter of personal faith in Jesus and has nothing to do with full visible union between separated churches that have mutually condemned each other and refuse to eat and drink together at the Lord's Table. Denominational purists fear that ecumenical dialogue will open the door to doctrinal relativism and indifferentism, and watering down the orthodox truths they confess *because* (*quia*, not *quatenus*) they are based solely on the Bible.

Eschatology has been a subject in dispute every since it arose in the belief system of late Judaism, between the two Testaments. The meaning of eschatology was a major topic of research in twentieth century theology. Karl Barth famously said, "Christianity that is not entirely and altogether eschatology has entirely and altogether nothing to do with Christ."[425] Albert Schweitzer

---

425. Karl Barth, *The Epistle to the Romans*, trans. by Edwin C. Hoskyns (Oxford University Press, 1933), 314.

and Johannes Weiss started a renaissance of interest in eschatology by a strict application of the methods of historical science. They agreed that eschatology lies at the heart of biblical faith and was central in the message of Jesus and early Christianity. However, they agreed that the eschatological outlook of the Bible is antiquated mythology. Systematic theologians do not have the privilege of following their example. If eschatology belongs to the essence of the first Christian theology but appears unacceptable to modern Christians, that is the definition of a crisis. Barth's attempt to renew the place of eschatology in an account of the Christian faith for today fittingly was called a "theology of crisis." Wolfhart Pannenberg and Jürgen Moltmann criticized Barth's purely dialectical eschatology because it lacked the time dimension of the future. Some of the theologians featured in this volume appropriated aspects of the new futurist interpretation of eschatology. The concept of "prolepsis" lies at the core of their understanding. Proleptic awareness is an anticipation in advance of a future happening. The gospel of Jesus Christ embodies ahead of time the future God has promised for the whole of the world and humanity. The future end of all things is already present in the life, death, and resurrection of Christ. This idea of the priority of the future sounds like gobbledegook to other theologians whose thinking is not guided by the apocalyptic eschatology of Jesus and the early church. This all can be demythologized, as Bultmann did, or it can be a first step in a new direction of theology. You, the readers of this book on Lutheran theology, are now in the position to have the last word.

Index

M

Major, Georg, 70, 280
Mandela, Nelson, 261
Mangina, Joseph L., 274
Mannermaa, Tuomo, 214, 216-217, 232-233, 280
Marcos, Ferdinand, 21-22
Marion, Jean Luc, 232
Maritain, Jacques, 249
Marshall, Robert, 272
Marty, Martin, 90
Martyn, J. Louis, 228
McFague, Sallie, 153
Mattox, Mickey, 224
Maximus the Confessor, 211
McGovern, W. M., 64
Menninger, Karl, 160
Melanchthon, Philip, 17, 33, 45, 51, 70, 207, 225
Meyer, Harding, 172
Moltmann, Jürgen, 150, 198, 228, 252, 282
Murphy, Nancy C., 164

N

Nash, Ogden, 93
Naumann, Michael, 90
Nestingen, James, 48
Neuhaus, Richard J., 83, 85, 90, 98, 107, 115, 205, 263, 272-273
Newton, Isaac, 205
Niebuhr, H. R., 93. 96
Niebuhr, Reinhold, 66-67, 79-80, 86, 98, 254, 262-263
Niemöller, Martin, 63, 65
Nissiotis, Nikos, 72
Noll, Mark, 92
Novak, Michael, 83
Nygren, Anders, 7, 57

O

Ockham, William of, 107
Ogden, Schubert, 142, 257
Origen, 39, 199, 206, 254
Ottaviani, Cardinal, 175
Otto, Rudolf, 188
Outka, Gene, 57

P

Pannenberg, Wolfhart, 90, 107, 123, 135, 138, 141, 147, 149, 156-157, 164, 198-199, 223, 249, 251-252, 254, 257, 263, 282
Pauck, Wilhelm, 54, 66
Paul the Apostle, 39, 71, 93, 112, 114-115, 227-228, 252-253, 259, 271
Paulson, Steven, 33-34, 47
Peacocke, Arthur, 123, 163
Pelikan, Jaroslav, 9, 11, 55, 105
Peters, Ted, 8, 144, 169, 257
Peterson, Cheryl, 274
Peuro, Simo, 214
Philip of Hesse, 61
Pinomaa, Lennart, 66
Pitcher, Alvin, 80
Plato, 107, 125, 146, 206, 236, 278
Plotinus, 206, 236, 278
Podhoretz, Norman, 83
Prenter, Regin, 66, 115, 233
Polak, Frederick L., 252
Preus, Herman, 13
Preus, Jacob, 25
Pusey, Nathan, 105

Q

Quenstedt, Johann, 208